D0488981

The Reign of Elizabeth

William Simpson

Series Editors
Martin Collier
Erica Lewis

Heinemann Educational Publishers
Halley Court, Jordan Hill, Oxford, OX2 8EJ
a division of Reed Educational & Professional Publishing Ltd
Heinemann is a registered trademark of Reed Educational & Professional
Publishing Ltd

OXFORD MELBOURNE AUCKLAND
JOHANNESBURG BLANTYRE GABORONE
IBADAN PORTSMOUTH NH (USA) CHICAGO

First published 2001

ISBN 0435 32735 6
03 02 01
10 9 8 7 6 5 4 3 2 1

Designed and typeset by Wyvern 21 Ltd

Printed and bound in Great Britain by The Bath Press Ltd, Bath

Picture research by Peter Morris

Photographic acknowledgements
The author and publisher would like to thank the following for
permission to reproduce photographs:
AKG: 19; Corbis: 7, 12 (all three), 23 (left), 90, 124; Hulton Getty: 11
(both), 23 (right), 46 (both), 63, 66, 69, 73, 90, 91, 115, 130, 131, 132,
136, 151 (both), 161

Cover photograph: © Coursham Court Collection

Written source acknowledgements
The author and publisher gratefully acknowledge the following
publications from which written sources in the book are drawn. In some
sentences the wording or sentence structure may have been simplified:
A.G. Dickens *The English Reformation* (Batsford, second edition, 1989):
143; G.R. Elton *The Parliament of England, 1559-1581* (Cambridge
University Press, 1986): 167-8; C. Haigh *Elizabeth I* (Longman, second
edition, 1998): 143, 168; J.E. Neale *The Elizabethan House of Commons*
(Cape, 1949): 167

Dedication
Thanks to Sheila for her encouragement and support.

CONTENTS

HOW TO USE THIS BOOK

This book covers the reign of Elizabeth I, 1558–1603, and is divided into three parts.

Part I serves as an introduction to the period and is designed especially for AS students who are encountering Tudor history for the first time. Chapter 1 sets the scene, describing the main features of Elizabethan England and outlining the problems Elizabeth inherited – both at home and abroad. Chapter 2 provides a brief summary of the main issues and events of the reign.

Part II contains a detailed and analytical treatment of Elizabeth's reign. Chapters 3 to 7 provide a chronological account of the main events of Elizabeth's reign both at home and abroad. Chapter 3 describes the establishment of the Elizabethan regime, particularly Elizabeth's system of government, the making of the religious settlement and early ventures in foreign policy. This is followed by an Assessment section, which gives advice on how to tackle different styles of essay question. Chapter 4 tackles the threats to the regime, particularly from the Catholic minority and Mary Queen of Scots in England. Chapter 5 covers foreign policy up to the outbreak of war with Spain. Chapter 6 deals with that war from 1585 to 1604. It also includes England's participation in the Dutch Revolt and the French Wars of Religion, and events in Ireland. Chapter 7 looks at the last years of the Elizabethan regime and the factional divisions that marked them.

Part III focuses on particular aspects of the Elizabethan regime: the religious settlement and the challenges to it from Catholics and Puritans (Chapter 8); the working of the system of government (Chapter 9); and the economic problems that demanded attention and the government's responses to them (Chapter 10).

The book has been written to meet the needs of both AS and A2 candidates, but the subject matter cannot be separated to correspond precisely to that division. Instead, at the end of each chapter from Chapter 3 onwards there is an Assessment section, divided into two parts. In the first part, there are summary questions designed to ensure that the material has been correctly understood and clearly grasped. In the second part, there are either AS-style questions, mainly of a descriptive character, and/or A2-style questions, which demand an analytical approach and in some cases familiarity with the relevant historiographical debates. There are suggested approaches to these questions, but they are not intended to act as model answers. It is recommended that readers consult these approaches after, rather than before, working out their own answers.

There is a selective bibliography that students are advised to consult. It is arranged by topics, and includes both recent interpretations of the reign of Queen Elizabeth and earlier works that are still valuable.

PART I: THE REIGN OF ELIZABETH I – INTRODUCTION AND BACKGROUND

CHAPTER 1

England in 1558

POPULATION

England's population appears to have grown steadily in the sixteenth century, following the decline that was associated with the **Black Death** in the fourteenth and fifteenth centuries. No precise figures are available before the first census in 1801, but at no time did the annual death rate exceed 2.68 per cent of the population. England was spared the demographic disaster that afflicted Ireland in the nineteenth century, when the Irish potato famine of 1845–8 caused over 1 million deaths.

Population of England (in millions)	
1525	2.25
1561	2.98
1601	4.10

Population of Wales	
1500	210,000
1603	380,000

Populations in England and Wales.

(Source: John Guy, *Tudor England*, OUP, 1990.)

Why did the population increase?

This increase appears to have been caused both by a rise in the **birth rate**, as a consequence of a fall in the age of marriage, and a reduction in the **death rate** as agricultural productivity improved. That is not to say that famine was unknown. There was a serious scarcity of food between 1593 and 1597 caused by a sequence of poor harvests.

Where did people live?

The majority of this population, some 90 per cent, lived in the countryside, three-quarters of them south and east of a line drawn between the Rivers Severn and Humber. The north and west of the country were underpopulated compared with the Midlands and the south-east.

At the start of the sixteenth century, London was the only substantial town, with a population of 60,000. This figure rose to 215,000 by 1603. Its closest rival was Norwich, which reached 18,000 until an attack of plague reduced its

Sixteenth-century England: where people lived.

population in 1579. Other towns, none of which had more than 12,000 inhabitants, were Bristol, York, Coventry, Salisbury and King's Lynn.

Comparisons with other countries

In terms of population, England was small compared with her international rivals. France had a population of about 15 million in 1500; Spain had a population of about 12 million.

THE ECONOMY

KEY TERMS

Open Field system Where arable land was divided into strips representing a day's ploughing and allocated to members of the village community. Meadow land was likewise divided until the hay harvest. The Common land was available to all for grazing, subject to a stint limiting the number of animals each villager might be allowed.

Enclosure This was not the only source of grievance. Engrossing (the amalgamation of farms) and the conversion of arable pasture for sheep rearing were also unpopular because of their effects on employment.

KEY EVENT

Kett's Rebellion A rebellion named after its leader, Robert Kett, which broke out in July 1549 in Norfolk. The rebels had a variety of economic grievances. It was suppressed with great violence by the Earl of Warwick.

Agriculture

Agriculture was the staple industry and source of wealth. The pattern of land use and ownership varied widely. In some parts of East Anglia and Kent, for instance, arable farming predominated. In the north and west, where the land was much less fertile, it was used to rear cattle and sheep. In the Midlands, where the land was equally suited to arable and pasture, mixed farming predominated. In over half of England the **Open Field system** survived until the eighteenth century.

The Open Field system was inevitably inefficient and, while suited to subsistence farming, little improvement in productivity could be expected while it endured. Thus, throughout the century, Open Fields were liable to be **enclosed**. In other words, land would be parcelled out on a permanent basis and individual holdings surrounded by hedges or fences. The process was a major source of friction. In 1548–9, for example, it helped to provoke **Kett's Rebellion**.

This led to many attempts by Tudor governments either to prevent enclosure or to regulate it. There are no accurate figures for the total acreage enclosed. Even in the worst affected counties it has been calculated that as little as 3 per cent of the total land area was enclosed between 1500 and 1600. That said, enclosure was a visible and identifiable grievance and, as such, attracted a great deal of attention. However, it is probably true to say that improvements in agriculture owed more to the gradual application of marl and lime and the manuring of fields than to enclosures.

According to one Tudor economic historian, Peter Ramsay, in *Tudor Economic Problems* (1963):

> *Whereas the best thirteenth-century farms had produced only six to twelve bushels to the acre, the Elizabethan farmer could expect at least sixteen.*

Industry

The cloth industry. By far the most important English industry in the sixteenth century was the production of woollen cloth. Whereas in the thirteenth century raw wool had been England's major export, by Henry VIII's reign the ratio of cloth exports to raw wool was 92 per cent to 8 per cent. In some parts of England – notably Gloucestershire, Wiltshire and East Anglia – the cloth industry was a major source of employment. Cloth made up four-fifths of English exports. Most of it was channelled through London to the port of Antwerp (in modern-day Belgium) until 1551, where it was used by the Flemish **finishing trades**. The decline of Antwerp as a port, initially as a consequence of financial instability and subsequently because of the outbreak of the Dutch Revolt in 1566, meant that finding fresh markets for English cloth became a major consideration from 1551 onwards.

Other important industries. Other important industries were food and drink (notably brewing), building and leatherworking. In the north-east, the coal industry expanded considerably. Annual production increased from 33,000 tons in 1564 to 252,000 in 1609. Over the same period, London increased its annual import of coal from 24,000 tons to 74,000 tons. There was a flourishing iron industry on the Sussex Weald and in Monmouthshire, Glamorgan and the Forest of Dean.

Economic growth. Though England did not experience anything like the **industrial revolution** of the eighteenth century, Tudor rule did provide the political stability required for economic growth. Without reliable statistics such growth is impossible to quantify in many areas.

However, what evidence there is suggests that England was a more prosperous country in 1600 than it had been in 1500.

THE STRUCTURE OF GOVERNMENT

The monarchy

The Tudor dynasty was established by **Henry VII** after the Battle of Bosworth in 1485. He was the unlikely claimant to the throne as a consequence of a series of struggles over the succession, better known as the **Wars of the Roses**.

The first of these struggles occurred in 1399 when Richard II was deposed by his cousin, Henry Bolingbroke (who became Henry IV). Once the succession had been upset, the stage was set for nearly a century of dynastic strife between the descendants of Edward III. The two main families involved were:

- the descendants of John of Gaunt (the House of Lancaster, whose emblem was the red rose)
- the descendants of Edward, Duke of York (the House of York, whose emblem was the white rose).

In brief, while Henry V and Henry VI (of the House of Lancaster) came to the throne without a struggle, Edward IV (of the House of York) succeeded in replacing Henry VI twice, each time after victory in battle:

- first in 1461, after the Battle of Towton
- second in 1471, following Henry VI's brief restoration after the Battles of Barnet and Tewkesbury.

Henry VI died in the Tower of London, almost certainly murdered in 1471. Edward V succeeded his father Edward IV, at the age of twelve, only to be deposed by his uncle, Richard III. It was this man, Richard Crookback of legendary evil reputation, whom Henry VII defeated at Bosworth.

Henry owed his own claim to his descent from John of Gaunt through the Beaufort line, and to the marriage of

KEY PERSON

Henry VII The first Tudor king who gave England much needed stability. During his reign, 1485–1509, he subdued the nobility, reorganised royal finances and won foreign recognition for himself and his dynasty.

KEY EVENT

Wars of the Roses The term has come to be used to describe the struggles over the succession that broke out in the reign of Henry VI. Most of the fighting was concentrated into three periods: 1455–61, 1469–71 and 1485. Thirty-eight peers were killed and the casualties at some battles, notably Towton in 1461, ran into thousands. Shakespeare's history plays – *Richard II*, *Henry IV*, *Henry V*, *Henry VI* and *Richard III* – give a vivid account of these events, and in their portrayal of a society at war emphasise the Tudor concern for order and stability.

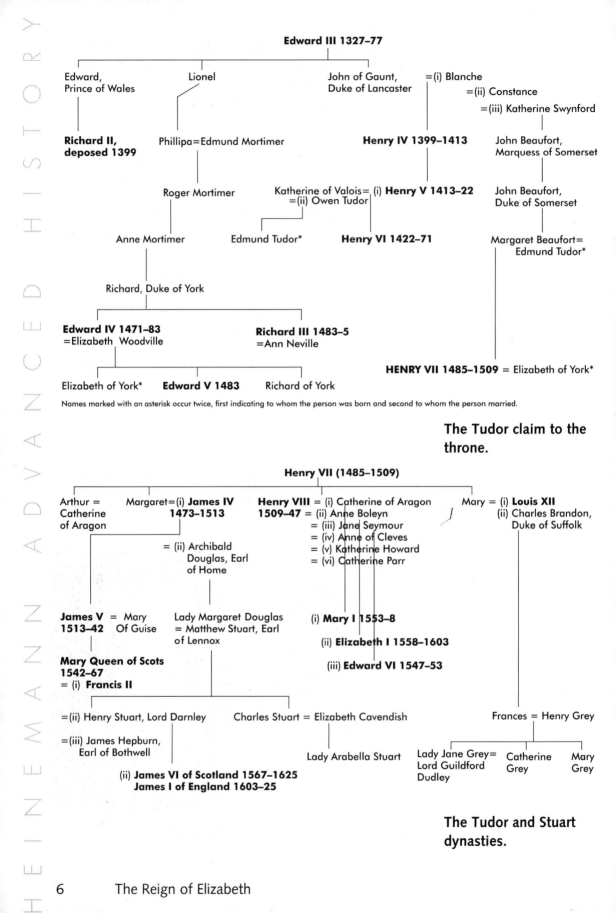

Edward III 1327–77

Edward,
Prince of Wales

Lionel

John of Gaunt,
Duke of Lancaster

=(i) Blanche

=(ii) Constance

=(iii) Katherine Swynford

**Richard II,
deposed 1399**

Phillipa=Edmund Mortimer

Henry IV 1399–1413

John Beaufort,
Marquess of Somerset

Roger Mortimer

Katherine of Valois=(i) **Henry V 1413–22**
=(ii) Owen Tudor

John Beaufort,
Duke of Somerset

Anne Mortimer

Edmund Tudor*

Henry VI 1422–71

Margaret Beaufort=
Edmund Tudor*

Richard, Duke of York

Edward IV 1471–83
=Elizabeth Woodville

Richard III 1483–5
=Ann Neville

HENRY VII 1485–1509 = Elizabeth of York*

Elizabeth of York*   **Edward V 1483**   Richard of York

Names marked with an asterisk occur twice, first indicating to whom the person was born and second to whom the person married.

The Tudor claim to the throne.

Henry VII (1485–1509)

Arthur =
Catherine
of Aragon

Margaret=(i) **James IV
1473–1513**

Henry VIII = (i) Catherine of Aragon
1509–47 = (ii) Anne Boleyn
= (iii) Jane Seymour
= (iv) Anne of Cleves
= (v) Katherine Howard
= (vi) Catherine Parr

Mary = (i) **Louis XII**
(ii) Charles Brandon,
Duke of Suffolk

= (ii) Archibald
Douglas, Earl
of Home

James V = Mary
1513–42 Of Guise

Lady Margaret Douglas
= Matthew Stuart, Earl
of Lennox

(i) **Mary I 1553–8**

(ii) **Elizabeth I 1558–1603**

(iii) **Edward VI 1547–53**

**Mary Queen of Scots
1542–67**
= (i) **Francis II**

=(ii) Henry Stuart, Lord Darnley

Charles Stuart = Elizabeth Cavendish

Frances = Henry Grey

=(iii) James Hepburn,
Earl of Bothwell

Lady Arabella Stuart

Lady Jane Grey=
Lord Guildford
Dudley

Catherine
Grey

Mary
Grey

(ii) **James VI of Scotland 1567–1625
James I of England 1603–25**

The Tudor and Stuart dynasties.

The Reign of Elizabeth

his grandfather, Owen Tudor, to Katherine, widow of Henry V (see the family tree on page 6). He had to face several challenges to his position from the Pretenders Lambert Simnel and Perkin Warbeck, but left an undisputed succession to his son Henry VIII.

But, while Henry VIII's accession was universally approved, his divorce from Catherine of Aragon (in order to marry Anne Boleyn, Elizabeth's mother) and the religious changes which accompanied it brought the succession into dispute once again. Elizabeth could not but be mindful of the plight of some of her forebears whose claims to the throne had been challenged:

- Richard II had been deposed and executed.
- Henry VI and Edward V were both murdered in the Tower.
- Elizabeth's sister Mary's claim to the throne had been challenged by Lady Jane Grey, at the bidding of the Duke of Northumberland in 1552.
- Elizabeth herself had, at one stage, been imprisoned in the Tower by Mary.

With hindsight it might look as though Elizabeth's claim to the throne was never in doubt. At the time, memories of the Wars of the Roses were still fresh, and the problem of

Henry VIII.

Anne Boleyn.

the succession continued to be a very pressing concern to Elizabeth and her advisers throughout her reign.

The power of the Crown

What powers did Elizabeth enjoy? This is still a matter of some dispute among historians and will be further discussed in Chapter 9. It is common ground that the Queen inherited the following rights:

- She could choose all her servants and ministers, both in her Household and her Council.
- She had the right to approve or refuse any policy initiatives suggested to her.
- Similarly, she had the right to assent to or reject any legislation from Parliament.
- Decisions on peace and war were finally hers.

Both Henry VIII and Edward VI had claimed supreme headship of the Church of England – a claim that Mary, as a devout Catholic, readily surrendered. Elizabeth was to follow her father's lead, though not in quite the same form, as we shall see.

The Crown also enjoyed an assured ordinary revenue, made up largely from the receipt of customs duties, the rents from Crown lands and **feudal incidents** such as the sale of wardships. It was accepted that in peacetime the Crown's ordinary revenue should suffice to meet its expenditure. However, in the event of war, Parliament would have to vote the extraordinary revenue needed to meet exceptional costs. In this respect, England was to differ significantly from France where the Estates General lost the right to vote taxes in the course of the sixteenth century. Because of the Anglo-Spanish war from 1585, Parliament met much more frequently in the final eighteen years of Elizabeth's reign than it did in the previous 26.

Thus, while the position Elizabeth inherited was potentially very strong, her power would still depend on the skill with which she exercised it. Her claim to the throne was never unchallenged. Her handling of political issues would be subject to sharp criticism from both

KEY TERM

Feudal incidents These arose out of the feudal rights of the Crown – for example, wardship, the right to manage estates and draw the income from them where there was no adult heir. This right ended when the heir or heiress reached the age of majority.

individuals and groups within her Privy Council. Through her dependence on Parliament for extraordinary revenue, and also for legislation, she could never rule without it.

The Royal Household and the Privy Council

At the centre of Elizabethan government were two overlapping and sometimes competing groups:

- the **Royal Household**
- the **Privy Council**.

The Royal Household. This included those of Elizabeth's servants who were in daily attendance upon her. They might have official titles, unrelated to the functions they actually performed, but the Lord Steward, the Lord Chamberlain, the Treasurer and Comptroller of the Household, the Captain of the Guard and the Master of the Horse fulfilled key elements of their post or delegated them.

Elizabeth's favourites were usually rewarded with positions in the Household. Robert Dudley, for instance, was made Master of the Horse in 1559. Membership of the Household carried with it the right of access to Elizabeth, but not necessarily any role in the making of policy.

The Privy Council. This was a much smaller and more tightly defined body. In Elizabeth's reign its membership fluctuated between nineteen in 1559 and thirteen in 1601. It would always have included the great officers of state, notably the Treasurer and the Secretary. Senior Churchmen were often included – for instance, **Stephen Gardiner** under Henry VIII and Mary. Elizabeth broke with this practice until 1583, when John Whitgift, the Archbishop of Canterbury with whom she was most in sympathy, became a member.

The Privy Council met on a regular basis, three or four times a week in the 1560s, and daily in the 1590s when the country was at war. Its responsibilities were all-embracing:

- the management of finance;
- the enforcement of religious conformity;

- defence;
- foreign policy;
- the maintenance of internal security;
- the regulation of economic affairs.

The Privy Council could act as an informal court of law. It had the authority to use torture to extract information. Indeed, this power was used in 53 cases in Elizabeth's reign.

The Privy Council followed the **Court**. It met most frequently at the royal palaces in London, Greenwich, Hampton Court and Whitehall. However, when the Queen was on one of her **royal progresses**, a select group of the Privy Council would accompany her.

The Queen's ministers

Elizabeth was peculiarly fortunate in her servants.

William Cecil. At the centre of affairs was William Cecil, elevated to the peerage in 1571 as Lord Burghley. Cecil had been the surveyor of Elizabeth's estates before she became queen, and was a natural choice to be her first Secretary. He held this position until 1572, when he succeeded the Marquis of Winchester as Lord Treasurer. He stayed in office until his death in 1598. Elizabeth personally attended his bedside during his final illness. He was her trusted servant in all matters and, while at times he became infuriated with Elizabeth's changes of mood and mind, he never wavered in his devotion.

Sir Francis Walsingham. Another highly competent minister was Sir Francis Walsingham, one of Cecil's protégés. He succeeded Cecil as Secretary, after a brief interlude, in 1573. A more committed Protestant than Cecil, Walsingham often disagreed with Elizabeth on matters of policy, but he provided an invaluable intelligence service to meet the internal and external threats to Elizabeth's security.

Other servants. Other men who gave loyal and devoted service to Elizabeth were Sir Francis Knollys, Sir Christopher Hatton, Sir Thomas Smith and Lord Howard of Effingham. In a different category to those already

KEY TERMS

The Court was both a series of places and a collection of people. Geographically it consisted of the royal palaces, mainly in London, where the Queen lived, but it might also move to the private houses of the great when Elizabeth went on royal progresses. Socially it was made up of all those nobility and gentry who sought office and royal favour. One recent calculation by Penry Williams suggests that the Court provided a total of 1250 positions, ranging from stablehand to Lord Chamberlain. Of these posts about 200 were suitable for a gentleman. (See Penry Williams, *The Later Tudors, England 1547–1603*.)

Royal progress English monarchs spent much of their time on the move. It was a way of acquainting themselves with their subjects and saving on domestic expenditure. Elizabeth loved to travel, though she did not stray far beyond the home counties.

William Cecil, Lord Burghley.   **Sir Francis Walsingham.**

mentioned were Elizabeth's favourites, men who charmed her without necessarily earning her respect. They were: Robert Dudley, Sir Walter Ralegh, and Robert Devereux, Earl of Essex.

Robert Dudley. The first in Elizabeth's affections was Robert Dudley, who became Earl of Leicester in 1564. For a time it looked as though she would marry him. However, the death of Leicester's wife, Amy Robsart, in suspicious circumstances (she was found dead at the bottom of a flight of stairs) in 1560, effectively ruled out that possibility. Leicester provided a counterweight to Cecil, usually arguing for a more ambitious foreign policy. Leicester's ambitions were military rather than political, though he made little of the opportunity given to him in 1585 when he was given command of the English army sent to the Netherlands. His death in 1588 swiftly followed his recall.

Sir Walter Ralegh. After Leicester's death, Elizabeth's attention was drawn to Sir Walter Ralegh, who became Captain of the Guard in 1587 and therefore gained access to Elizabeth. His wit won him her favour, but she never admitted him to the Privy Council. He was even imprisoned briefly in 1591, having made one of Elizabeth's maids in waiting, Bess Throckmorton, pregnant. Though

Ralegh was released, he had to return to the sea-faring career in which he had made his early reputation.

Earl of Essex. The young Earl of Essex, Leicester's stepson, coincidentally arrived at Court at the same time as Ralegh. Essex was only nineteen in 1586 when Elizabeth first met him. He was soon her constant companion and she would gladly have entrusted him with greater responsibility had he been more deserving of it. As it was, she gave him military commands in France in 1591, the command of a huge expedition to Cadiz in 1596 and command of the army sent to subdue the Irish Rebellion in 1599. While the Cadiz expedition was a success, Essex failed miserably in Ireland. He also over-played his hand with disastrous consequences in 1601 when he engineered a plot to seize London. Elizabeth made no attempt to save him from the death sentence that followed his conviction for treason.

Robert Dudley, Earl of Leicester.

Robert Cecil. More important than either Ralegh or Essex, though not a favourite, was Robert Cecil, Burghley's son. Cecil was admitted to the Privy Council in 1592 at the age of 29. On the death of Walsingham in 1590, Burghley assumed the duties of Secretary, but in practice his son performed them, and he secured the office himself in 1596. When Burghley died in 1598, Robert Cecil assumed his father's role, but the last years of Elizabeth's reign were marred by factional disputes between the supporters of Essex and Robert Cecil.

Sir Walter Ralegh.

Thus, while Elizabeth gave her fullest confidence to her most reliable advisers, she was not immune to the charms of mercurial figures like Ralegh and Essex. Their influence on policy was usually slight, but it added an upsetting dimension to the world of politics.

Parliament
As we have seen, Parliament had an essential role to play both in the passage of **legislation** (see key terms on page 13) and the voting of taxes. By Elizabeth's reign the two Houses (the House of Lords and the House of Commons) had assumed the structure and composition they were to have until the 1832 Reform Act.

Robert Devereux, Earl of Essex.

The House of Lords. This House was made up of the lay **hereditary peers** who had an automatic right of summons, and the spiritual peers, now the two archbishops of Canterbury and York, and the other bishops of the Church of England. Until 1536, heads of the greater religious houses had also enjoyed membership of the Lords, but with the dissolution of the monasteries between 1536 and 1539 that privilege obviously came to an end. This meant that, for the first time, lay peers outnumbered spiritual peers – a matter of some significance when it came to the Elizabethan settlement.

The House of Commons. This House was recruited from both the counties and the boroughs of England. Each of the counties had the right to send two knights of the shire to Parliament, as did any borough with a royal charter. While the county membership remained unchanged, new boroughs were constantly being created. In Elizabeth's reign, membership rose from 402 in 1559, to 438 in 1571, and 462 in 1586. The significance of these changes is discussed in Chapter 9.

Parliaments were summoned automatically at the beginning of every reign, and thereafter at the discretion of the sovereign. One Parliament might last for several sessions, in which case it was **prorogued** at the end of each session. If the monarch wanted a new Parliament, the old one would be **dissolved**.

The inconvenience and cost of attending Parliament were considerable. Elizabeth's view, as expressed by Lord Keeper Puckering in 1593, was probably shared by a good many Members of Parliament (MPs).

> *Her majesty hath evermore been most loth to call for the assembly of her People in Parliament, and hath done the same but rarely and only upon most just, weighty and great occasions.*

In fact, during Elizabeth's reign, ten Parliaments were elected. These Parliaments sat for thirteen sessions in all. In a reign of 44 years, Parliament was in session for only 126 weeks, an average of three weeks a year. Its importance rested in the first place on the taxes voted. Every one of Elizabeth's Parliaments voted subsidies, except for that summoned in 1572, when no subsidy was requested.

Parliament also passed a very large number of bills. Some of these were promoted by the Privy Council (public bills). Others were promoted by individual Members of Parliament, usually acting on behalf of their localities (private bills). In the course of Elizabeth's reign, 272 public bills were passed along with 166 private bills. Thus Parliament played a critical role in the nation's affairs even if it was not yet part of the day-to-day machinery of government. While Elizabeth might have been loth to summon it, in practice she proved herself extremely adept at handling it.

THE LEGACY OF RELIGIOUS CHANGE

Between 1529 and 1558, England experienced three major upheavals in the beliefs, forms and practices of the prevailing religion, Christianity. From the standpoint of the twenty-first century it is not easy to appreciate why these changes were so momentous. In the sixteenth century practically all English people would have defined themselves as Christian, though there were occasional exceptions such as the Elizabethan playwright, **Christopher Marlowe**. Figures for church attendance are elusive, but everyone was expected to attend Sunday services and to receive **Communion** at least once a year.

The Church was a major landowner and its bishops were often significant figures in the state as well as the Church. Universities and schools were dominated by the clergy. The annual calendar was punctuated by religious festivals such as Christmas, Easter, Ascension Day and Whitsun.

Perhaps most difficult to appreciate is the importance attached to the next life in contrast to this one. Prior to the Reformation it was a well-accepted practice for wealthy men to found **chantries**. At death, so it was believed, every soul went to Purgatory, from whence it would go either to Heaven or to Hell. The length of time spent in Purgatory

Christopher Marlowe
Author of many fine plays. He gained a dangerous reputation for atheism and was due to answer charges on this account before the Privy Council in 1593. He was killed in a tavern brawl before he could answer the summons.

KEY TERMS

Communion Also known as the Lord's Supper, the Eucharist or the Mass (its Catholic title), the re-enactment of the Last Supper that Christ had with his disciples. Each of the gospels repeats the words Christ then spoke to his disciples in slightly different ways. The first gospel to be written, St Mark's, has this form: During supper he took bread, and having said the blessing he broke it and gave it to them, with the words: "Take this; this is my body." Then he took a cup, and having offered thanks to God he gave it to them; and they all drank from it. And he said, "This is my blood of the new covenant, shed for many.'" Communion became the central act of Christian worship, but it was also a source of bitter theological controversy.

Chantries Small chapels where masses might be said for the soul of the founder. Chantry priests were employed for this purpose. They frequently undertook other tasks as well, including teaching.

Indulgences Pieces of parchment sold by Papal licence. Their purchase would help to reduce the length of time spent in Purgatory by one's dead relatives. It became a money-raising device for the Papacy, and it was against this practice that Luther launched his famous protest in 1517.

Heresy The denial by a professed, baptised Christian of a revealed truth, or of that which the Roman Catholic Church claimed to be a revealed truth. Excommunication from the Church was the usual penalty, but in extreme cases heretics were put to death.

might be reduced by the good works performed on earth and, according to later Catholic doctrine, by the purchase of **indulgences**.

While Protestantism attacked Catholic teaching both on indulgences and on chantries, its sixteenth-century adherents believed as fervently in Heaven and Hell as any Catholic. At a time when the consequence of **heresy** was eternal damnation, religious belief became, literally, a matter of life and death. Thus the changes in religious belief and practice experienced between 1529 and 1558 were bound to be contentious, and inevitably brought with them a crop of martyrs, both Catholic and Protestant.

Religious changes under Henry VIII
Under Henry VIII four momentous changes took place.

- Henry broke with the Papacy.
- The Pope's authority was replaced by that of Henry.
- Between 1536 and 1539, all the religious orders in England were dissolved.
- The Bible was translated into English and a copy was placed in every parish church.

Breaking with the Papacy. Because of the Pope's refusal to grant him a divorce from his first wife, Catherine of Aragon, Henry broke with the Papacy. The process took several years to accomplish, but the key stages were achieved between 1533 and 1536. Under the Act in Restraint of Appeals to Rome, passed in 1533, Henry abolished the Pope's right to intervene on any matter affecting the English Church. The Pope's authority was finally ended in 1536, by the Act Extinguishing the Authority of the Bishop of Rome.

Replacing the Pope's authority. In the Act of Supremacy, passed in 1534, Henry and his successors were to be 'taken, accepted and reputed the only supreme head in earth of the Church of England called *Anglicana Ecclesia*'. In so far as the Act was passed by Parliament, it could be argued that Henry's power over the Church rested on Parliament's approval, and this was to become a critical bone of contention in Elizabeth's reign. What was not in dispute was Henry's power to legislate for the Church as he saw fit, providing he could secure Parliament's approval.

Dissolving religious orders. This change reflects the power now gained by Henry VIII over the Pope. Between 1536 and 1539, all the religious orders in England were dissolved and their possessions annexed by the Crown. Some 7000 monks and 2000 nuns were forcibly removed from their religious houses, though most of the monks received pensions or employment as clergy.

Henry's motives were primarily financial, but he was also concerned to eliminate an important source of opposition to the royal supremacy. Indeed, neither he nor his chief minister, **Thomas Cromwell**, had any sympathy for the monastic ideal. As a consequence, the Crown acquired a huge increase in its real estate, together with the rental income to be derived from monastic lands. Unfortunately, from the point of view of Henry's successors, much of this wealth was dissipated (frittered away) in Henry's expensive wars against France in the 1540s.

By 1547, almost two-thirds of monastic property had been sold off, mostly to neighbouring landlords. Purchasers of monastic lands had a vested interest in resisting any re-establishment of monasticism, as Mary Tudor found to her cost. Another consequence of the dissolution (as we have seen on page 13) was the disappearance of the heads of religious houses from the House of Lords.

Translating the Bible. The final significant religious change effected in Henry's reign was the translation of the Bible into English and the requirement in one of Thomas Cromwell's Injunctions of 1538 that a copy should be placed in every parish church. Several translations were made, but the official version was mainly the work of **Miles Coverdale**.

The original intention had been to make the Bible accessible to everyone, but in 1543 an act was passed to restrict Bible reading to the upper and middle classes. Such an act could not easily be enforced and such evidence as there is suggests it had little impact. Once the Scriptures

Thomas Cromwell Henry VIII's chief servant from 1531 to 1540. A self-made man, he was the efficient executor of all Henry VIII's religious changes during these years. He was responsible for the ruthless destruction of the monasteries, but also ensured that English bibles were placed in all parish churches, and that births, marriages and deaths were properly recorded in each parish.

Miles Coverdale A notable Biblical scholar, he started life as a monk. He became a reformer and moved to Zurich, where he produced the first complete translation of the Bible into English. He became Bishop of Exeter under Edward VI, and took refuge in Denmark during Mary's reign.

Thomas Cranmer When he first came to Henry VIII's attention, Cranmer was a Fellow of Jesus College, Cambridge. He lent his support to Henry's divorce, and was appointed Archbishop of Canterbury in 1532 – a position he held until his deprivation by Mary in 1552. His religious views continued to evolve during his life and he was essentially a scholar and theologian rather than a man of action or religious zealot. He believed that all worship should be conducted in English rather than in Latin, but he was anxious to incorporate traditional rites in the new service book and to allow a degree of latitude in matters of belief.

were available, the **laity** could read and draw inspiration from them directly. On the other hand it would only be a matter of time before rival interpretations of specific terms (for example, bishop) and texts would fuel religious controversy.

Religious initiatives in the final years of Henry's reign

The final years of Henry's reign witnessed a confusing series of religious initiatives. In 1539, Henry introduced the Act of Six Articles, designed to ensure that the English Church retained many of its Catholic features. Clerical marriage was forbidden, obliging Archbishop **Thomas Cranmer** to send his wife back to Germany. **Auricular confession** was approved. Most significantly, the doctrine of **transubstantiation** was made mandatory (compulsory). Denial would result in the death penalty.

In 1540, Henry had his loyal servant, Thomas Cromwell, executed on a trumped-up (made up) charge of treason. At the same time, Henry sent three Catholics to the block and had three Protestants burned for heresy. The last of his wives, Catherine Parr, whom Henry married in 1543, had Protestant sympathies. Additionally, Anthony Cooke, John Cheke and Richard Cox, the tutors whom Henry appointed for the royal children, showed reformist tendencies. When Henry died in 1547, though the breach with Rome and the royal supremacy were not in doubt, it was far from clear where the Anglican Church was heading.

Religious changes under Edward VI

Edward's reign brought a rapid shift towards a more Protestant Church. Edward was only ten at his accession. So the kingdom was ruled first by Protector Somerset (Edward's uncle), and then by the Duke of Northumberland who ousted Somerset in 1549. Both men were sympathetic to Protestantism and Archbishop Thomas Cranmer was given a relatively free hand to shape the Anglican Church along the lines he wished.

The first English Prayer Book. In 1549, Cranmer introduced the first English Prayer Book. Based on a variety of sources, it retained the main Sacraments of the Church – Baptism, Communion, Confirmation, Marriage and Ordination. The Litany and forms of service for Matins and Evensong were also retained. An Act of Uniformity, passed the same year, made use of the new Prayer Book compulsory in all churches.

The Act of Uniformity was generally observed, though there was a strong adverse reaction in Devon and Cornwall, where a rebellion broke out. The rebels described the new Prayer Book as 'but like a Christmas game … and so we Cornish men (whereof certain of us understand no English) utterly refuse this new English'. The rebels in their turn wanted a return to traditional Catholic practices, and those refusing them to die as heretics.

The Second Prayer Book. A number of Protestant **theologians** were also welcomed into England, notably Peter Martyr, Martin Bucer and Paul Fagius. Their influence is reflected in the Second Prayer Book, introduced in 1552, which drew a more explicit line between the Anglican Church and Catholic tradition. At the Communion service the use of **vestments** was forbidden and a simple table was to replace the Altar. At the administration of the elements of bread and wine, the words to be used were changed from 'The Body of Our Lord Jesus Christ which was given for thee preserve thy body and soul unto everlasting life' to 'Take and eat this *in remembrance* that Christ died for thee, and feed on him in thy heart by faith with thanksgiving'.

There was controversy, too, over the **rubric** directing that the people should communicate 'meekly kneeling upon your knees', because it might imply adoration of the elements of bread and wine. Cranmer refused to modify the rubric, whereupon the Council then inserted the so-called 'Black Rubric', denying any intention to adore the elements by kneeling, or any natural presence of Christ's body therein.

Further steps towards Anglicanism. A further step towards Anglicanism was taken with the formulation of the Forty-Two Articles, which were approved by the Privy

Council, but not by Convocation, on 12 June 1553, a month before Edward's death. The Articles had to be signed by a cleric wishing to preach. They are distinctly Protestant in tone and condemn many Catholic beliefs and practices – transubstantiation, purgatory, the worship of relics and images for instance.

Attack on the Church's wealth. Edward's reign also saw a further attack on the Church's material wealth. Under the Chantries Act of 1548 all chantries, free chapels, colleges, hospitals, **fraternities** and guilds in England and Wales were assigned to the Crown. According to the **Valor Ecclesiasticus** made in 1535, there were 2374 chantries, 90 colleges and 110 hospitals, but these figures are probably an underestimate. In practice, all hospitals were exempted and, where a chantry had served a useful as well as a purely religious purpose, it was usually allowed to continue. Most of the Edward VI grammar schools derived from chantries. The picture is inevitably mixed where such a variety of localities and institutions is concerned, but certainly another significant feature of medieval England had disappeared.

The changes reversed: the reign of Mary

Edward VI died on 6 July 1553. The Duke of Northumberland, knowing of Mary's zeal for the Catholic faith, realised that his own position depended on preventing her accession. He arranged for his own son, Lord Guildford Dudley, to marry Lady Jane Grey, who could trace her descent back to Henry VII. He persuaded the Council to recognise Lady Jane Grey as queen. But Mary gained strong local backing in Norfolk and, when she arrived in London on 3 August, Northumberland's supporters had melted away. Her accession was generally popular and, initially, she faced little opposition.

Mary, the Catholic. As the daughter of Catherine of Aragon, Mary was both a devout Catholic and proud of her Spanish forebears. She was determined to restore England to the Catholic fold and to marry Philip II, the recently widowed King of Spain. The two ambitions proved a fatal combination.

KEY TERMS

Fraternities Lay groups of Christians who came together both for self-help and burial clubs, for instance, and for charitable and religious functions such as the organisation of religious processions or the performance of Miracle Plays.

Valor Ecclesiasticus A detailed assessment of all clerical incomes and monastic assets, put together by Thomas Cromwell and his officials in 1535. Its purpose was to record the church's wealth with a view to taxing or confiscating it.

The return to Catholicism proceeded with a deceptive smoothness. In her first Parliament in 1553, Mary secured the repeal of all the Edwardian religious legislation, though 80 MPs out of 350 opposed the repeal of the Act of Uniformity.

In her third Parliament, which lasted from November 1554 to January 1555, all the anti-Papal legislation since 1529 was repealed and the heresy laws revived.

In November 1554, **Cardinal Pole** arrived from Rome to become Archbishop of Canterbury and Papal Legate. He came, he said, 'not to pull down but to build, to reconcile, not to censure; to invite but without compulsion'.

However, in practice Pole did nothing to mitigate the religious persecution that began in February 1555. Mary herself urged the strict enforcement of the heresy laws, and she was probably encouraged in this by her **Spanish confessors**, Bartolome Carranza and Alonso a Castro.

At least 282 so-called heretics were burned at the stake between February 1555 and November 1558, and a further 40 died in prison. The majority came from London and the south-east, five from the south-west, and three from Wales. The majority were of humble birth because committed **Protestants** who had the means to do so went abroad. Among those to die were five bishops (Nicholas Ridley, Hugh Latimer, John Hooper, Robert Ferrar and Thomas Cranmer) and sixteen clergy.

It has been claimed that, by the standards of the age, Mary's persecutions were not unduly harsh and certainly her father had been equally ruthless with his Catholic opponents. But the scale of the burnings was unprecedented and the courage with which the victims met their end gave to Protestantism a moral stature that it had hitherto lacked. Furthermore, the martyrs had a propagandist of great skill and conviction: John Foxe.

Foxe's *Acts and Monuments*, better known as the *Book of Martyrs*, was first published in its English edition in 1562 and soon became a bestseller. Elizabeth's government

Cardinal Pole Opposed Catherine of Aragon's divorce and left England in 1536. As Papal Legate he was given authority to restore England to the Catholic Church. When war broke out between Philip II and Pope Paul IV in 1556, Pole was put in a very difficult position.

Mary's Spanish confessors Spiritual advisers. Bartolome Carranza and Alonso a Castro had both been concerned with the discovery and punishment of heretics in Spain.

Protestants The term was first used to describe the followers of Martin Luther in 1529. It came to mean any Christian who did not belong to the Roman Catholic Church.

encouraged the provision of a copy in all cathedrals and collegiate churches. Meanwhile, the stories of the deaths of Ridley, Latimer and Cranmer became part of English folk culture.

Mary's Spanish connections. If the persecutions severely damaged Mary's reputation, the Spanish marriage had equally dire consequences. It led directly to the one rebellion of the reign, known as **Wyatt's Rebellion**, led by Sir Thomas Wyatt in January 1554.

Mary's marriage also involved England in a wasteful war with France, which saw the loss of the coastal town Calais, England's last continental possession. By a final irony, Philip II was also fighting Pope Paul IV in Italy, where the Papal States adjoined Philip's Spanish territories. Pole even had his **legatine commission** revoked in April 1557.

The situation when Elizabeth became queen. Because of these events, the religious situation that Elizabeth inherited was incredibly confused. The Catholic Church had supposedly been fully restored, but only at the cost of severe persecution. Relations with the Papacy had been renewed, only to be suspended. Some 800 Protestants had fled to the continent and were now determined to return, many of them strengthened in their **Calvinist** convictions. The great majority of the English people had kept their heads down, but religious allegiance varied greatly from one part of the country to another. In Cornwall, men rebelled at the new Prayer Book. In London and the home counties they died because they would not accept the Catholic faith.

A DISUNITED KINGDOM

In the sixteenth century, it still made sense to talk of England rather than Britain. Though England laid claim to Wales, Scotland and Ireland, her authority over these parts of the British Isles had still to be established and the nature of the relationship differed in each case.

HEINEMANN ADVANCED HISTORY

Wales

So far as Wales is concerned, the situation had become reasonably clear cut by Elizabeth's accession. After the campaigns of Edward I (1277–84), Wales was annexed to the English Crown in 1284. In practice, the establishment of English rule was a lengthy process. It was punctuated by rebellions, the last of which, led by **Owen Glendower**, lasted from 1400 to 1412.

The Tudor dynasty had strong links with Wales. Henry VII had landed at Milford Haven in 1485 to launch his bid for the throne and this may have helped to reconcile the Welsh to English rule. Thomas Cromwell was anxious to integrate Wales more closely into England and by two significant acts of Parliament, passed in 1536 and 1543, Wales acquired a judicial and political system similar to England's.

The Welsh shires. Twelve Welsh shires were created, each of which had the right to send two MPs to Parliament. English officials – Justices of the Peace, Sheriffs, Constables and Lords Lieutenant – were introduced. The English legal system was extended to Wales, with circuit judges going round on **assizes** to enforce English laws.

Wales and the Reformation. The Reformation met with little opposition in Wales, which proved naturally receptive to Protestant ideas. Thus, compared with other parts of her realm, Wales gave little difficulty to Elizabeth, and though the Welsh language and sense of identity survived, at this stage cultural differences did not provoke serious conflict.

Scotland

The Tudor record in Scotland prior to 1558 was not nearly so constructive as in Wales. Henry VII treated his fellow monarch, James IV, as an equal and was glad to arrange the marriage of his eldest daughter Margaret to the Scottish king.

The two kingdoms remained on reasonably good terms throughout Henry's reign. But with Henry VIII's accession matters changed. A contemporary quip neatly summarises the situation: 'Who that intendeth France to win, with

KEY PERSON

Owen Glendower A Welsh nobleman and initially a supporter of Henry Bolingbroke (later Henry IV) against Richard II. Convinced that his fellow Welshmen were being exploited and over-taxed, Glendower led a rebellion against Henry IV in 1400 and by 1404 controlled most of Wales. He summoned an independent Welsh Parliament, but was defeated several times by Henry IV's son, the future Henry V, and by 1409 his main strongholds had been taken. He remains a heroic figure in the history of the Welsh nation.

KEY TERM

Assizes Though the royal courts of justice were based in London, it had long been the practice for royal judges to travel throughout England to try serious criminal cases. Such cases were heard at the local assizes, which took place at county towns.

Scotland let him begin.' Any war with France was almost certain to encourage a Scottish invasion, and Henry was bent on war.

Scotland and the French. When war broke out between England and France in 1512, the Scottish army crossed the border in force, led by their king, James IV. The army was destroyed at the Battle of Flodden in 1513. The king, many of his nobles and 10,000 men died in the battle.

The French offered their support to Scotland. James V, heir to James IV, married Madeleine, daughter of the French king, Francis I. Then, on her death, he married Mary of Guise. The 'auld alliance' as it came to be known, was now firmly in place. In 1542, prior to his final war with France, Henry VIII launched a raid on Scotland. James V retaliated with another invasion of England, which was halted at the Battle of Solway Moss, another severe defeat. James reputedly died of grief, leaving the kingdom to his six-day-old daughter Mary and the regency in the capable hands of his widow, Mary of Guise.

Henry sought to exploit his victory. Under the Treaty of Greenwich signed in 1543, his son Edward was pledged to marry Mary, now Queen of Scots.

James V, King of Scotland.

Mary of Guise.

The **rough wooing** did not work. Mary was crowned Queen of Scotland and the French alliance was reaffirmed. In 1544, Henry ordered Edward's uncle, the Earl of Hertford (the future Protector Somerset) to invade Scotland and destroy Holyrood Palace (in Edinburgh), plus every house and village within seven miles of Edinburgh. Hertford did not carry out his instructions to the letter, but the raid was still very damaging. It was repeated the following year, with equally devastating effects.

KEY TERM

Rough wooing How contemporaries described the efforts made by Henry VIII to win the hand of Mary Queen of Scots for his son, Edward.

England's attempt at permanent conquest of Scotland.

When Hertford became Protector in 1547, he embarked on the most ambitious of Tudor policies towards Scotland. His aim was permanent conquest. He invaded Scotland with a large army, won the Battle of Pinkie, and established garrisons in the borders and beyond the Firth of Forth. Such a policy was too expensive to maintain, and it simply had the effect of strengthening the French alliance.

Mary Stuart was sent to France in 1548 where she was betrothed to the Dauphin, heir to the French throne. The garrisons were withdrawn in 1550 under the Treaty of Boulogne. Thus the policy of integrating Scotland into England met with humiliating failure.

Ireland

Tudor policy towards Ireland prior to 1558 was equally ambitious, and little more successful. At the outset of the Tudor period, English authority was effective only within a narrow coastal strip on the east coast, known as the Pale. The rest of Ireland was ruled indirectly through the Earls of Kildare.

In 1534, the Eighth Earl was summoned to London and then imprisoned in the Tower. This sparked off the first of many rebellions against Tudor rule. It was successfully suppressed, and Henry and Thomas Cromwell decided that aristocratic delegation should be replaced by direct rule.

Henry's plan for direct rule of Ireland. In 1541, Henry changed his royal style from 'Lord' to 'King' of Ireland, partly because of the fear that the Pope's authority might be preferred to his. Having claimed the royal title, Henry's relationship to the Irish chieftains also changed. From now on, ruling Ireland would no longer simply be a matter of negotiating with powerful local families. By the end of the century it would require a regular garrison, and a policy of settlement and conquest.

There was a further complication. Whereas in Scotland a spontaneous native Protestant reformation was about to occur, in Ireland the bulk of the population, aristocracy as well as peasantry, remained committed to the Catholic faith. Attempts to impose a Protestant Church in Ireland for the majority, were doomed to fail. Thus, while the Reformation brought England and Scotland more closely together, in Ireland it had the opposite effect. Both the Papacy and Spain were to offer their support to Elizabeth's Catholic opponents in Ireland. As her reign progressed, Ireland became an increasing worry and the greatest burden on her financial resources.

THE INTERNATIONAL ARENA

In the sixteenth century, Europe was dominated by three powers:

- France
- Spain
- the Holy Roman Empire.

In each of these powers there was an established dynasty and government, capable of raising sufficient taxes to supply armies and warships, and therefore to conduct war against its neighbours.

France. In France, the Valois dynasty ruled without dispute until the death of Henry II in 1559. Charles VIII (1494–8), Louis XII (1498–1515), Francis I (1515–47) and Henry II (1547–59) all came to the throne unchallenged by serious rivals.

Spain. In Spain, the union of Aragon and Castile was achieved by the marriage of Ferdinand of Aragon to Isabella of Castile in 1469. This marriage gave to Spain the unity that was needed for her to play the dominating role she assumed in the latter part of the sixteenth century.

The Holy Roman Empire. This Empire extended over most of present-day Germany and Austria, but also included parts of Italy. Though, in theory, the Emperor was elected by seven German princes and bishops, in practice the ruling house of Habsburg had established an invincible claim to the imperial title in the fourteenth century. Two areas of Europe attracted the predatory attentions of these three powers because of their relative wealth and military weakness: northern Italy, where the city states of Florence, Milan and Venice were no match for a French or Spanish army; and ducal Burgundy (present-day Belgium and Holland), equally vulnerable to more powerful neighbours.

A concentration of power

By a series of dynastic marriages and untimely deaths, Spain, the Holy Roman Empire and Burgundy all came under the rule of one man, Charles V.

- The Emperor, Maximilian, married Mary of Burgundy in 1477.
- Their son, the Archduke Philip, married Joanna, daughter of Ferdinand and Isabella of Spain in 1496.
- This marriage produced Charles V in 1500.
- From his father Charles V inherited Burgundy in 1506; from his Spanish grandfather, Ferdinand, he inherited Spain in 1516; and on Maximilian's death he was elected Holy Roman Emperor in 1519.

Rivalries

Partly in consequence of this concentration of power in one ruling house, international relations in the sixteenth century were marked by the rivalry between France and Spain. Fought out mainly in Italy during the first half of the century, the focus of conflict later shifted to Burgundy. This rivalry was a source of strength to England, whose support was sought by each side. and who encouraged rulers to pursue a more ambitious foreign policy than their resources warranted.

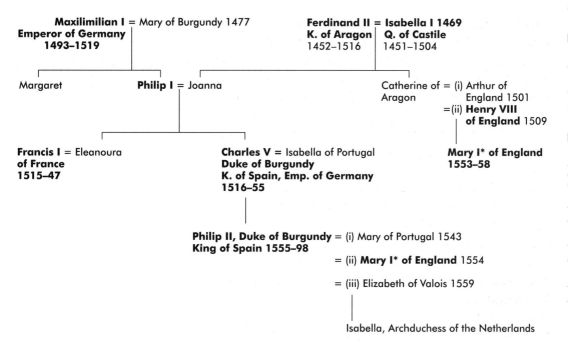

Names marked with an asterisk occur twice, first indicating to whom the person was born and second to whom the person married.

The Spanish connection.

After the English Reformation there was always the danger that the Catholic powers of Europe might unite against a Protestant threat. Such a danger nearly materialised in 1540. Fortunately for England, secular rivalry usually took precedence over ideology. However, her rulers had to be very conscious of the need not to antagonise both France and Spain at the same time.

Foreign policies, and war

Henry VII. The first Tudor, Henry VII, pursued for the most part a realistic foreign policy, tailored to England's needs and resources. He sought foreign recognition of his dynasty by marrying his children into other royal houses.

- His eldest son, Arthur, married Catherine of Aragon in 1501.
- On Arthur's death in 1502, negotiations were opened for Catherine to marry his second son, Henry. These eventually bore fruit on Henry's accession in 1509.
- As we have seen, he married his first daughter, Margaret, to James IV of Scotland.

- His youngest daughter, Mary, was married to Louis XII of France, though this marriage did not take place until 1514.

Henry VIII. Henry VIII enjoyed the **panoply** of war for its own sake. He wanted to extend England's possessions on the French coast, and in his most ambitious moments renewed England's claim to the French throne. He fought three wars against France, usually as the ally of Spain, in 1512–14, 1523–5 and 1543–6. The only tangible gain was Boulogne, which, in any case, had to be given up in 1550.

Somerset. Protector Somerset continued Henry's anti-Scottish, and therefore anti-French, policy in 1547 with disastrous results. When Mary came to the throne her foreign policy was governed by her marriage to Philip II, king of Spain.

Philip. Philip succeeded his father in 1556 as King of Spain and almost immediately became embroiled in a war with France, now allied to the Papacy. In 1557, under Philip's persuasion, England also joined in the war against France. Unexpectedly the French laid siege to Calais throughout the winter of 1557, and in January 1558 it fell.

Thus, when Elizabeth came to the throne she found, in the words of Armigil Waad, former Clerk to the Privy Council, 'the French king bestriding the realm, having one foot in Calais and the other in Scotland'.

KEY TERM

Panoply Literally means 'suit of armour'. Henry relished the glamour of war as his many surviving suits testify.

SUMMARY QUESTIONS

1 Describe the main features of the English economy and system of government in 1558.

2 What problems confronted Elizabeth I at her accession, both at home and abroad?

CHAPTER 2

The reign of Elizabeth I: main issues and events

INTRODUCTION

The purpose of this chapter is to give a bird's eye view of the reign of Queen Elizabeth I. It will:

- introduce the main issues that dominated the period
- highlight the particular events that had a significant bearing on those issues.

It is hoped that, having read this chapter, students will know what to expect in subsequent chapters and will be able to place events within their overall context.

THE CHARACTER OF ELIZABETH'S REIGN

Elizabeth I's reign lasted for 44 years – from 17 November 1558 until 24 March 1603. The dates are significant in that they mark two important boundaries:

- the transition from a Catholic to a Protestant England
- the change from the Tudor to the Stuart dynasty.

It is also true that Elizabeth's reign had characteristics of its own, stemming from the character of the Queen. In an age of personal monarchy, all political life revolved around the sovereign and all policy decisions relied on Elizabeth's consent. Thus her views, whether on religion, foreign policy, or the treatment of rivals and opponents, mattered. She chose all her ministers, who in turn transmitted her wishes.

Length of reign
The length of Elizabeth's reign was also a source of stability, giving England a long period of internal peace,

compared with the upsets that had taken place between 1547 and 1558, and in notable contrast to France, where the Wars of Religion created bitter divisions between Catholics and Protestants and led to periods of anarchy.

POLICY ISSUES

The problems that Elizabeth and her ministers had to face were inherited, and they continued after her death. Though they were not confined to her reign, the Queen and her Privy Council affected the outcome of these problems, often with lasting consequences. There were real choices to be made in the following areas of policy:

- the settlement of religion
- opponents to the settlement and their treatment
- foreign policy issues
- the conduct of war
- relations with Scotland and Ireland
- the operation of government
- the working of the economy.

The settlement of religion

The first question to be settled was: 'Would England return to the Protestant fold?' If so: 'To what variety of Protestantism?' Though the decision for Protestantism was made in principle in 1559, the second part of the question, 'To what variety?', remained unresolved for much of the reign and continued to be a source of controversy. The Anglican Church was slow to take shape and did not take root easily in many parts of the country. Its evolution is described in Chapters 3 and 8.

Opponents to the settlement

No sooner was the Anglican Church established than it came under attack from two sources:

- those who adhered to the Catholic faith;
- those who wanted to 'purify' the Anglican Church from all its Catholic features.

KEY TERM

Recusants Those who refused to attend Anglican services. It was the duty of Justices of the Peace (JPs) to record their absence and to fine them for non-attendance. Within this group were a small minority who were prepared to carry their opposition to the religious settlement as far as rebellion against the Queen.

KEY PEOPLE

Purifiers, or 'Puritans' as they became known, mounted a series of challenges to the Elizabethan Church settlement. These ranged from demands for changes in clerical attire in the 1560s to attacks on the Church liturgy and structure in the 1570s and 1580s (see page 134 for a fuller definition).

Adherents to Catholicism. Those who adhered to the Catholic faith were not willing, in many cases, to be won over to Anglicanism. In 1570, Elizabeth was excommunicated and an irreconcilable Catholic minority emerged, supported by missionary priests from the Continent. The presence of these **recusants**, as they came to be known, created a considerable problem when their loyalty to Elizabeth was called into question. It was the task of government to decide how this Catholic opposition was to be treated; much hinged on the government's response.

Anglican 'purifiers'. The second source were those who wanted to **purify** the Anglican Church from all its Catholic features. The more extreme members of this group would have swept away the Church's liturgy and abolished its bishops. Here, too, the treatment of opponents would have lasting consequences. Opposition to the Elizabethan settlement is considered in Chapters 4 and 8.

Foreign policy issues

England was peculiarly linked to the European continent during Elizabeth's reign because of the religious divisions that afflicted Europe as well as England. They were important in two ways.

- England's previous friendship with Spain was affected by Philip II's commitment to Catholicism.
- England's support was sought by Protestant groups in France and the Netherlands.

Anglo-Spanish relations. Both the Papacy and Philip II of Spain wished to see the return of England to the Catholic faith. At various times they supported steps to remove Elizabeth from the throne, whether by rebellion, assassination or conquest. Thus Anglo-Spanish relations took on a new significance and, though war was delayed until 1585, it threatened to break out much earlier.

Protestants vs. Catholics. England's aid was also sought by Protestant elements in Europe. Throughout much of

Elizabeth's reign there were two power struggles in which Catholics were pitted against Protestants:

- the Dutch Revolt, which lasted from 1566 until 1609;
- the French Wars of Religion, which took place at varying intervals between 1562 and 1598.

Elizabeth and her ministers had to decide whether or not to lend England's support and, if so, where and in what form. Foreign policy is considered in Chapters 3 and 5.

The conduct of war

From 1585 until the end of the reign of Elizabeth, England was at war with Spain. When the Spanish Armada sailed in 1588, England faced the most serious threat of invasion since **the Norman Conquest of 1066**. Its defeat did not end the threat. English forces were deployed in France and the Netherlands; naval expeditions were sent to Spain and the Indies. Forces had to be raised and paid for, and choices had to be made about commanders and where forces were to be deployed. The war is the subject of Chapter 6.

Relations with Scotland and Ireland

Scotland. Relations with Scotland were complicated by the long-standing Scottish alliance with France. Fortunately for Elizabeth, Scotland experienced a Protestant reformation in 1559. By allying with the Protestant parties, England was able to secure the removal of French influence in 1560, but there was always the danger of a Catholic pro-French faction reasserting its authority and, with the arrival of Mary Queen of Scots in 1561, Scotland had a Catholic queen. Even after Mary's flight to England in 1568, the danger was not over. Furthermore, she was Elizabeth's presumed heir, in Catholic eyes the present legitimate queen, after 1570.

Ireland. England's relations with Ireland were aggravated by the Reformation. The Irish were generally unwilling to accept Protestantism, especially when it was associated with an alien ruling class. Conversely, the Papacy and Philip II saw Ireland as a possible bridgehead from which an invasion of England might be launched.

KEY EVENT

1066, the Norman Conquest It is perhaps worth noting that William the Conqueror's army at the Battle of Hastings in 1066 numbered some 5000 men. It was better equipped and trained than Harold's. The Duke of Parma's army, had it successfully crossed the Channel in 1588, would have included over 17,000 battle-hardened soldiers. To counter them, the English could only muster the inadequately trained and poorly armed militia. There was a French raid on the Solent in 1545 involving 200 French ships, but it was not intended as a full-scale invasion.

Foreign troops landed in Ireland in 1579 and 1601. Thus, Elizabeth was faced with a potentially rebellious province, liable to be invaded by her enemies. Relations with Scotland and Ireland are examined in Chapters 3, 5 and 6.

The operation of government

Elizabeth inherited a set of political institutions that worked both at national and local level, as we have seen. It was her task to make sure that the ministers she appointed at the centre advised her wisely, and that the Lords Lieutenant and Justices of the Peace (JPs) in the localities did her bidding. She needed to win the co-operation of her Parliaments, both for the passage of legislation and, especially after the outbreak of war, the voting of taxes. She needed, above all, to maintain her authority and retain her people's loyalty. Chapters 7 and 9 consider these questions.

The working of the economy

Sixteenth-century governments, like their successors, were expected to:

- provide employment and keep prices stable;
- maintain order at home and relieve poverty;
- encourage trade and promote economic progress;
- provide for the country's defence without burdensome taxes.

Elizabeth's ministers had to respond to these challenges. How well they did so is examined in Chapter 10.

Placing issues in context

While all these issues are addressed in the course of the book they cannot always be treated in isolation. Events at home are closely linked to events abroad. To get the feel of Elizabeth's reign it is necessary to see events in the order in which they happened, and policy decisions need to be placed into their context. Thus, before proceeding with the detailed analysis there follows a brief account of the reign.

SUMMARY OF THE MAIN EVENTS

In order to help you with a summary of the main events covered in this book, a chronological table is provided on pages 36 and 37. This table can be looked at in two ways.

- Read vertically, each column summarises landmarks in the particular area that it covers – for instance, religious developments or relations with Spain.
- Read horizontally, the table lists what is happening in each year of Elizabeth's reign.

This brings out the links between events, and underlines the varied concerns that came before the Queen and her ministers at any one time. In 1559, for instance, peace negotiations were being conducted with France, while the religious settlement was being put through Parliament. Once peace was signed there was less need to conciliate Catholic sentiment. At the risk of over-simplification, Elizabeth's reign can be seen to fall into three main periods:

- 1558–67
- 1568–85
- 1586–1603

Events and persons highlighted are referred to in the table, and are more fully explained elsewhere in the text (see index, pages 191–5).

1558–67

Establishing a system of government. For her first eight years in power, 1558–66, Elizabeth and her ministers were concerned with the recognition of her claim to the throne and the establishment of her system of government. A new religious settlement was needed, once the decision to break with Catholicism had been taken. Peace had to be made with France and Scotland. In brief, Elizabeth's accession was generally welcomed. She appointed a new group of Protestant Privy Councillors, while retaining some of Mary's Catholic peers. The first Parliament of her reign passed the Acts of Supremacy and Uniformity, making Elizabeth Supreme Governor of the Church of England and introducing a new Prayer Book, based on those of 1549 and 1552.

The international front. On the international front, peace was made with France at the Treaty of Cateau-Cambrésis in 1559, England having to surrender Calais. Meanwhile, in Scotland, a religious reformation began with the arrival of John Knox at Perth. This had enormous significance for Anglo-Scottish relations. By giving aid to the Protestant forces in Scotland in 1560, England was able to build up a pro-English party there and bring to an end the French presence through the Treaty of Edinburgh.

The accession of the Catholic Mary Queen of Scots in 1561 complicated the situation, but Mary's brief reign came to an unhappy end in 1567 and from then on, with brief exceptions, power rested with the Protestant pro-English faction, supported when necessary by English intervention.

English troops were also sent briefly to France to support the Protestant cause there in 1562 (the Treaty of Hampton Court) but had to be withdrawn in 1563 without achieving anything.

Marriage and succession. The two serious policy issues during these early years were the questions of Elizabeth's marriage and the succession. Her own position was unchallenged, and partly for that reason Elizabeth's ministers were very anxious to ensure that she should have an heir as soon as possible, and, if not, at least a suitable successor should be recognised. Elizabeth had to face challenges both from the Privy Council and from Parliament on these issues. She refused either to marry or to nominate a successor, but the argument did not go away.

1568–85

From 1568 to 1585, Elizabeth faced growing challenges to her authority, both at home and from overseas.

Challenges at home. Catholics proved to be an increasingly recalcitrant minority. Pope Pius IV ordered them not to attend Anglican services in 1564, thus ending the hope that they might gradually be absorbed into the established Church.

THE REIGN OF QUEEN ELIZABETH
CHRONOLOGY

Date	HOME Politics	Religion	Society/economy	ABROAD France	Spain/Netherlands	Scotland	Ireland
1558 Nov	Accession New Privy Council						
1559	First Parliament	Acts of Supremacy and Uniformity Parker Abp of Canterbury		Treaty of Cateau Cambrésis June death of Henry II (of France)		John Knox to Perth Reformation begins	
1560				Death of Francis II		English fleet to Leith	
1561						Arrival of Mary Queen of Scots	
1562		Jewel's Apology		Treaty of Hampton Court			
1563	Succession issue	39 Articles raised in Parliament	Act for Poor Statute of Artifices	Peace of Amboise			
1564				Treaty of Troyes			
1565						Mary marries Darnley	
1566	Succession and subsidy linked	Parker's *Advertisements*			Dutch Revolt begins	Birth of James I	O'Neill's rebellion
1567					Alva to Netherlands	Mary marries Bothwell.	
1568					Spanish treasure confiscated	Battle of Langside	
1569	Norfolk Plot Rebellion of Northern Earls					Mary to England	
1570		Elizabeth excommunicated					
1571		Ridolfi Plot Treasons Act					
1572		*Admonition to Parliament*		April Treaty of Blois August Massacre of St Bartholomew	Sea Beggars capture Brill and Flushing		
1573	Walsingham made Secretary						
1574							
1575					Spanish bankruptcy		
1576		Grindal Abp. of Canterbury			Pacification of Ghent		
1577		Suspension of Grindal			Renewed Spanish offensive Loans to Netherlands Drake's circumnavigation		
1578							
1579				Alencon's visit	Union of Arras	Esmé Stuart arrives	Fitzmaurice to Smerwick in Ireland
1580					Annexation of Portugal by Spain		Desmond's rebellion

THE REIGN OF QUEEN ELIZABETH
CHRONOLOGY

Date	HOME Politics	Religion	Society/economy	ABROAD France	Spain/Netherlands	Scotland	Ireland
1581		Laws vs. Catholics Recusancy fines raised		Alencon's visit			
1582					Alencon to Neths		
1583	Throckmorton Plot	Whitgift appointed Abp of Canterbury					
1584	Bond of Association			Treaty of Joinville	Assassination of W. the Silent		
1585	Parry Plot	Legislation vs. seminary priests		Loans to Henry of Navarre	Treaty of Nonsuch	Pension to James 1	
1586	Babington Plot					Treaty of Berwick	
1587	Feb. Execution of Mary Q. of Scot	Cope's Bill and Book			Raid on Cadiz Resignation of Leicester		
1588					First Spanish Armada		
1589				Aid to Henry IV	Raid on Santander		
1590					Naval raids		
1591							
1592							
1593		Execution of Barrow, Greenwood and Penry		Henry IV Catholic			
1594							
1595					Ralegh to Guiana		Outbreak of Irish Rebellion
1596	Robert Cecil Secretary			Treaty of Greenwich	Essex raid on Cadiz Second Spanish Armada		
1597	Essex Earl Marshal		Harvest failures		Exped. to Azores Third Spanish Armada		
1598	Death of Burghley	Act vs. Sectaries	Vagabonds Act Poor Law	Edict of Nantes Treaty of Vervins	Death of Philip II		Essex to Ireland
1599					Fourth Armada planned		Essex's return from Ireland
1601	Essex Rebellion Monopolies debate		Poor Law		Spanish troops land at Kinsale		
1602							Defeat of Irish rebels
1603	24 March Death of Elizabeth						
1604					Treaty of London		

In 1568, William Allen founded the first of several seminaries at Douai in the Netherlands. They were to train over 450 missionary priests who came to England during Elizabeth's reign. Also in 1568, Mary Queen of Scots lost her last battle in Scotland at Langside, and fled over the border. She then became the focus of various plots, initially to have her claim to the throne recognised and then, more seriously, to place her on the English throne.

In 1569, the first such plot – to marry Mary to the Duke of Norfolk – came to nothing, but was followed later that year by the Rebellion of the Northern Earls. This attracted some popular Catholic support and encouraged Pope Pius V to issue a Papal bull of excommunication against Elizabeth in 1570, depriving the Queen of her title to the throne, and absolving her subjects from their duty of obedience to her. This was a vital landmark in the reign. Not only did it encourage English Catholics to engage in plots against Elizabeth, it also gave official approval to the Catholic powers of Spain and France to support such plots. The subsequent Ridolfi, Throckmorton and Babington plots all received foreign backing.

The English government responded with a series of acts:

- the Treasons Act of 1571;
- the Act of 1581 designed to prevent the saying or hearing of Mass, entitled an Act to retain her Majesty's Subjects in their True Obedience;
- the Act of 1585, banishing seminary priests on pain of death, entitled an Act against Jesuits, seminary priests and such other like disobedient persons.

The Babington Plot in 1586 finally persuaded Elizabeth to bow to pressure from her ministers and Parliament to have Mary Queen of Scots executed. In February 1587, Mary went to the block.

Paradoxically it was during this period, too, that the Puritans mounted their strongest attack on the Anglican Church. In 1572, the first *Admonition to the Parliament* was printed, calling for an end to use of the Prayer Book and the abolition of bishops. This was only the first of a number of such attacks. In 1587, a Puritan Member of Parliament (MP), John Cope, introduced a bill into Parliament that would have implemented the changes called for in the *Admonition.*

Challenges from overseas. The international situation also became more threatening. In 1566, the Revolt of the Netherlands began. Spanish rule there was challenged and in 1567 the Duke of Alva arrived with an army of 10,000 well-trained Spanish soldiers. From this point until the end of Elizabeth's reign, this potential invasion force was stationed just across the Channel. Relations with Spain deteriorated for other reasons as well. In 1568, Elizabeth confiscated a ship-load of silver intended to pay Alva's army. A trade embargo (ban) followed. From 1568 onwards, English privateers began raiding Spain's colonies in the New World, with the covert approval of Elizabeth. In 1577, Sir Francis Drake began his historic voyage round the world, using the opportunity to prey on Spanish shipping on the Pacific coast of America. In 1579, Spanish troops landed at Smerwick in Ireland.

Both Philip II and Elizabeth were reluctant to go to war.

- Philip, because he had other commitments;
- Elizabeth, because of the expense and uncertainty about the outcome.

What finally turned the scales was the English decision to send aid to the Dutch rebels in 1585 under the Treaty of Nonsuch. Orders to prepare an Armada were given in October 1585.

These events brought the period of uneasy peace to an end, and thus began the final phase of Elizabeth's reign.

1586–1603

The last eighteen years of Elizabeth's reign were dominated by the Anglo-Spanish war. Operations are fully covered in Chapter 6. At this point all that will be done is to indicate their extent and scale. The war was fought at sea and on land.

The war at sea. At sea, the Spanish launched three Armadas – in 1588, 1596 and 1597. Of these, only the first presented a serious challenge. It included a fleet of 130 ships, which carried an army of 17,000 men. Had a junction with Parma's 17,000 troops taken place, England would have confronted an invasion force of 34,000 well-trained soldiers.

In response, the English mounted a series of raids on Spanish coasts, the most extensive of which, the attack on Cadiz in 1596, involved over 100 English ships and 15,000 men. There were several unsuccessful attempts to intercept Spanish silver fleets and privately conducted raids on Spanish shipping.

War on land. On land, English troops were sent to the Netherlands, Normandy and Brittany between 1585 and 1603. The largest contingent, however, was the army of 20,000 sent to subdue the Irish rebellion between 1598 and 1601.

This long period of warfare had important consequences at home.

- It caused unprecedented demands for money.
- It led to the more frequent summoning of Parliament.
- It caused the loss of traditional markets for England's cloth exports.
- Its conduct led to serious divisions within the Privy Council, made worse by the rivalry between the Earl of Essex and Robert Cecil. (It was this rivalry that led to the last protest against Elizabeth's rule, the Essex Rebellion of 1601 – fully covered in Chapter 7.)

OVERALL SUMMARY OF ELIZABETH'S REIGN

The reign of Elizabeth has attracted enormous historical interest, and continues to do so. This has partly been inspired by the Queen herself, whose personality and character continue to attract biographers. She remains one of the most remarkable rulers to have sat on the English throne.

Her achievements. There are also the positive achievements to record.

- The Spanish Armada was defeated, both by superior English sailing and navigation skills, and the weather.
- The Church of England was successfully re-established, to become a national institution, but also with its own distinctive blend of Protestant and Catholic beliefs.
- Scotland, the hereditary enemy, became a Protestant ally and its king the first of the Stuart dynasty to accede to the English throne.
- The first steps towards a national system of poor relief were taken.
- The challenges of a rising population and rising prices were successfully met.
- New markets were found for English cloth, and English traders moved into the Mediterranean, down the coast of Africa and across the Atlantic.
- The East India Company was founded in 1600, preparing the way for English expansion into the Far East.

Cultural development. Space does not allow for more than a bare reference to the cultural flowering that took place in literature and music in Elizabeth's reign. The plays of Christopher Marlowe and many of those by **William Shakespeare** were written and first performed in Elizabethan London. Tudor Church music reached a very high standard, with works by William Byrd and **Thomas Tallis** showing exceptional quality.

The problems. There was, inevitably, a downside to this record of achievement. The religious divisions created by the Reformation and the Counter Reformation persisted, and were aggravated by the international quarrels to which they were linked. Anti-Catholicism became a combustible element, always likely to explode when ignited by events like the Gunpowder Plot in 1605 or the Irish Rebellion in 1641. The Puritan threat to the Anglican Church was contained, but would take a new and radical form in the reign of Charles I.

KEY PEOPLE

William Shakespeare (1564–1616) England's greatest dramatist. He wrote at least 36 plays, including tragedies, comedies and history plays. There is little evidence to suggest that Elizabeth took a great interest in the stage, but she was sensitive to any threats to her position. The performance of *Richard II* in 1601 at the time of the Essex Rebellion was seen as a deliberate challenge to her authority.

Thomas Tallis (1510–85) Employed in the Chapel Royal from about 1542 onwards. He was one of the first composers to provide musical settings for Anglican services; and wrote a wide range of other church music and composition for the keyboard. He was an expert in counterpoint, writing one anthem for 40 different voices. He is best known for Tallis's canon.

The most damaging legacy of Elizabeth's reign was perhaps what happened in Ireland. The Irish Rebellion of 1595 was successfully suppressed, but only at the expense of worsening the relationship between rulers and ruled.

A golden age. When Queen Elizabeth II was crowned in 1952, comparisons were deliberately drawn with the reign of Elizabeth I and the hope expressed that Britain would once again enjoy a golden age.

It is one of the historian's tasks to explore the gap between myth and reality. How glorious was the reign of Gloriana, as Elizabeth became known? Was she a great queen, as **David Starkey**, one of her most recent biographers, would still claim in *Elizabeth I: Apprenticeship* (2000), or might she be more aptly entitled 'Elizabeth the Fortunate', as another recent historian, **Wallace MacCaffrey**, has argued in *Elizabeth I, War and Politics, 1588–1603* (1992)? The following chapters will, it is hoped, shed light on these and other questions.

PART II: THE REIGN OF ELIZABETH, 1558–1603

CHAPTER 3

The settlement of the kingdom, 1558–66

INTRODUCTION

Elizabeth was faced with several immediate tasks when she came to the throne in November 1558.

- She had to make sure that her claim to the throne was recognised by the ministers she inherited from Mary, by Parliament, by the people at large, and by the rulers of France and Spain.
- She had to choose her own Privy Councillors.
- She had to settle the affairs of the Church and appoint a new bench of bishops.
- She had to end war with France and with Scotland.
- Above all, she had to restore harmony to a realm that had witnessed three rebellions (Kett's Rebellion and the Cornish Rebellion in 1549, and Wyatt's Rebellion in 1554) in the space of eleven years.

In addition to these tasks, Elizabeth had to face demands from both her Councillors and Parliament that she should marry or, at the very least, nominate her successor. This chapter considers these challenges and how they were met.

ELIZABETH BECOMES QUEEN

Before she became queen

Elizabeth's claim to the throne was far from watertight (refer back to the genealogy chart in Chapter 1, page 6). The Papacy had never recognised Anne Boleyn's marriage to Henry VIII. This meant that Elizabeth was technically illegitimate in Catholic eyes. Her claim to the succession had been removed in 1536 by Henry VIII when Anne Boleyn was executed on the trumped-up grounds of her adultery. It was only restored in 1544 by the **Succession Act**, which placed Elizabeth third in line to the throne after Edward VI and Mary. Elizabeth's route to the throne had been tortuous, to say the least.

Conspiracies involving Elizabeth. Throughout Mary's reign, Elizabeth was kept under house arrest and spent two months in the Tower of London after Sir Thomas Wyatt's rebellion in 1554 (see Chapter 1, page 21). Elizabeth was interrogated by the Council and accused of complicity. She defended herself vigorously and Wyatt swore that she had not known about the rising in advance. Nothing could be proved and Elizabeth was moved to a house at Woodstock, where she was kept under careful supervision.

There was a further conspiracy in 1555–6 in which the French ambassador, Antoine de Noailles, plus members of Elizabeth's household, were involved. It came to nothing and, on Philip II of Spain's advice, Elizabeth herself was not questioned.

Attempts at finding a suitor. Philip also did his best to bring about a marriage between Elizabeth and Emmanuel Philibert, Prince of Piedmont, who was Philip's cousin. Elizabeth refused to consider the marriage, and at one point even contemplated flight to France. (To refresh your memory on 'the Spanish connection', you might like to refer back to the genealogy chart in Chapter 1, page 27.)

The impact of Mary's infertility. Once it became clear to Mary that she was not going to have a child (there had been two phantom pregnancies, in 1554 and 1557), she reluctantly recognised Elizabeth as her heir. However, this was only on the understanding (on Mary's side) that Elizabeth would keep England Catholic. In practice, this recognition was enough to ensure that, when Mary died on 17 November 1558, Elizabeth's accession was unchallenged, either by Catholics or Protestants.

Philip's approval of Elizabeth. At this stage, Philip II also welcomed Elizabeth's accession. Still engaged in a war with France, he much preferred Elizabeth to Mary Stuart, now married to the French Dauphin. At this time, Catholics had no rival around whom to rally, while Protestants were only too glad to welcome an English-born queen, whose Protestant sympathies they probably exaggerated.

Elizabeth's accession

Elizabeth received a tumultuous welcome when she first arrived in London, from **Hatfield Palace**. At her coronation in January 1559, a number of pageants were staged in her honour, two of which drew significant historical parallels.

- In one, her accession was likened to the uniting of the two houses of York and Lancaster, the marriage of Henry VII to Elizabeth of York, bringing unity to the realm.

Hatfield Palace
Granted to Elizabeth in 1550, it had formerly belonged to the Bishop of Ely. She returned to Hatfield in 1555 after her detention, first in the Tower and then at Woodstock, following Wyatt's Rebellion.

- In another, the Queen was compared to the Old Testament prophetess Deborah, who had inspired the Israelites to throw off the rule of the Canaanites and whose counsel had guided the people for the next 40 years.

Image of Elizabeth as queen. Elizabeth was to show herself as a past master in the field of public relations. Both at Court and on her royal progresses she played up to the image that was expected of her. Partly because she was so good at performing the role of queen, it has taxed the minds of historians and biographers to discover the real person beneath the surface. She left little, after she died, in the way of personal letters or diaries. Her views have often to be interpreted through her public speeches – for instance, to Parliament – her recorded remarks and her occasionally decisive interventions in policy. Some aspects of her personality and character are generally agreed, however.

Elizabeth's personality and character

No one disputes Elizabeth's intellectual ability. Her tutor, Roger Ascham, gave the following report of her to a friend when Elizabeth was sixteen:

> *The constitution of her mind is exempt from female weakness, and she is endowed with masculine power of application. No apprehension can be quicker than hers, no memory more retentive. French and Italian she speaks like English, Latin, with fluency, propriety and judgment; she also spoke Greek with me, frequently, willingly and moderately well …*

Her authority. Elizabeth's natural authority was clear from the start. Though only 25 years old when she came to the throne, she was clear in her own mind about the powers she enjoyed and had no doubts about using them when it seemed necessary.

Her indecision. All Elizabeth's biographers concede that she took a long time to make up her mind, and that she was reluctant to take decisions. Opinions differ as to whether this was the result of her native caution and an unwillingness to take needless risks, or whether it arose from a tendency to prevaricate (be misleading or evasive).

Her religious views. Finally, while Elizabeth's own religious views are hard to pin down, she had no wish to impose them on others. Unlike her father, who once presided at a heresy trial in person (that of **John Lambert** in 1538) or her sister, whose commitment to Catholicism necessarily entailed the extinction of heresy, Elizabeth did not see it as part of her role to 'make windows into men's hearts and secret thoughts' (the phrase comes from **Francis Bacon**). Elizabeth sought outward

---

KEY PEOPLE

John Lambert
Tried for heresy in 1538 because he had argued that since Christ had bodily ascended into heaven he could not, in a corporeal sense, be in the sacrament, though he could be 'figuratively, sacramentally or significantly'. Henry VIII, clad in white, presided at the trial and, anxious at the time to obtain the approval of the Catholic powers in Europe, ordered Lambert's death.

Francis Bacon
The younger son of Sir Nicholas Bacon, one of Elizabeth's Privy Councillors. He was a lawyer, a Member of Parliament and a scholar. He rose to prominence under James I.

The young Elizabeth.

Elizabeth in coronation robes.

conformity for the sake of good order, but would not persecute her subjects for false beliefs.

The influence of Elizabeth's gender

It is arguable whether Elizabeth suffered because she was a woman. The conventional view of a woman's place, whether in the home or the state, was that expressed by St Paul in his first letter to Timothy.

A woman must be a learner, listening quietly and with due submission. I do not permit a woman to be a teacher, nor must woman domineer over man; she should be quiet. For Adam was created first, and Eve afterwards; and it was not Adam who was deceived; it was the woman who, yielding to deception, fell into sin. Yet she will be saved through motherhood – if only women continue in faith, love and holiness, with a sober mind. (1 Timothy, 2, 12–15)

In 1558, the Scottish reformer **John Knox** published his *First Blast of the Trumpet against the Monstrous Regiment* [rule] *of Women*, which he condemned as 'monstriferous'. Knox was thinking primarily of Mary Tudor and Mary of Guise. He was therefore embarrassed when he found himself having to deal with Elizabeth. He was prepared to make an exception in her case, because God had raised her to restore the Gospel.

Elizabeth certainly had to overcome a strongly felt prejudice against women rulers. But she also exploited her femininity to the full. She wooed her courtiers such as the Earl of Leicester and Walter Ralegh.

KEY PERSON

John Knox Little is known of Knox's early life or parentage. He was born about 1514, trained for the priesthood at St Andrews and was converted to Protestantism by George Wishart. In 1547, he was arrested by the French at St Andrews and spent nineteen months as a slave in French galleys. In 1549, his release was secured by Protector Somerset and he returned to England. On Mary Tudor's accession he escaped to the Continent and spent most of the next five years in Geneva. Here he became a devoted admirer of John Calvin and the system of Church government he found there. In 1559, he returned to Scotland at the invitation of the Protestant Lords of the Congregation.

She could also call upon an extra degree of loyalty from her trusted servants, who were aware of her vulnerability. Perhaps most importantly, she was able to establish a rapport with her subjects:

> She meant it when she said late in life that she had kept the goodwill of her people as though they were all her husbands, 'for if they did not rest assured of some special love to them, they would not yield me such obedience' (cited in J.M. Levine, *Elizabeth I*, 1969).

Elizabeth's choice of ministers

Elizabeth swiftly surrounded herself with men she could trust.

- William Cecil, who had been overseer of her estates, and a member of the Privy Council under Protector Somerset and the Duke of Northumberland, became her Secretary.
- Cecil was joined by Sir Nicholas Bacon, Francis Russell (second Earl of Bedford), Sir Francis Knollys, William Parr, Sir Thomas Parry and Sir Edward Rogers (Thomas Cranmer's brother-in-law) in the Privy Council. All were Protestants.
- She retained some of Mary's officers, such as the Marquis of Winchester, and several Catholic peers, including the Earls of Arundel, Derby and Pembroke, on whose loyalty she could count.

Cecil's personal abilities, his phenomenal work rate, and the coincidence of his views with those of Elizabeth on fundamental issues, ensured that he became her chief adviser as well as the centre of her administration from the outset of her reign. When disagreements arose, as they did over the succession and Mary Queen of Scots, the relationship survived.

The settlement of religion

Reversing Mary's settlement. Elizabeth's own inclinations and the Protestant sympathies of her Councillors made a reversal of Mary's religious settlement inevitable. This is not the place to discuss the likely success of Mary's attempts to restore Catholicism had she lived longer. Suffice to say that, while she had created a loyal and devoted episcopate, and at Oxford University sowed the seeds that would bring many Catholic priests back to England to face death in the 1570s, in 1558 the heresy trials and the loss of Calais created a climate of opinion in which a return to some form of Protestantism was the only realistic policy.

The form of Elizabeth's settlement. There has been much debate about why the Elizabethan settlement took the form it did. **J.E. Neale** argues that a Protestant-inclined House of Commons pushed Elizabeth further than she meant to go. **Norman L. Jones** argues that it was opposition from the Catholic bishops and lay peers in the House of Lords whose resistance had to be overcome and conciliated where possible.

KEY DEBATE

Neale vs. Jones
J.E. Neale's views are expressed at length in the first part of his *Elizabeth and Her Parliaments*, published in 1953. Norman Jones, in an important essay 'Elizabeth's first year' (included in *The Reign of Elizabeth I* ed. Christopher Haigh, 1984), succeeds in showing the strength of Catholic opposition and finds little evidence of the group of committed Protestant MPs that Neale claimed to have discovered.

Progress towards Protestantism. The chain of events shows a continuous, if at times interrupted, progress to a more Protestant Church. Elizabeth began by suspending the heresy laws in December 1558, and releasing those awaiting trial for heresy. Catholic rites and ceremonies were to continue 'until consultation may be had by Parliament'.

Rejection of transubstantiation. Elizabeth made plain her own rejection of transubstantiation at Mass on Christmas Day, when she ordered that the Host (the elements of bread and wine) should not be elevated, and left the service when the celebrant, Bishop Owen Oglethorpe, refused to obey her instructions. When Parliament assembled on 25 January 1559, Elizabeth was met by a procession of monks at Westminster Abbey with lighted tapers, incense and holy water. She cried: 'Away with these torches, we see very well.' The monks then had to endure a sermon from **Richard Cox**, a returned Protestant exile. In it, he attacked the monks for their part in the heresy persecutions and urged the Queen to destroy idolatry.

A new bill. Several bills were introduced into the House of Commons, which were combined into a single bill on 21 February. This bill would have made Elizabeth head of the English Church and provided a Protestant form of worship. Though it passed the Commons, the Lords forced the bill into a committee of fifteen, eight of whom were Catholic sympathisers. The changes in worship were removed, and the peers refused to endorse the royal supremacy, although they admitted Elizabeth's right to take it. The Lords also refused to repeal the heresy laws. In what might seem a bid for toleration rather than Protestant ascendancy, the Commons then voted that 'no persons shall be punished for using the religion used in King Edward's last year'.

The Parliamentary recess. Rather than dissolve Parliament with so little achieved, Elizabeth prorogued it over Holy Week and Easter. During the recess, a **Disputation** was held in Westminster Abbey. Three propositions were listed for debate.

- The first of these asserted that 'it was contrary to the Word of God to use a tongue unknown to the people in worship'.
- The second asserted that 'every Church had authority to change its ceremonies, so long as the changes were edifying'.
- The third asserted that 'it cannot be proved by the Word of God, that there is in the mass offered up a sacrifice propitiatory for the quick and the dead'.

The Catholics were hardly given a fair opportunity to state their case. Indeed, in the end, they refused to continue the debate. Two Catholic

Dr Richard Cox
One of Edward VI's tutors. A committed Protestant, he escaped to Frankfurt in 1555, where he clashed violently with John Knox. Cox was committed to the kind of Anglicanism associated with Cranmer and the Prayer Book, whereas Knox was a full-blown Calvinist. On his return to England in 1558, Cox lent his support to the Acts of Supremacy and Uniformity, and he was rewarded for his loyalty in becoming Bishop of Ely.

KEY TERM

Disputation This took place during the Parliamentary recess on 31 March and 3 April 1559. It was designed to force the Catholic bishops into opposition, while depriving them of the right to claim that they had been silenced without a hearing. The terms of the debate were framed by the Protestants, and after two days the Catholics refused to participate further.

bishops were subsequently arrested and charged with disobedience to common authority.

The Acts of Supremacy and Uniformity, 1559

When Parliament reconvened it considered two separate bills:

- the Act of Supremacy;
- the Act of Uniformity.

Act of Supremacy, 1559. This made Elizabeth Supreme Governor of the Church, rather than Supreme Head. John Jewel, later Bishop of Salisbury, wrote commendingly: '[Elizabeth] seriously maintains that this honour is due to Christ alone, and cannot belong to any human being soever.' In practice, Elizabeth had as much power over the Church as her predecessors, certainly so far as appointments and the enforcement of the religious settlement were concerned. Unlike her father, however, she did not pronounce on matters of doctrine.

Additionally, the Act:

- repealed the heresy laws;
- guaranteed freedom of worship for Protestants, in case the Act of Uniformity failed;
- provided for Communion in both kinds – that is, the laity would receive the wine as well as the bread. It was Catholic practice for only the clergy to receive the wine.

The Act passed the House of Commons easily. In the House of Lords it was opposed by all the bishops who attended and by one Catholic layman.

Act of Uniformity, 1559. The new Act of Uniformity was modelled on the Second Prayer Book of Edward VI (1552). As a concession to Catholics, both sentences used at the administration of Communion were now to be used (see Chapter 1, page 18). The Act required the following.

(see Chapter 1, page 18)

KEY TERM

Iconoclasm The deliberate destruction of images, stained glass windows, wall paintings and so on, because they are seen as idolatrous (to be worshipped).

- The Prayer Book was to be used in all churches.
- There were penalties for those refusing to use it.
- Everyone was to attend church on Sundays and holy days.
- Those who did not might be fined one shilling per Sunday.
- The ornaments of the church and the dress of the clergy were to be the same as in the second year of Edward VI's reign 'until other order shall be taken therein by the Queen's Majesty'. This gave Elizabeth a certain discretion where church furnishings and vestments were concerned, and discouraged the **iconoclasm** that had marked the final years of Edward VI's reign.

The Act had a relatively easy passage through the Commons. However, it was opposed by nine bishops and nine temporal peers in the House of Lords. Twenty-one temporal peers voted in favour. Had the two Catholic bishops detained in the Tower of London been free to vote, and had the Abbot of Westminster and the Bishop of St Asaph also been present, the Act would have been defeated.

There were further changes. The few monasteries and chantries Mary had restored were dissolved, and their assets transferred to the Crown. Elizabeth also restored **First Fruits and Tenths** to the Crown.

Decisions regarding the settlement. When Parliament was dissolved in May 1559, the main features of the Elizabethan religious settlement had been decided. Because of its repudiation of the Papacy, it could never be acceptable to orthodox Catholics. However, it might satisfy those who attached little importance to the Papal supremacy. Equally, it would not satisfy those English people who looked to Calvin's **Geneva** as the model of a Christian commonwealth.

On the positive side, the Anglican Church retained its traditional structure of bishops, priests and deacons. It also had its own Prayer Book, written in Cranmer's felicitous English.

Of Mary's bishops, only one – Anthony Kitchin of Llandaff, who had been made a bishop under Henry VIII – was prepared to accept the Elizabethan settlement. All those who refused were deprived of their posts and met with varying treatment. None suffered the deaths endured by Hugh Latimer, Nicholas Ridley, John Hooper and Thomas Cranmer.

- Nicholas Heath, Archbishop of York, was allowed to retire to his house at Chobham after three years in the Tower.
- Edmund Bonner was committed to the Marshalsea Prison, where he died in 1569.
- Owen Oglethorpe, Ralph Bayne and Cuthbert Tunstall all died in 1559.
- Others served various terms of imprisonment or were placed under house arrest.

It is impossible to know exactly how many of the Marian clergy refused to accept the new order. **John Guy** has discovered that 400 of them were deprived or resigned between 1559 and 1564. He estimates that 200 of these went because they refused to accept the Acts of Supremacy and Uniformity (*Tudor England*, 1997). As there were between 8000 and 9000 parishes in England and Wales, the great majority must have conformed.

Royal injunctions

The main features of the Elizabethan settlement were contained in the Acts of Supremacy and Uniformity. Many details still needed to be decided, however, and the settlement had to be enforced.

In 1559, Cecil drafted injunctions to deal with some of the contentious issues still outstanding. The injunctions covered matters such as images and relics, which were attacked, but not forbidden.

- The Bible was to be placed in all churches, without restriction on who might read it.
- There was to be a pulpit and an alms chest in every church.
- Clergy might marry, but only with the consent of their bishop and two JPs.
- Clergy were to wear the **surplice**.
- Altars might be replaced by Communion tables, if the minister and church wardens so wished.

Enforcing the injunctions. A visitation to enforce the settlement and the injunctions took place in the summer and autumn of 1559. As a result, most of the Marian (Catholic) additions to church furnishings were removed and English parish churches reverted to the plainness of the Edwardian years. Where Catholic sympathies were strong, as in Lancashire and Yorkshire, this process took a good deal longer.

Elizabeth clearly had a problem in finding a loyal and effective bench of bishops. She made a good start with Matthew Parker, a scholarly don from Cambridge, who became her first Archbishop of Canterbury. Paradoxically, her most diligent clerics were those who had left England for the sake of their own consciences during Mary's reign but with whose advanced Protestant views Elizabeth had least sympathy. Only time would tell whether the new Anglican Church would be able to claim an authenticity of its own, with an effective leadership and its own body of devoted members.

MARRIAGE AND SUCCESSION

Marriage

Elizabeth's foreign policy, her possible suitors and the succession were all closely linked. Her marriage might determine England's relationship to Europe, as it most obviously had done in Mary's case. Also, it would be a useful diplomatic bargaining counter to be used with potential suitors. The naming of a successor to the throne might have similar repercussions.

In the eyes of her Councillors, and to her early Parliaments, England's security depended upon Elizabeth contracting a suitable marriage. If that could not be managed, then at least a successor should be nominated. What they feared above all was that, in the event of her untimely death, the realm would be plunged into strife between rival contenders. Elizabeth, on the other hand, was always reluctant to commit herself in either respect.

Many reasons have been advanced for **Elizabeth's unwillingness to marry**. In a speech to her first Parliament she reputedly said:

> *And to me it shall be a full satisfaction both for the memorial of my name, and for my glory also, if when I shall let my last breath, it be engraven upon my Marble Tombe,* Here lyeth ELIZABETH, *which reigned a Virgin, and died a Virgin.*

Psychologically, Elizabeth may have recoiled from marriage for the following reasons.

- She was aware of the fate her mother had suffered.
- At the age of eight, she was made aware of the execution of Catherine Howard, Henry VIII's fifth wife.
- At the age of fifteen, she had experienced the amorous attentions of Thomas Seymour (uncle to Edward VI), which were described by one recent biographer, **David Starkey**, as bordering on child abuse.
- It is possible that she was physically incapable of having sexual relations, but no firm evidence of this has been found.
- More plausible is the suggestion that she enjoyed power and was unwilling to share it with a consort.

A Scottish emissary, James Melville, alleged that in 1564 Elizabeth had said to him: 'I am resolved never to marry, if I be not therefore necessitated by the Queen my sister's [Mary Queen of Scots] harsh behaviour toward me.' Melville reportedly replied: 'Your Majesty thinks that if you were married you would be but Queen of England, and now you are both king and queen!' (C. Haigh).

Whatever her motives, Elizabeth refused all opportunities for matrimony, though it was not until the 1580s that the impossibility of her marrying was finally recognised.

The succession

Elizabeth's refusal to name an heir had a more specific explanation. In a message to the House of Commons in 1559, responding to a suggestion that she name Mary Queen of Scots as her successor, she said:

KEY DEBATE

Elizabeth's unwillingness to marry The authenticity of this speech has been questioned. It dates from William Camden's history of Elizabeth's reign which was not published until 1615. Whatever her views in 1559, Elizabeth rejoiced in the title of Virgin Queen in later years.

When my sister Mary was Queen, what prayers were made by many to see me placed in her seat ... Now then, if the affections of the people grow faint ... what may we look for when evil-minded men shall have a foreign prince appointed the certain successor to the crown? In how great a danger shall I be ... when a prince so powerful, so near unto me, shall be declared my successor? Assuredly, if my successor were known to the world, I would never esteem my state to be safe.

Potential successors and suitors. Elizabeth's advisers were convinced that England's security rested on there being an assured successor. However, Elizabeth saw the absence of a known successor as the best guarantee of her security (see the Tudors and the Stuarts genealogy chart, which appears in Chapter 1, page 6).

In the first eight years of Elizabeth's reign these issues played a significant part in her foreign and domestic policy. In 1559, Philip II made a tentative offer of marriage. Clearly he could not marry a heretic, as Elizabeth pointed out, but she did not dismiss the offer outright and was clearly anxious to retain Philip's friendship.

Among other foreign suitors to be considered was the Archduke Charles, Philip II's cousin and heir to the Holy Roman Emperor, Ferdinand. Charles IX of France was also briefly in the frame.

In 1560, **Robert Dudley**, future Earl of Leicester, appeared to be a likely candidate, and he retained Elizabeth's affection until the end of his life. But the death of his first wife in suspicious circumstances put paid to any thought of marriage, so far as Elizabeth was concerned. The marriage was also strongly opposed by Cecil, and a potential rivalry between the two men was thus avoided.

Parliament and succession. The issue of the succession came up twice in Parliament, in 1563 and 1566. Elizabeth suffered an attack of smallpox in 1562, and the Commons implored her to name a successor in the next session of Parliament. They renewed their plea in 1566, and even tried to tie the voting of subsidy to Elizabeth's compliance in this respect. But she refused Parliament's wishes in magisterial terms: 'It is monstrous that the feet should direct the head.' From then on, her wishes were unwillingly respected, and even on her deathbed she hesitated to name her successor.

FOREIGN POLICY

Developments in France and Scotland

Foreign policy during these years saw a significant development in Anglo-Scottish relations and the first unsuccessful attempt to intervene in Europe.

Extricating England from war. Elizabeth's first task was to extricate England from the disastrous war with France. This was achieved through the Treaty of Cateau Cambrésis, signed on 1 April 1559. Under its terms, England surrendered Calais for eight years. With hindsight, the loss of Calais was almost certainly to England's benefit. It turned the eyes of the English to the east and across the Atlantic. At the time it seemed an affront that must be reversed.

A postscript to the Treaty of Cateau Cambrésis was the death of the French King, Henry II, at a joust on 30 June to celebrate the peace. His eye was pierced by a lance. This left his wife, Catherine de Medici, as the unpopular Regent of France. None of her surviving children were yet adults. Francis II (married to Mary Queen of Scots) who succeeded Henry II was just fifteen years old.

Instability in France. Henry's death led to a period of great instability in France, as the great noble families jostled for control of the monarchy. The situation was worsened by the rise of the **Huguenots**, the French Protestants, as Calvin's influence spread from Geneva.

The Scottish situation. Equally significant was the progress of the Scottish reformation. Protestantism had begun to make some headway there and two Protestant martyrs, Patrick Hamilton and George Wishart, had been burned at the stake in 1528 and 1546 respectively.

- In 1546, a Protestant minority had seized the town of St Andrews after the murder of Cardinal David Beaton and held it for a year.
- In 1557, a group of Protestant Lords signed a Covenant 'to apply our whole power, our substance and our very lives to establishing the reformed faith'.
- On 11 May 1559, John Knox, who had recently returned from Geneva, preached an inflammatory sermon in St John's Kirk, Perth. This provoked a wave of iconoclasm in neighbouring religious houses and an outbreak of similar protests throughout the lowlands of Scotland.
- On 21 October 1559, Protestant Lords 'suspended' the regency of Mary of Guise. The arrival of French troops to restore her emphasised the link that now existed between Catholicism and foreign rule.

KEY TERM

Huguenot The origin of this term is uncertain. It may have come from one of the early leaders, Besancon Hugues. Alternatively, it may be a corruption of the German word *eidgenossen*, meaning 'those bound together'. It was generally used to describe all French Protestants.

English intervention

This presented an opportunity that was not lost on Cecil. He persuaded the Privy Council to send English assistance to the Protestant forces in Scotland. Elizabeth was reluctant to agree. Cecil asked to be removed from responsibility for Scottish affairs if she would not comply with his wishes. Elizabeth gave way.

Aid was covert to begin with, but in December an English fleet was sent up to the Firth of Forth where it divided French forces in Fife from those stationed at Leith. Though a military expedition sent north in March 1560 failed to capture Leith, the French now also faced problems nearer home.

- On 15 March, Huguenots raised the first sign of resistance to the French monarchy at the Tumult of Amboise.
- On 11 June, Mary of Guise died.

On 6 July, the Treaty of Edinburgh was signed, providing for the evacuation of all French troops and the recognition of the Protestant faith in Scotland. This was a remarkable *coup* for English foreign policy, and a turning point in Anglo-Scottish relations.

When Mary Queen of Scots arrived in Scotland in 1561 it was to find an **Anglophile** group in power. And though the Auld Alliance with France was not yet dead, provided there was a Catholic party in Scotland, it was no longer as threatening.

Intervention in France

Perhaps because of the success of English intervention in Scotland, when an apparently similar opportunity arose in France, Elizabeth showed no reluctance to intervene.

Involvement of the Huguenots. In March 1562, a group of Huguenots were massacred at Vassy, on the instruction of the Duke of Guise. This provoked a second wave of Huguenot opposition. One English observer, Henry Killigrew, wrote from Le Havre: 'It lies in [Elizabeth's] hands to banish idolatry from France.' Meanwhile, the English ambassador in Paris, Nicholas Throckmorton, urged Cecil to 'animate and solicit the Princes Protestant with speed by all means you can, not to suffer the Protestants in this realm to be suppressed'.

Elizabeth had no great sympathy for the Protestant cause in Europe, but saw the opportunity to recover Calais. By the Treaty of Hampton Court signed between Elizabeth and the Prince of Condé on 19 March 1563, 6000 troops were sent to aid the Huguenots with a loan of £30,000.

Le Havre and Dieppe were to be held as pledges for the restoration of Calais. In the event, Condé was defeated at Dreux, plague broke out at Le Havre and the war ended at the Peace of Amboise. The French had united against the English; Le Havre was besieged and had to be abandoned.

England's claim to Calais was finally forfeited by the Treaty of Troyes, signed in April 1564. English intervention thus brought no benefit, and Elizabeth took the lesson to heart. She would need much more persuading to lend her support to Protestants abroad in future.

The effect on Anglo-Spanish relations. Partly because of English support for the Huguenots, Anglo-Spanish relations deteriorated. Margaret of Parma, Philip II's Regent in the Netherlands, imposed a ban on the export of English cloth to Antwerp and all other Flemish ports. Fortunately, English merchants found another outlet at Emden, and the ban was lifted in January 1565. At the time it did no serious damage, but it demonstrated the important link between England's commercial interests and relations with Spain.

Strengths and weaknesses in the early years of Elizabeth's reign

Elizabeth's position undoubtedly strengthened at home and abroad in the first eight years of her reign. Her claim to the throne was universally accepted after the Treaty of Cateau Cambrésis. The religious settlement met with tacit consent, if not active approval. The Privy Council, headed by Cecil, worked effectively. But there were clouds on the horizon.

- The arrival of Mary Queen of Scots in Scotland in August 1561 meant that there was now a Catholic successor to Elizabeth close at hand.
- The outbreak of unrest in the Spanish Netherlands in 1566 sparked a struggle in an area of crucial strategic importance to England that would last throughout the rest of Elizabeth's reign.
- Most importantly, the religious divisions between Catholic and Protestant were to become more acute, both in England and on the Continent.

SUMMARY QUESTIONS

1 Attempt a character sketch of Elizabeth I on the basis of her actions between 1558 and 1566.
2 What were the Catholic and what were the Protestant features of the Acts of Supremacy and Uniformity?
3 What important initiatives did Elizabeth and her ministers take in foreign policy between 1558 and 1566?

ASSESSMENT: GENERAL PRINCIPLES

INTRODUCTION

You are likely to be faced with a variety of questions, depending on the examination board for whose papers you have been prepared, and the level – AS or A2 – of the examination. Currently there are three main variants:

- essays in the form of a single question, or statement for discussion;
- structured questions that are divided into two sub-questions;
- questions based on documentary material, which may be drawn from original sources and from the writings of later historians.

Advice is given at this point on how to tackle essay questions in general. In later chapters you will find examples of structured questions and document-based questions.

PRINCIPLES OF WRITING GOOD HISTORY ESSAYS

The principles of any good history essay remain the same, whether you are writing an answer to an AS or A2 level question. The differences lie in the kind of question you may be asked and in the depth of knowledge you may reasonably be expected to have.

These principles may be summarised as follows.

- Your answer should be aimed directly at the question asked.
- It will be given a structure that corresponds to the question.
- It will demonstrate a sound grasp of relevant factual knowledge. Accuracy is the first requirement of the historian. Any argument you put forward needs to be supported by evidence.
- Your answer will be expressed in clear and grammatically correct English.

These principles are easy to state, but less easy to practise. It should help you to observe them if you go through a regular procedure in preparing and writing your answers.

SUGGESTED PROCEDURE FOR WRITING GOOD ESSAYS

Step 1
Read carefully. Read the question carefully and underline the key words that indicate what kind of question it is. Does it ask you to describe,

explain, assess, compare or discuss? If you are not quite sure, try rephrasing the question in your own words.

Examples of essay questions. The following examples on the reign of Elizabeth I illustrate each kind of essay question.

1 What were the main features of the Elizabethan religious settlement reached in 1559?

2 Explain why England went to war with Spain in 1585.

3 How serious a threat was Mary Queen of Scots to Queen Elizabeth?

4 Compare the threat posed to the Elizabethan Church by Catholics and Puritans.

5 'The Elizabethan religious settlement was designed to satisfy all shades of opinion.' Discuss.

Step 2

Plan your answer. It is vital that the structure of your plan fits the question. With practice, it may be enough to jot down your headings for each section of your essay. Initially it is good to plan the essay paragraph by paragraph. It is also a good idea to list the kind of evidence you intend to cite to support your arguments. If you are writing the essay under exam conditions, you will not have time to do more than remind yourself of what needs to be included.

Step 3

Express yourself clearly. When writing your answer try to express yourself clearly and simply. Short words, and sentences, are better than long ones.

Obey the rules of grammar and punctuation. Watch out for the use of commas and apostrophes. Make sure that sentences have a main verb.

Spelling. Try to avoid misspelling of words that history students ought to know – for example, monastery, Parliament, government.

Step 4

Again, read carefully. Read through what you have written with care.

Before attempting any question, whether for an assignment or for an examination, it is essential that you have a sound grasp of the relevant factual background – otherwise your answer will be either woolly or wrong.

CHECKING YOUR UNDERSTANDING

As a way of checking how well you have understood and grasped the main features of Elizabeth's reign and the issues that they raise, summary questions have been included at the end of each chapter (with the exception of Chapter 2). It would be sensible to look at them first.

Specimen questions have also been included from Chapter 3 onwards. While in each case there is a suggested approach, this should not be viewed as a model answer. Rather, it is an attempt to ensure that the answer has a framework relevant to the question and has the right kind of factual support.

These principles will not be re-stated in advance of every specimen question, but should be applied each time you attempt an answer.

AS QUESTION

Why were Elizabeth's ministers so anxious for her to marry, or at least to nominate a successor, and why did Elizabeth refuse to do either between 1558 and 1566?

Suggested approach to answering this question
This is a four-part question that requires you to give reasons under each part. Each part should be given equal weight.

Reasons for Elizabeth to marry
- A marriage would provide an heir to the throne.
- The rule of a woman on her own was unnatural. Elizabeth needed a consort.
- A diplomatic marriage might provide a useful ally – for example, the Archduke Charles, Charles IX of France.

Reasons for Elizabeth to nominate a successor
- In the event of Elizabeth's death there would be a struggle for the succession – the lesson of the Wars of the Roses, Lady Jane Grey and Wyatt's Rebellion. Elizabeth's attack of smallpox in 1562 made the issue more urgent.
- There was fear that, if Elizabeth did not nominate another heir, Mary Queen of Scots would claim the throne in her own right, saddling England with another foreign Catholic ruler.

Elizabeth's reasons not to marry
There are a variety of possibilities.

- She might have disliked the idea of marriage on principle (her experiences with Thomas Seymour).
- If she could not marry Robert Dudley, she would not marry anybody.
- She did not want to share power with anyone else.
- She felt her position would be strengthened if she remained a Virgin Queen.
- By remaining single she could use her marriage potential as a bargaining power.

Elizabeth's refusal to nominate her successor
- A successor would become a focus around whom opposition could rally (as had happened with Elizabeth and Mary Tudor).
- The succession was a matter of Elizabeth's prerogative.
- Elizabeth was reluctant to take any irrevocable step.
- There was no suitable candidate, though she would not exclude Mary Queen of Scots.

A2 QUESTION

What main considerations determined the religious settlement reached in 1559?

Suggested approach to answering this question
The key word in this question is 'considerations'. You need to decide in your own mind what the word means in this context. You will also have to show your familiarity with the details of the religious settlement if you are to produce a convincing answer.

Considerations. Begin your answer by discussing the considerations. These might include:

- the political and religious situation in 1558–9;
- Elizabeth's own religious views and those of her ministers;
- the views of each House of Parliament;
- the international situation.

The political situation in 1558 saw the return to Catholicism associated with the burning of heretics, an unpopular foreign marriage and an unsuccessful war. A return to Protestantism would be popular.

The religious situation was very complicated because of all the changes of the previous three reigns. There were committed Catholics and committed Protestants, and all shades of opinion in between. Thus the Church should be as inclusive as possible.

Elizabeth believed in the royal supremacy, in a modified form. She did not share the Catholic belief in transubstantiation (see her opposition to the elevation of the Host on Christmas Day, 1558, Chapter 3, page 48). Her chief minister, William Cecil, shared her moderate Protestant views. However, there were several Catholic peers in the Privy Council.

The House of Lords still contained Catholic bishops and several Catholic peers and would oppose too Protestant a settlement.

England was still at war with France when the first legislation was introduced and so could not afford to antagonise Spain.

How are these considerations reflected in the settlement? The political and religious situation demanded a return to the royal supremacy, and Elizabeth was ready to see a return to the Second Prayer Book of Edward VI. Opposition from the House of Lords forced changes in the first uniformity bill (February, 1559).

Parliament was thus prorogued, disputations were held over Holy Week, and two Catholic bishops were imprisoned. By the time Parliament reconvened, the peace of Cateau Cambrésis had been signed and a more Protestant settlement could now be forced through.

The Act of Supremacy recognised Elizabeth as Supreme Governor, not Supreme Head, which was a concession to Catholic sensibilities. In the Act of Uniformity, both 1549 and 1552 sentences at Communion services were permitted. Ornaments and dress of clergy were to revert to what they had previously been in 1549. Use of the Prayer Book was made compulsory and there were limited fines (one shilling per Sunday) for non-attendance. The Act was opposed by nine bishops and nine peers in the House of Lords, and got through by 21 to eighteen votes.

Conclusion. Thus the settlement reflected Elizabeth's religious views, modified by conservative opposition in the House of Lords, and the need to embrace as wide a spectrum of opinion as possible.

CHAPTER 4

Catholic threats to Elizabeth's security ✓

INTRODUCTION

The arrival of Mary Queen of Scots in England in 1568, the Rebellion of the Northern Earls in 1569 and the excommunication of Elizabeth by Pope Pius V in 1570 signalled a complete change in Elizabeth's position. In Catholic eyes, she was now a heretic and a **usurper**. Mary Queen of Scots was an accessible Catholic successor, with a better claim to the throne than Elizabeth. With the arrival of seminary and Jesuit priests trained at Douai (in the Netherlands), Rheims (in France), Valladolid (in Spain) and Rome (in Italy), the Catholic community in England was given sustenance and encouragement, ensuring its survival.

KEY TERM

Usurper Someone who wrongfully takes another's position.

The threat to Elizabeth's security arising from within her realm was made more serious because of the possibility of external support. Both King Philip II of Spain and the Guise party in France were ready, albeit at different times, to lend their support to plots to remove the Queen and to invade her kingdom. Once it became clear that Elizabeth would not change her religious allegiance, the Papacy gave its approval to rebellion, conspiracy and foreign conquest.

A series of plots gave substance to the government's fears. Indeed, between 1571 and 1603, both lay and ordained Catholics faced imprisonment and execution. Mary Queen of Scots, the focus of most of the plots, suffered increasingly harsh treatment, culminating in her execution in February 1587.

This chapter considers the nature of the threats and the government's response to them. Among the issues raised are:

- whether the dangers to Elizabeth were as great as they were perceived to be;
- where responsibility lay for the policies adopted;
- whether they were justified.

THE THREAT FROM MARY QUEEN OF SCOTS: SCOTLAND ✓

Mary's early life

Mary was born on 8 December 1542, just at the moment when English armies were about to invade and occupy the Scottish Lowlands (see Chapter 1, page 23). For her own security she was moved first to Stirling Castle, and then to Inchmaholm Priory on the Lake of Menteith.

In 1548, following the rough wooing, Mary was sent to France where she spent the next twelve years. She enjoyed life at the French court, and her education rivalled that of Elizabeth's. Mary, too, learned six languages. She was raised as a Catholic and, while never as single-minded in her beliefs as Mary Tudor, her personal faith was equally strong.

In April 1558, Mary was married to the Dauphin, Francis (heir to the French throne) in Notre Dame Cathedral in Paris. By a secret agreement between Mary and Henry II, her claim to the English throne was recognised in preference to that of Elizabeth's, whom the French still regarded as illegitimate. Mary began to display her title to the English throne on her coat of arms.

At the age of nineteen, a succession of deaths propelled Mary into a situation for which she was quite unprepared.

- First, Henry II of France died in June 1559.
- He was followed by Mary of Guise, Regent in Scotland, in June 1560.
- Then, worst of all from Mary's point of view, the Dauphin, now Francis II, died in December of the same year.

Mary's mother-in-law, the formidable Catherine de Medici, made it clear that there was no home for Mary in France. So, in August 1561, Mary arrived in Scotland. Nothing had prepared her for the reception by the Protestant Lords and John Knox, which she now had to face. Mary made no secret of her Catholicism and, while she was prepared to tolerate Protestant worship in Scotland, she insisted on Catholic services in her own chapel. This uneasy compromise worked for a time, and had Mary married more discreetly she might have survived.

Mary's marriages to Darnley and Bothwell

Mary was married twice more:

- first, to Henry Darnley
- then, to the Earl of Bothwell.

Mary Queen of Scots as a girl.

Henry Darnley. In July 1565, Mary made what seemed at the time an unwise choice that turned out disastrously. She chose as her consort

Henry Darnley, a handsome but feckless and unprincipled young man. He was bound to arouse Elizabeth's distrust because of his indirect, but none the less authentic, claim to the English throne (see the Tudor and Stuart dynasties genealogy chart, which appears in Chapter 1, page 6). Darnley's one significant accomplishment was to father Mary's only child, James, who was born in 1566. On 9 March 1566, while Mary was still pregnant, Darnley orchestrated the murder, in her presence, of her Italian Secretary, **David Rizzio**. Darnley had wrongly suspected Rizzio of having a liaison with his wife. Mary never forgave her husband for this, though for the sake of outward appearances they did not formally separate.

The Earl of Bothwell. Some of Mary's supporters, including the **Earl of Bothwell**, plotted to get rid of Darnley. Indeed, on 9 February 1567, Darnley was found strangled in the garden of his house in Edinburgh. The house had also been blown up. Mary's subsequent actions sealed her fate in Scotland. On 19 April, Bothwell secured the approval of 28 fellow nobles and prelates to his projected marriage to Mary. They all signed a document known as the Ainslie Bond promising to promote the marriage. On 24 April, and with 800 men, Bothwell intercepted Mary on her way back to Edinburgh from Stirling, where she had been visiting her infant son. Mary was persuaded to accompany Bothwell to Dunbar Castle. Whether she was raped there by Bothwell or whether she simply agreed to marrying him is still disputed. There could be no doubt about her next actions.

- On 3 May 1567, Bothwell was divorced from his wife, Lady Jean Gordon.
- On 12 May 1567, Mary created him Duke of Orkney.
- On 15 May 1567, Mary married Bothwell according to Protestant rites. For the rest of their brief life together (the marriage lasted only a month), she showed him every favour.

Mary's conduct continued to be the subject of much speculation. In 1571, Elizabeth released the so-called Casket letters between Mary and Bothwell. If genuine, these prove Mary's complicity in Darnley's murder. Much doubt surrounds the authenticity of the letters, but the rapidity of Mary's marriage to Bothwell, the chief suspect, even though he was formally acquitted by the Scottish Parliament, made Mary guilty by association.

Mary's defeat and flight to England

The evidence against Mary regarding Darnley's murder was sufficiently damning to lose her the support of both Catholic and Protestant nobles.

Her surrender and imprisonment. On 15 June 1567, there was a trial of strength at Carberry Hill, just outside Edinburgh. Bothwell rode off to

David Rizzio (or Riccio) A young adventurer who had joined Mary's service from that of the Savoy ambassador.

Earl of Bothwell James Hepburn, Earl of Bothwell, was a Protestant supporter of Mary of Guise. He had met Mary Queen of Scots in 1560 in Paris and, after various adventures, returned to Scotland in 1564. He was a forceful man, ready to take any initiative that would advance his prospects.

ADVANCED HISTORY HEINEMANN

raise support. Meanwhile, Mary surrendered herself to her opponents, expecting that there would now be a full investigation of Darnley's murder. Instead, she was imprisoned on an island on Lochleven.

Her resignation. In isolation, and suffering from the effects of a miscarriage, she was induced to sign a letter of resignation. On 29 July 1567, the infant James was crowned king of Scotland, and Mary's half-brother, the Earl of Moray, became regent. Bothwell escaped to Scandinavia, only to be imprisoned by the King of Denmark. He died, insane, seven years later.

Her bid for the throne again. Mary made one more bid for the Scottish throne. On 2 May 1568, she escaped from Lochleven and managed to raise another army. She reached Hamilton, near Glasgow, and assembled an army of about 6000 men. On 13 May, this force was defeated by Moray's troops at the Battle of Langside. This time, Mary evaded capture.

Her flight to England. In desperation, Mary took refuge in England, from where she hoped her cousin Elizabeth would aid her return to Scotland.

THE THREAT FROM MARY IN ENGLAND ✓

Elizabeth's prisoner

For the next nineteen years, Mary was Elizabeth's unwanted guest and prisoner. The story of their relationship has often been told and has, on the surface, all the elements of romantic drama. The contrast between the women has attracted countless authors and provides the basis for one very good play, *Mary Stuart*, by the German eighteenth-century author, Friedrich Schiller.

- Mary was beautiful, headstrong, devout and thrice-married. (She also had an estranged son.)
- Elizabeth was plain (although striking), worldly wise and a spinster.

Conflict between the two. But, even without this clash of personalities, conflict between the two queens was inevitable. So long as Mary was alive, she provided an alternative focus around whom Catholic opposition to Elizabeth could rally. Furthermore, Mary never abandoned her hopes of returning to Scotland and succeeding Elizabeth as Queen of England in the fullness of time. Fatally for Mary, her more militant supporters were not prepared to wait this long, even if this entailed internal rebellion, foreign invasion and, in the final resort, Elizabeth's assassination.

It is hardly surprising that the Privy Council and both Houses of Parliament frequently pressed Elizabeth to put her rival to death – as they did in 1572, 1576, 1585 and 1586. While Elizabeth had little sympathy for her cousin, she was reluctant to shed the blood of a relative, or subject a fellow monarch to the humiliation of a public trial. Mary's death would be irrevocable and might simply replace one potential Catholic heir with another – as, in fact, it did in 1587 when Philip II took Mary's place. Elizabeth's natural caution and innate distaste for such a ruthless act kept Mary alive much longer than most of Elizabeth's advisers thought prudent, but it may well have been the wisest policy.

The Rebellion of the Northern Earls, 1569

The first overt challenge to Elizabeth's authority came in 1569. It arose from a complicated series of manoeuvres at the English court. One possible answer to the threat posed by Mary was to see her married to a trustworthy Englishman. The Earl of Leicester and several other courtiers suggested the **Duke of Norfolk** for this role. Elizabeth got wind of the suggestion, and Norfolk was summoned to Court and lodged in the Tower. Catholic supporters of the marriage included:

- the Earl of Westmorland (who was married to Norfolk's sister, Jane; she urged her husband to act);
- the Earl of Northumberland.

When they were also summoned to Court they refused to go, and instead summoned their tenants to arms. Their aims were to see Mary married to a Catholic and recognised as heir to the throne. They had a force of 4000 foot soldiers and 1500 horses, and marched unimpeded as far south as Selby in Yorkshire.

The work of the rebels. Catholic services were restored wherever these rebels went. In Durham Cathedral, English bibles and prayer books were destroyed. The Earl of Sussex, President of the Council of the North, chased the rebel army north as it disintegrated. Westmorland and Northumberland fled to Scotland. Northumberland was sold back to the English by the Scots for £2000 and was executed in 1572, while Westmorland reached the Netherlands. He died in exile in 1601 and his estates were forfeited.

The government's response. Meanwhile, the Privy Council raised an army of 12,000 men who arrived in the north after the main rebellion had disintegrated. There was a brief flurry of opposition in Cumbria, led by Leonard Dacre in February 1570, which resulted in the only pitched battle of the Rebellion.

The punishment. Though no further threat existed, Elizabeth insisted on harsh punishment. Examples were to be made of every village represented

Duke of Norfolk
Thomas Howard, fourth Duke of Norfolk, belonged to a distinguished old family. His grandfather had been one of Henry VIII's chief ministers. Though nominally a Protestant, he may have had secret Catholic sympathies.

The Duke of Norfolk.

in the rising, and 700 rebels were to be summarily hanged. Local commanders moderated these figures, but it seems that about 450 were executed, compared with the 90 executed after Wyatt's Rebellion (see Chapter 1, page 21).

Elizabeth's excommunication

One of the most serious consequences of the Northern Rising was the Papal response to it. By this time, Pius V had lost all hope of Elizabeth's return to the Catholic faith. When he received an appeal from the Northern Earls in February 1570 (the appeal had been despatched in November 1569), he determined to put Papal authority behind the Rebellion. At the end of the month he signed the Papal Bull *Regnans in Excelsis*. It began with a ringing assertion of Papal authority:

> *[The Pope] alone hath [God] made Prince over all People and all Kingdoms, to pick up, destroy, scatter, consume, plant and build; that he may preserve his faithful people … in the Unity of the Spirit and present them spotless and unblamable to their Saviour.*

The Bull continued with a savage attack on Elizabeth, 'the pretended Queen of England, the Servant of Wickedness', accusing her of reducing 'the Said Kingdom into a miserable and ruinous condition, which was so lately reclaimed to the Catholic Faith and a thriving condition'. In consequence,

> *We do … declare the aforesaid Elizabeth as being an Heretick and a Favourer of Hereticks, and her Adherents in the matters aforesaid, to have incurred the Sentence of **Excommunication** and to be cut off from the Unity of the Body of Christ.*

The Bull concluded by depriving Elizabeth of her title to the throne and, most damagingly, absolving the Nobility, People and Subjects of the said Kingdom of 'all manner of Duty of Dominion, Allegiance and Obedience'. Furthermore, they were 'not to obey her or her Orders, Mandates and Laws: and those which shall do the contrary, We do include them in the like Sentence of **Anathema**'.

The significance of the Bull. It is hard to exaggerate the significance of this Bull. It placed devout Catholics in an impossible position. They could not at the same time be loyal to the Pope and to the Queen. When the first Jesuit Mission to England was planned in 1580, its leaders sought guidance on whether Catholics who obeyed the Queen in civil matters were really obliged to consider themselves under anathema, and were given the answer that the Queen's Catholic subjects might continue to recognise her until means were found to overthrow her. It was not much of a concession.

For her part, Elizabeth tried initially to play down the impact of the Bull. She was still anxious to retain the allegiance of her Catholic subjects. In a public statement, read by Lord Keeper Sir Nicholas Bacon in the summer of 1570, she said that she wished all her loving subjects to understand that,

> As long as they shall openly continue in the observation of her laws and shall not wilfully and manifestly break them by their open actions, her Majesty's meaning is not to have any of them molested by an inquisition or examination of their consciences in causes of religion; but will accept and entreat them as her good and obedient subjects.

Parliament was not inclined to be so tolerant. When it met in 1571, all members had to take, for the first time, the Oath of Supremacy. It also passed a Treasons Act, which made it treasonable to write or signify that Elizabeth was not lawfully queen, thereby making spoken words treason. However, Elizabeth still rejected a rider attached to the bill, which would have excluded Mary from the succession.

Conspiracies against Elizabeth ✓

While the great majority of Elizabeth's Catholic subjects did continue to observe her laws, a small number sought her overthrow. There were at least five more conspiracies that had as their objective the replacement of Elizabeth on the English throne by Mary Queen of Scots – two of these aimed for her assassination. The key people involved in these conspiracies and assassination attempts included:

- **Roberto Ridolfi**
- William Allen and Robert Parsons
- the Duke of Guise
- William Parry
- Anthony Babington

Mary may not have been the chief conspirator, but she *was* the catalyst. In the secret world of conspiracy, penetrated by double agents, these are muddy waters. But enough hard evidence has survived to implicate the main principals at least in condoning and supporting the plotters' intentions, as the remainder of this section shows.

The Ridolfi Plot

The first plot, hatched in 1571, seems to have been the brainchild of a Florentine banker, resident in London, called Roberto Ridolfi.

The plan. Ridolfi's intention was to secure Mary's release, have her married to the Duke of Norfolk and brought to the throne. This was to

Roberto Ridolfi
Born into a Florentine banking family. He came to London as a business agent in 1555. His ardent Catholicism drew him into the Northern Rebellion, and its failure convinced him of the need for foreign support.

be achieved with the aid of Spanish troops, brought over from the Netherlands under the command of the Duke of Alva. Ridolfi visited Brussels, Rome and Madrid. But, while his intentions were approved, Alva never gave his support to the plot.

The outcome. The government got wind of the plot through Mary's ambassador, John Leslie, former Bishop of Ross, who revealed all he knew under interrogation. The involvement of Mary and Norfolk was clear. In January 1572, Norfolk was tried and sentenced to death. His execution, demanded by Parliament, took place in June. Ridolfi was still abroad when the plot was discovered and thus escaped arrest.

The coming of seminary priests

Following the death of Norfolk there was a lull in conspiratorial activity, but towards the end of the decade there was a revival. This was due partly to:

- changes in the international scene;
- the actions of two politically-minded Catholic priests, William Allen and Robert Parsons.

The original plan. In 1568, William Allen founded a seminary at Douai in the Netherlands. By 1576, it had 120 students. Allen's intention was to keep the Catholic faith alive in England by sending in trained priests who would minister in secret to the Catholic faithful. In 1575, an English college was opened in Rome, under direction of the **Jesuit order**, with the same purpose in mind. Both Allen and Parsons would have seen keeping the Catholic faith alive as their first priority, but each was prepared to use political means to that end. In his book *A True, Sincere and Modest Defence of English Catholics* (published in 1584 in response to a publication by Burghley entitled *The Execution of Justice*, justifying putting priests and their helpers to death on the grounds of treason, rather than religion), Allen explicitly justified the Bull *Regnans in Excelsis* and its implications: 'Therefore let no man marvel that in case of heresy the Sovereign loseth his superiority and right over his people and kingdom ...' In 1580 the first Jesuit priests, **Edmund Campion** and **Robert Parsons** arrived.

The outcome. In response to the threat posed by seminary priests, as they were dubbed, two further acts were passed:

- an Act to Retain the Queen's Majesty's Subjects in their True Obedience;
- an Act against Seditious Words and Rumours.

Cardinal William Allen.

The terms of the Act to Retain the Queen's Majesty's Subjects in their True Obedience were as follows:

- Any persons attempting to 'absolve, persuade or withdraw' any of Elizabeth's subjects from their 'natural obedience', or *'for that intent'* (these words were inserted at Elizabeth's insistence) to leave the Church of England for the Church of Rome were to be adjudged as traitors. (It would be treason to persuade someone to become a Catholic, but not treason to be one.)
- Saying Mass was now punishable by a fine of 200 **marks** and a year in gaol; hearing Mass was punishable by a fine of 100 marks.
- The fines for non-attendance at church were raised from one shilling for each Sunday missed to £20 per month.

Under the second Act seditious words now carried the death penalty for a second offence.

Further consequences. The government embarked on a determined campaign to track down the seminary priests. The first four of them were subsequently put to death that year. As the treatment of Catholics became harsher, so the removal of Elizabeth, in the eyes of Allen and Parsons at any rate, became more necessary.

In 1579, Esmé Stuart, Sieur d'Aubigny and a cousin of James VI, arrived in Scotland from France. He won the confidence of James, now thirteen, who created him Duke of Lennox. In 1581, the pro-English Regent Morton was arrested, put on trial for his part in Darnley's murder, and executed. Lennox converted to Protestantism to win the support of the Scottish nobility but attracted Catholic support through his willingness to see Mary restored. A Jesuit, Father William Holt, was sent to Scotland to spy on the situation. He reported cautiously, but plans went ahead. They involved Lennox, Mendoza (the Spanish ambassador in London), the Duke of Guise in France, Mary (now in Sheffield Castle) and de Tassis, the Spanish ambassador in France.

The Throckmorton Conspiracy. In April 1582, another Jesuit, William Creighton, arrived in Paris with news of Lennox's readiness to co-operate in a design to restore Catholicism and liberate the Queen of Scotland. He would need an army of 20,000 men plus 20,000 crowns. Robert Parsons assured de Tassis that the English Catholics in the north would rally to the support of an invading Scottish army. The Duke of Guise proposed to make a diversionary landing on the Sussex coast.

The result. Before the plot could get off the ground, a Protestant *coup d'état*, led by the Earls of Angus, Gowrie and Mar on 22 August 1582 seized James, and Lennox was forced to retire to France. But this did not end the conspiracy.

Edmund Campion An Oxford graduate of great intellectual ability. He had doubts about the legitimacy of the Church of England, went to Douai in 1572 and joined the Jesuit order in 1573. He became Professor of Rhetoric at Prague University in 1574 before coming to England in 1580. He saw his main purpose as ministering to English Catholics and keeping the Catholic faith alive. He was captured in July 1581, refused an offer of preferment in the Anglican Church, and was hung, drawn and quartered (the death for traitors) in December.

Robert Parsons Also an Oxford graduate, he went to study medicine at Padua in 1575 but joined the Jesuit movement instead. After Campion's arrest he escaped from England and spent the rest of his life abroad. Together with William Allen he took the view that Elizabeth must be deposed and supported the plots to remove her.

A plan to assassinate Queen Elizabeth ✓

In 1583, the Duke of Guise turned his attention to the possibility of assassinating Elizabeth, not for the first time. The Catholic Church, if not the Pope in person, had already given its approval to this weapon. In 1580, the Cardinal of Como, who was Papal Secretary of State at the time, conveyed the official feeling on the possible assassination of Elizabeth in a reply to Cardinal Sega, the Papal Nuncio in Madrid:

> *Since that guilty woman of England rules over two such noble kingdoms of Christendom and is the cause of so much injury to the Catholic faith, and loss of so many million souls, there is no doubt that whosoever sends her out of the world with pious intention of doing God service, not only does not sin but gains merit, especially having regard to the sentence pronounced against her by Pius V of noble memory.*

The details. Walsingham was aware that something was afoot, but he did not get to know the details until one of Mary's chief agents, Francis Throckmorton, was arrested in November 1583. Under torture he revealed what he knew, including the involvement of the Spanish ambassador Mendoza, who was consequently expelled. This event precipitated the formation in England of the **Bond of Association**. The signatories bound themselves to avenge any attempt on the life of their most gracious sovereign lady Queen Elizabeth, never to accept any pretended successor 'by whom or for whom any such detestable act shall be attempted or committed', and 'to prosecute such person or persons to the death and to take the uttermost revenge on them'. In other words, should Elizabeth be assassinated, Mary Stuart would be killed whether she had been implicated or not. Elizabeth denied all knowledge of the Bond until it was shown to her. It was superseded by the Act for the Queen's safety passed in 1585.

The results. The Bond of Association was watered down in the Act for the Queen's Safety, passed in 1585, which provided that only after an investigation of the facts might vengeance be pursued after invasion, rebellion or a plot against the state. Should Elizabeth be killed, her 'pretended successor' – in other words, Mary Queen of Scots – would be disabled from the succession. This Act was accompanied by one directed specifically at the Jesuits and priests trained abroad, entitled an Act against Jesuits, seminary priests and such other like disobedient persons. Any Catholic priest ordained after 1559 was given 40 days to leave the kingdom. Should he be discovered in England after that date he would be deemed guilty of treason. It has been calculated that under the legislation of 1571, 1581 and 1585, some 250 Catholics were put to death or died in captivity, among them 180 priests. (For further discussion of this question, see Chapter 8.)

KEY TERMS

Mark The equivalent of two-thirds of a pound; 200 marks would be equivalent to £14,400 in today's currency.

Bond of Association Drafted by the Privy Council in the autumn of 1584, following the Throckmorton Plot and the assassination of William the Silent. Thousands of people signed the pledge to revenge themselves on Mary Queen of Scots in the event of Elizabeth's untimely death, whether Mary had been involved or not.

There were plans for two further assassination attempts on Queen Elizabeth:

- the Parry Plot
- the Babington Plot.

The Parry Plot

The first, the so-called Parry Plot, is still a mystery.

What happened. William Parry had been employed by Lord Burghley as a secret service agent, to try to penetrate foreign plots against the Queen. He returned to England in 1584 and made a full report on what he had found. He was returned to Parliament later in the year, but in February 1585 was accused by Sir Edmund Neville of suggesting a scheme to kill the Queen 'as she rode abroad to take the air'.

The outcome. When interrogated, Parry admitted the facts but insisted he had been trying to uncover further designs against her life. He was not believed and was sentenced to death. A letter to Parry from the Cardinal of Como was also discovered in which Parry was urged to 'Put therefore your most holy and honourable purposes in execution, and attend your safety'.

The Babington Plot

The final plot against Elizabeth was the one that brought about Mary's execution.

In 1585, Walsingham managed to introduce an agent, Gilbert Gifford, into Mary's confidence. A chain of communication was established between Mary and the French embassy, which Walsingham was able to tap (obtain information from). Every letter from and to Mary was concealed in beer barrels to which Walsingham's men had access.

In July 1586, Anthony Babington, a Catholic gentleman with connections at the French embassy, suggested to Mary another conspiracy to place her on the throne. However, this time Babington offered to despatch the usurper and claimed to have six Catholic friends 'who for the zeal they bear unto the Catholic cause and your Majesty's service will undertake that tragical execution'.

The outcome. Mary replied, fatally, to the suggestion, including the phrase: 'Then shall it be time to set the six gentlemen to work, taking order upon the accomplishment of their design …'

The trial. In August, Walsingham pounced. He now had all the evidence he needed. Mary was tried at Fotheringhay Castle before thirty six

William Parry
The career of Parry is still a mystery. He was employed by Burghley and Walsingham to spy on Catholic exiles. He became an MP in 1584, and attracted hostile attention by attacking the bill against Jesuit and seminary priests in December 1584. He was pardoned for this indiscretion but was then accused of plotting to kill the Queen. One view is that he had outlived his usefulness and was therefore expendable. He may also have been a double agent, pretending to work for the government, while secretly planning the Queen's assassination.

commissioners. She denied all knowledge of the plot, but the evidence of the Babington correspondence was supported by her two secretaries, Claude Nau and Gilbert Curle.

The verdict. As with most Tudor treason trials, the verdict was a foregone conclusion. Mary was found guilty as 'not only accessory and privy to the conspiracy but also an imaginer and compass of her majesty's destruction'. But Mary's demeanour and resolution in her defence made a lasting impact. On 29 October 1586, Parliament was summoned to lend its weight to the verdict. It duly gave its approval and added a fervent plea for Mary's execution.

The sentence. Elizabeth reserved for herself the right to impose sentence. She delayed for nearly four months, seeking to anticipate foreign reaction.

This picture was painted after Mary's death and was intended to show her as a Catholic martyr.

When reassured that Mary's son, James, would not change his policy – he was now receiving a pension from England – to save his mother's life, Elizabeth finally made up her mind. She may also have been influenced by rumours sweeping the country that Spanish troops had landed in Wales and that Mary had escaped. On 1 February 1587, she signed the death warrant. The Privy Council at once put in train the arrangements for Mary's execution. Elizabeth made one final effort to distance herself from the deed. She wrote to Mary's jailer, Sir Amyas Paulet, suggesting that Mary be privately killed. To his lasting credit, Paulet replied:

> God forbid that I should make so foul a shipwreck of my conscience, or leave so great a blot on my posterity, to shed blood without law or warrant.

The execution. The execution finally took place in the Great Hall at Fotheringhay Castle on Wednesday 8 February 1587. Elizabeth reacted with fury when she heard the news. It is impossible to say whether this was feigned or genuine. She refused to speak to Cecil for a month, and Davison, who had sent the warrant, was imprisoned in the Tower for eighteen months. Elizabeth, as much as Mary, was a victim of circumstance, though her fate was not such a cruel one.

CONTINUING PERSECUTION OF CATHOLICS

Persecution of Catholics did not cease with Mary's death. If anything, the situation became worse as the international climate darkened. Mary had already announced her intention to bequeath her claim to the English throne to Philip II. In a letter dated 20 May 1586, she wrote to Mendoza that she was about to 'cede and grant by **Will** my right to the succession to this crown to the king, your master'. Allen, now a cardinal in Rome, urged him to accept.

Priests continued to be hunted down and those aiding them were also at risk.

- Some 88 Catholics were put to death between 1590 and 1603.
- Of these, 53 were priests.
- The remaining 35 were lay people.

In 1593, the Privy Council introduced a very severe measure against Catholics, which, if passed, would have taken children aged seven away from recusant parents and had them brought up as Protestants. On this occasion, Parliament showed itself more lenient than the Privy Council. Indeed, the only significant addition to the legislation against Catholics

KEY DOCUMENT

Mary's will This has never been found, but Mary's letter was intercepted by English agents, and passed on to James VI.

was the provision that those convicted of recusancy were to reside within five miles of their usual dwelling place.

It needs to be remembered that during these years Philip II launched three Armadas against England – in 1588, 1596 and 1597. A fourth was planned in 1599. The treatment of Catholics in Elizabeth's reign inevitably reflected the international context in which it was conducted.

SUMMARY QUESTIONS

1 Describe the events leading to Mary Queen of Scots' flight to England, and explain the failure of her rule.

2 Summarise the various plots and intrigues which led to the execution of Mary Queen of Scots in 1587.

3 How and why did Catholics become a threat to Elizabeth?

AS QUESTION IN THE STYLE OF OCR

How serious a threat did Mary Queen of Scots pose to Queen Elizabeth?

Suggested approach to answering this question

The key words in the question are 'how serious'. You are asked to gauge the seriousness of the threat posed by Mary Queen of Scots. This means defining the nature of the threat, analysing the degree of support on which Mary could rely, and examining the likelihood of success of the various plots and conspiracies in which Mary was involved.

The nature of the threat
- Mary was a threat to Elizabeth because she had as good a claim to the English throne as Elizabeth.
- She could also trace her descent back to Henry VII, and her marriage to Darnley strengthened that claim.
- After the Papal Bull of Excommunication in 1570, in Catholic eyes Mary was the legitimate queen, with Elizabeth the heretic and usurper.
- Mary was a willing participant in the plots to place her on the English throne.

The strength of Mary's supporters
- Mary forfeited the support of her Protestant Scottish subjects through her indiscretions and support for Catholicism.
- After 1568 she was a virtual prisoner in England.

- On the other hand, she could rely on some support from the English Catholic community – for example, the Earls of Northumberland and Westmoreland in 1569 – and those prepared to take parts in plots against Elizabeth, such as Babington.
- There was also the possibility of foreign support from the Papacy, the Guise party in France and Philip II in Spain.

The likelihood of success
This can best be judged by examining the particular plots and conspiracies in which Mary was involved. You should mention:

- the Northern Rebellion, 1569;
- the Ridolfi, Throckmorton and Babington plots between 1571 and 1586;
- the threats to assassinate Elizabeth made by men such as William Parry.

Factors to take into account might include:

- the lukewarmness of foreign support;
- the high quality of Walsingham's intelligence service.

On the other hand, many of Elizabeth's contemporaries were assassinated, notably Henry III and William the Silent. Certainly Elizabeth's ministers and Parliament were convinced of the seriousness of the threat.

CHAPTER 5

Foreign policy, 1566–85

INTRODUCTION

The second half of the sixteenth century was dominated in western Europe by the clash between Catholics and Protestants. As the Catholic Church revived, so it sought to bring back to the fold its lost members and to combat heresy wherever it was found. Protestants in Germany, England, Scotland and France sought the right to practise their various faiths and, where they were in a majority, to ban Catholic worship.

We have already seen the clash at work in England. Throughout most of Elizabeth's reign it was happening in the Netherlands, France and Scotland. Elizabeth's excommunication in 1570 might seem to have placed England firmly in the Protestant camp. This is indeed how it seemed to committed Protestants like the Earl of Leicester and Sir Francis Walsingham. But other issues were at stake as well as religion.

- In the Netherlands, the struggle was a rebellion against a lawful ruler.
- The French Wars of Religion were also clashes between rival noble factions for control of the monarchy.

Thus, while there was a Protestant interest to be served, it was frequently mixed with other motives. Neither Elizabeth nor Philip II of Spain viewed the national interest exclusively in terms of the fate of their co-religionists. For both, war was a burdensome expense they would have preferred to avoid.

This chapter considers the complicated European context in which foreign policy had to be conducted. It seeks to explain why England, which had been the ally of Spain in 1558 and the enemy of France and Scotland, had become the ally of France in 1572 and the patron of James VI in 1585. Also it:

- outlines the slow and uneven progress towards war with Spain;
- examines where responsibility for the final breach lay;
- asks what the war was ultimately about.

THE EUROPEAN CONTEXT

Revolt of the Netherlands

The Netherlands, also known as the Low Countries, comprised most of present-day Belgium and Holland. They were part of Philip II's inheritance when he succeeded Charles V in 1556 as King of Spain. Thereafter, they came under Spanish rule.

- Trouble began in 1566, when there was a wave of protest at ecclesiastical reforms that threatened **vested interests** and the spread of Calvinism. Violence broke out in many cities, and Philip decided on tough action.
- In 1567, the Duke of Alva arrived with an army of 10,000 Spanish infantry, soon to be joined by many other recruits. From this point until 1609 there was a large Spanish military presence in the Netherlands.

The Revolt lasted another 40 years. It went through many phases. When Spanish fortunes were at their lowest, after the army mutinied in 1576, it looked as though the whole area might win its independence. At other times, as in the 1580s, the Duke of Parma might well have crushed all resistance, had he not been faced with other distractions. For our purpose, the main landmark to note is the **Pacification of Ghent**, agreed to in 1577, and its subsequent breakdown between 1578 and 1579. Thereafter the Netherlands were divided into two halves:

- the Catholic Union of Arras in the south;
- the Calvinist-dominated Union of Utrecht in the north.

The Catholic south tolerated a Spanish presence and it was to the Union of Utrecht that Elizabeth now turned her support, such as it was.

French Wars of Religion

The French Wars of Religion began in 1562 and continued intermittently until 1598. On one side were the Catholics; on the other side were the Calvinists. The degree of toleration to be accorded to the Huguenots (see Chapter 3, page 54) was always at stake and was the subject of each peace treaty. But the wars were also between rival factions.

- On the Catholic side was the Guise family.
- On the Protestant side were nobles such as the Prince of Condé and the kings of Navarre.

Holding the balance was a group of nobles known as the *politiques* whose aim was to find an acceptable compromise. So far as Elizabeth was concerned, the danger to be feared was a victory for the Guise faction, which was not only linked to Mary Queen of Scots but was also ultra-Catholic. Thus, Elizabeth could not ignore the power struggles in France any more than those taking place in the Netherlands.

One landmark needs to be noted. In August 1572, the infamous Massacre of St Bartholomew took place. It was so-called because it began on the eve of the saint's day. The origins of the episode are still obscure, but this much is known.

- A plot to assassinate Admiral Coligny, a notable Huguenot, failed. However, he *was* wounded.
- Possibly to cover up the Crown's involvement in the crime, Catherine de Medici persuaded her son, Charles IX, to order an attack on all Huguenots in the city of Paris. Many were there to celebrate the marriage of Catherine's daughter Margaret to Henry of Navarre, a leading Protestant. Some 3000 Huguenots in Paris alone were put to the sword.
- Estimates for those killed elsewhere in France vary between 500 and 20,000.

Pope Gregory XIII struck a medal to celebrate the event. Needless to say, Protestant opinion was appalled.

- In France it led to a further outbreak of warfare.
- In England it sowed suspicion of the French alliance.
- More generally, the massacre raised the ideological temperature, and deepened the rift between Catholics and Protestants.

Scotland

After the departure of Mary Queen of Scots in 1567, there was always the danger that a pro-Catholic faction would seize control of the young James VI. Such a danger surfaced twice:

- first in 1570;
- then in 1579.

1570. In 1570, the Regent Moray, trusted by Elizabeth, was assassinated by members of the Hamilton clan. A struggle between the King's men and Mary's supporters ensued. It was ended only when Elizabeth sent troops and artillery to Edinburgh in 1573.

1579. Morton, one of the Protestant Scottish lords responsible for Darnley's murder, now became Regent. But his rule came to an end in 1579 with the arrival of Esmé Stuart. Morton was put on trial for Darnley's murder and executed in 1581. As we have seen in

Chapter 4, page 70, Esmé Stuart was prepared to support the Throckmorton conspiracy.

Thus, Elizabeth was inevitably drawn into the internal affairs of the Netherlands, France and Scotland. In each area there was a Catholic–Protestant divide that impinged on Elizabeth's own security, and on her relations with England's old ally, Spain.

Trade and warfare in the New World

There was a further source of friction arising out of England's growing interest in the New World. Under a Papal ruling of 1493, the world that was being explored by the Portuguese navigator Vasco da Gama and the Italian explorer Christopher Columbus was divided into two spheres of interest:

- the western half going to Spain;
- the eastern half going to Portugal.

The dividing line was to run from North Pole to South Pole, 100 leagues west of the Cape Verde islands (1 league is approximately 5.5 kilometres).

In 1494, under the Treaty of Tordesillas signed by Spain and Portugal, this line was moved 370 leagues west. It meant that the American continent, apart from present-day Brazil, was now reserved to Spain for conquest and settlement. Other European countries never recognised the validity of the treaty, but so far as the Spanish were concerned any non-Spanish traders or colonists were regarded as trespassers. When men such as **John Hawkins** began to trade with the Spanish colonies they were certain to encounter official resistance. From there it was a short step to raids on Spanish shipping, which, in Spanish eyes, were no better than piracy.

England's convoluted diplomacy between 1566 and 1585 was thus conducted in a rapidly shifting context in which religious allegiances sometimes cut across, and sometimes coincided with, national interests.

THE EUROPEAN CONTEXT: ENGLISH POLICY

Main considerations

Elizabeth, in so far as one can interpret her goals from her actions, was concerned above all with her own security on the throne. This explains:

- her savage repression of the Rebellion of the Northern Earls (see Chapter 4, page 66);
- her reluctance to get involved in a war she might not win.

John Hawkins
He played many parts in England's sea-faring history. He was initially a trader and was the first Englishman to carry slaves to the New World in 1562–3, selling his cargoes in the Spanish West Indies, contrary to official Spanish policy. This led to the attack mounted on his ships in 1569 at San Juan de Ulloa. In 1577 Hawkins succeeded his father-in-law, Benjamin Gonson, as Treasurer of the Navy, and did much to improve the quality and design of English fighting ships prior to the Armada in 1588. He played a leading role in the defeat of the Armada, commanding one of the English squadrons, and was an important influence on English naval policy thereafter, until his death on his final expedition to the New World in 1595.

KEY TERM

Calvinism This
form of
Protestantism
broke much more
decisively than
mainstream
Anglicanism with
the Catholic
Church in terms of
its form of worship
and system of
Church
government (see
Chapter 8).

She was also permanently short of money, and war was the quickest route
to insolvency and dependence on Parliament. Whether she felt any
concern for the Protestant cause in Europe seems less likely. She had
little sympathy for **Calvinism** – be it in Scotland, France or the
Netherlands.

Elizabeth was naturally reluctant to support rebels against fellow
monarchs. After her first intervention in France in 1562–3, she was wary
of getting involved in further adventures. Her chief minister, William
Cecil, shared this view. After all, England's internal peace depended on
Elizabeth's security. As Lord Treasurer, which Cecil became in 1572, he
was only too aware of the need to limit expenditure. And while he was
certainly a Protestant, he placed political needs before religious
considerations. Other members of the Privy Council – Leicester and
Walsingham in particular – were more committed to the Protestant
cause, in Leicester's case because a foreign expedition carried with it the
prospect of military command. Thus, there were divisions over policy,
and while Elizabeth's word was final she was sometimes persuaded into
courses of action that went against her instincts.

The phases of policy

At the risk of making some artificial divisions, the period between 1566
and 1585 divides into three obvious phases:

- phase 1, from 1566 to 1574;
- phase 2, from 1574 to 1580;
- phase 3, from 1580 to 1585.

From 1566 to 1574, Anglo-Spanish relations steadily deteriorated for a
variety of reasons to the point where all trade between the countries was
cut off and war threatened. From 1574 to 1580, there was an easing of
tension, trade was resumed and England was able to pursue a policy of
defensive neutrality. The international balance of forces changed in 1580
when Philip II acquired the Portuguese throne, and from that point on
war became increasingly likely, finally breaking out in 1585.

Phase 1: 1566–74

A set of unrelated incidents caused an initial cooling of relations
with Spain.

1568. In 1568, Elizabeth's ambassador in Spain, Dr John Mann, was
expelled, supposedly for likening Pope Pius V to 'a canting little monk' at
a gathering in Madrid. By chance, the conciliatory Don Guzman de Silva
was replaced at the same time as the Spanish ambassador in London by
Guerau de Spes, who was much more ready to dabble in conspiracy.

Also in 1568, John Hawkins, who had been trading illegally with **Spanish possessions in the New World**, was set upon treacherously, so he claimed, by Spanish ships while at harbour in the Mexican port of San Juan de Ulloa. Then, a ship carrying a load of silver from Genoese banks, intended to pay the Duke of Alva's troops in the Netherlands, was forced by bad weather to take refuge in Southampton. Elizabeth took steps to safeguard the silver. However, declaring that it was a loan, she decided to borrow the money herself. In response, Alva seized all English ships and goods in the Netherlands. Elizabeth retaliated, and before long all Anglo-Spanish and Anglo-Netherlands trade came to a standstill.

1569. In May 1569, Alva imposed fresh taxes in the Netherlands, causing further unrest there.

1570. The year 1570 saw the Papal Bull of excommunication.

1571. This was followed in 1571 by the Ridolfi Plot (see Chapter 4, page 68).

1572. Partly because of these threats, Elizabeth decided to mend her fences with France. In April 1572, a defensive alliance was sealed by the Treaty of Blois. A marriage with the Duke of Anjou, the future Henry III, was envisaged. The 'realm and state of Scotland' was included in the treaty, thus tacitly indicating that France had now abandoned the cause of Mary Queen of Scots. Despite the Massacre of St Bartholomew, which caused Walsingham to remark 'I think less peril to live with them as enemies than as friends', the alliance survived, though not the projected marriage. Philip had also his hands full with subduing the **Moorish revolt** that had broken out in 1568. Alva would not act without support from Spain. Elizabeth, too, was prepared to be conciliatory. In 1572, she expelled from English ports the 'Sea Beggars' (Dutch rebels), who had been preying on Spanish commerce. A reconciliation with Spain was under way. In October 1572, Spain opened the way for negotiations.

Leading into phase 2, 1573–4. In the spring of 1573, trade was renewed and, by the Convention of Bristol signed in August 1574, the claims and counter claims arising from the seizures of ships and cargoes in 1569 were eventually settled.

Phase 2: defensive neutrality, 1574–80
For the next six years England was able to steer clear of foreign entanglements, though there was no let-up in diplomatic activity.

Spain's empire in the New World
By 1558 Spain had already acquired the bulk of her empire in the New World. Following Columbus's first crossing of the Atlantic in 1492, the Spanish established their hold over the islands of Hispaniola (present-day Haiti) and Cuba. In the 1520s Hernan Cortes and his Conquistadors occupied the Mexican empire, and in the 1530s the Pizarro brothers conquered the Inca empire in Peru. As remarkable as these feats was the process by which the Spanish empire was brought under centralised control and exploited for the benefit of the mother country. The most important product was the silver mined in Mexico and Peru. From 1564 onwards two fleets a year would be despatched to Mexico and the Isthmus of Panama to bring shiploads of silver back to Spain.

KEY EVENT

Moorish revolt

Spain contained many people of Moorish descent, known as the Moriscoes. Most of them were Muslims. When the practice of Islam was forbidden in 1526 the Moriscoes continued to observe their faith in private. In 1566, Philip II determined to ban Moorish customs, language and costume, and provoked a revolt that lasted until 1570. The revolt was another distraction from his concern with the Netherlands, and illustrates Philip's determination to enforce Catholic orthodoxy throughout his dominions. All Moriscoes were eventually expelled from Spain between 1609 and 1614.

KEY TERM

States General

Consisted of representatives from each of the provinces in the Union of Utrecht. It had full responsibility for foreign and military affairs.

Trying to solve the Netherlands problem. Elizabeth's main aim during these years was to find a settlement to the Netherlands problem. The Earl of Sussex expressed the dilemma succinctly:

The case will be hard with the Queen and with England if either the French possess or the Spaniards tyrannize in the Low Countries.

Cecil (created Lord Burghley in 1571) stated the objective in 1572 as:

Necessary for England that the State of the Low Countries should continue in their ancient government, without either subduing it to the Spanish nation or joining it to the Crown of France.

To that end, Elizabeth interceded with Spain to assist in getting the Pacification of Ghent accepted in 1577 and supported this initiative with the offer of a loan. She made a further offer of mediation in 1578 without success.

War breaks out again. When war between Spain and the Netherlands was resumed in 1578, the **States General** turned to another possible source of assistance, the **Duke of Anjou**. Anjou signed an agreement in August 1578 whereby he was to provide financial and military assistance to the States General 'as defender of Belgic liberties'. In return he would have the right to conquer lands east of the Meuse for himself and would be considered as a possible sovereign.

Elizabeth's solution. Elizabeth was worried that such a solution would place the Netherlands too firmly under French control. However, another solution might be to marry Anjou herself. His elder brother had been a candidate in 1572, but the Massacre of St Bartholomew had put a halt to that negotiation. In August 1579, Anjou visited England for twelve days, and formal articles were agreed in November. Elizabeth still refused to commit herself, but kept the offer open.

Elizabeth's involvement with 'piracy'. Another initiative supported by Elizabeth during these years was **Francis Drake**'s voyage to the Spanish Indies and his circumnavigation of the globe. Elizabeth gave her approval to Drake's next venture in 1577. Indeed, she and members of the Privy Council invested in the enterprise. Elizabeth's secret instructions have not survived. In the event, Drake captured a Spanish silver galleon, the *Cacafuego*, on the Pacific coast, which yielded a huge profit. When Elizabeth knighted Drake in April 1581 on the poop of his own ship, she condoned what was an act of piracy.

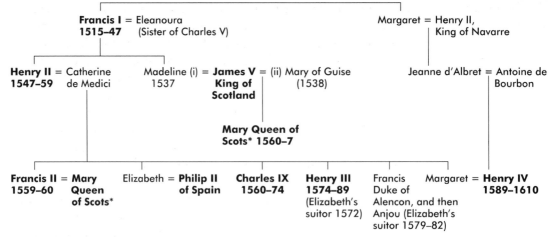

The French connection.

Names marked with an asterisk occur twice, first indicating to whom the person was born and second to whom the person married.

Phase 3: Years of crisis, 1580–5

These years of crisis were dominated by a number of key events, including:

- the conquest of Portugal;
- Parma's conquests in the Netherlands;
- the Treaty of Joinville;
- the Treaty of Nonsuch.

The acquisition of Portugal. From 1580 onwards, the international threat to Elizabeth's position grew steadily more acute.

The first serious change followed the chance death of King Sebastian of Portugal in 1578 at the Battle of Alcazar in North Africa. Philip had a strong hereditary claim to the Portuguese throne, which he acquired in 1580. The opposing candidate, Don Antonio (who was illegitimate), was forced to take refuge first in France, then in England. Spain now had the Portuguese navy and the profits accruing to the Crown from Portugal's lucrative eastern trade to support his naval and military power. Elizabeth clearly felt that Philip needed to be checked. She wrote:

> *We think it good for the King of Spain to be impeached both in Portugal and his Islands and also in the Low Countries, whereto we shall be ready to give such indirect assistance as shall not at once be a cause of war.*

KEY PEOPLE

Duke of Anjou
Catherine de Medici's youngest son. His first title was the Duke of Alencon. His elder brother, Henry, became King of France in 1574. Alencon succeeded to his title as Duke of Anjou in 1576.

Francis Drake
One of England's greatest seamen. Born in Devon, his father was a Protestant preacher and Drake grew up a committed Protestant. He was on John Hawkins's voyage to the Mexican port of San Juan de Ulloa.

Then, in 1572, he organised his own expedition to Central America where he intercepted a mule train carrying a huge quantity of silver.

William of Orange

Sometimes better known as William the Silent, he was a substantial landowner in the Netherlands. He initially found favour with Philip II, but opposed religious persecution and joined the opposition to Alva's rule in 1567. He supported the Pacification of Ghent in 1577. When that broke down, he was recognised as leader of the northern provinces of Holland and Zeeland. His importance may be gauged by the fact that, in 1579, Philip II offered a reward for his assassination.

The Netherlands, or Low Countries.

She allowed Drake to prepare an expedition in Don Antonio's name to secure the Azores as a base for operations against Spain, but would not allow him to sail unless she was guaranteed French support. When Philip made it clear that support of Antonio would be treated as a cause for war, she countermanded Drake's expedition. But she was still ready to support Anjou with subsidies in the Netherlands, sending him £30,000 to pay his troops in August 1581. In October 1581, Anjou made a second visit to London, this time staying for three months. When he departed in February 1582, it was without Elizabeth's hand in marriage, but with £10,000 in cash and the promise of £50,000 to follow.

Parma's conquests in the Netherlands. Elizabeth's support of Anjou made little difference. He quarrelled with the Union of Utrecht, and a bid to seize power for himself in January 1583 failed. In June he retired from the Netherlands leaving the rebels to fight on their own. In 1583–4, the Duke of Parma overran much of Brabant and Flanders, and threatened Antwerp and Ostend. The cause of Dutch independence was also severely threatened by the assassination of **William of Orange**, the only recognised leader, in July 1584.

The Treaty of Joinville. In November 1583, it will be remembered, the Throckmorton Plot was discovered, linking the Guise party and Philip II. This link was greatly strengthened in 1584. The death on 31 May of the Duke of Anjou, the last of Catherine de Medici's children, left the Protestant Henry of Navarre as the next direct heir to the throne. In December 1584, the Guise party signed the secret Treaty of Joinville with Philip II, under which he promised to aid them with 50,000 crowns a month in order to assist them in disinheriting Henry of Navarre. Thus a Guise-Spanish alliance came into operation. In June 1585, by the Treaty of Nemours, Henry III submitted to the Guise-dominated Catholic League and promised to expel heresy from France and to disinherit Henry of Navarre. There ensued what became known as the War of the Three Henries, between:

- Henry III;
- Henry of Guise;
- Henry of Navarre, later Henry IV.

In the event, all three of them were **assassinated**:

- Henry of Guise in December 1588;
- Henry III in July 1589;
- Henry of IV in 1610.

With France in a state of turmoil, Philip knew that he was safe from further French intervention in the Netherlands. Meanwhile, for Elizabeth, France could no longer be a counterweight to Spanish power.

The Treaty of Nonsuch. With Anjou's departure in June 1583 and William of Orange's assassination in 1584, the Union of Utrecht now turned to England. From the autumn of 1584 until the summer of 1585, a prolonged debate took place within the Privy Council on whether England should come to its aid, and if so in what form.

- Burghley urged caution, arguing that England's security would be better served by concentrating on her own defences rather than meddling in the Netherlands.
- Walsingham and Leicester advocated intervention.

When news of the Treaty of Joinville reached England in March 1585, Walsingham's hand was strengthened. In May, Philip II suddenly seized all English ships in Spanish ports and it seems to have been this action that precipitated the decision to intervene.

In June 1585, a Dutch embassy arrived to offer Elizabeth the sovereignty of the Netherlands. She declined the offer, but did agree to take the

Assassination of the three Henries
Each of the three Henries was assassinated for religious or political reasons. Henry of Guise was stabbed to death by Henry III's guards in December 1588. Henry III himself died at the hands of Jaquues Clement, a fanatical friar, in 1589. And Henry IV of France was stabbed by another Catholic fanatic, Ravaillac, in 1610.

Netherlands under her protection. By the Treaty of Nonsuch, signed on 10 August 1585, she offered to pay for, and send, a force of 6400 foot soldiers and 1000 cavalry. The commander of the force was to be an Englishman of quality and rank, who would sit with the Council of State. As security for the eventual repayment of her expenses, Elizabeth was to garrison at her own cost the ports of Flushing and Brielle.

The first English forces reached the Netherlands later that month. In September, Elizabeth's old favourite, the Earl of Leicester, was named as their commander. At the same time, Drake was sent to ransack Spanish towns on the north-west coast of Spain before setting off on a privateering voyage to Spain's possessions in the New World. Not surprisingly, in January 1586 Philip II instructed his senior admiral, Don Alvaro de Bazan, Marquis of Santa Cruz, to prepare an Armada to invade England. Such a scheme had already been advocated by Santa Cruz in August 1583. Now it was to become a reality. England and Spain were currently in a state of open, if still undeclared, war.

The one bright spot on the horizon was Scotland. While negotiating with the Dutch in the summer of 1585, Burghley was also negotiating with James VI. In July, James accepted an immediate grant of £4000, to be followed by an annual pension of £4000 in return for a defensive alliance, and by implication Mary's continued captivity. This arrangement was confirmed by a formal league the following year, known as the Treaty of Berwick. At least England's northern frontier was secure.

SUMMARY QUESTIONS

1 How did relations between England and Spain change between 1558 and 1585?

2 How did relations between England and Scotland and England and France change between 1559 and 1585?

A2 QUESTION IN THE STYLE OF AQA

Assess the importance of the Revolt of the Netherlands, English raids on the Spanish Indies and Philip II's support for Mary Queen of Scots in causing the breach between England and Spain.

Suggested approach to answering this question

This question requires you to examine each of these episodes, and to weigh them against each other as reasons for the breakdown of relations between England and Spain. It might be sensible to decide in advance which, in your view, is the most important. This is what has been done in the following.

Introduction. All three factors contribute, but English assistance to the Dutch rebels is the one issue on which Philip would not compromise. He refused to rule over heretics.

English raids on Spain. The trouble began with John Hawkins's slave trading ventures to the Caribbean. This was followed by Drake's interception of silver mule convoys (1572), his circumnavigation in 1577–80, and his raid on the Spanish colonies in 1585. Only the last episode was really serious, by which time the war was imminent.

Support for Mary Queen of Scots. Following the Papal Bull of 1570, Philip prepared to support Mary's claim to the throne, as seen in the Ridolfi Plot (1571) and Throckmorton Plot (1582–3). But note the gap between the two plots. Trade was renewed in 1573, and Elizabeth tried to negotiate a settlement of the Netherlands problem. The Babington Plot occurred after the Armada had been planned, as did Mary's execution.

The Revolt of the Netherlands. You should explain England's interest in this strategic area and the preferred solution – to keep the Netherlands 'in their ancient government' without being subjected to Spain. This solution became less and less likely after the breakdown of the Pacification of Ghent, Parma's reconquests and the assassination of William of Orange in 1584. If the northern provinces were to survive, they needed English assistance.

In August 1585, Elizabeth signed the Treaty of Nonsuch offering military aid to the Netherlands. In October, Drake landed on Spanish coasts and raided the Caribbean. Philip began to plan the Armada.

Conclusion. Weigh various factors – all contribute, but if Elizabeth had not intervened in the Netherlands, Philip would probably have continued the uneasy peace.

CHAPTER 6

War with Spain, 1585–1604

INTRODUCTION

From 1585 until 1604, England was at war with Spain. For nearly 30 years Elizabeth had managed to avoid that outcome, and she accepted it only with reluctance. The war went on for a long time, however. Its glorious moments were few and far between, and nothing after 1588 matched the defeat of the Spanish Armada. But in one sense the Armada settled nothing.

The struggle for supremacy at sea continued until the end of Elizabeth's reign. The threat of invasion recurred in 1596, 1597 and 1599. The fate of the 1588 Armada had little bearing on the Revolt of the Netherlands or the French Wars of Religion, apart from acting as a useful diversion of the Duke of Parma's army. Thus, English forces continued to be deployed in the Netherlands from 1585 until the end of the reign. Additionally, there were numerous expeditions to Normandy and Brittany, where Henry of Navarre, the Protestant claimant, needed support if a Spanish-sponsored candidate was not to succeed to the French throne. Finally, the Irish Rebellion, which lasted from 1595 to 1603, made the greatest claim on England's resources.

These events have been the subject of two major works in recent years, **W.T. MacCaffrey's** *Elizabeth I, War and Politics, 1588–1603*, published in 1992, and **R.B. Wernham's** *After the Armada, England and the Struggle for Western Europe*, published in 1984. They raise serious questions about the conduct of the war.

- Was Philip II of Spain really aiming to be the 'lord, commander of all Christendom', as Lord Burghley believed in 1590?
- Were the strategies employed at sea (for instance, the attempts to intercept Spanish silver convoys) realistic?
- How much difference did the presence of English troops make to the outcome of the Dutch Revolt or the French Wars of Religion?
- Could the Irish Rebellion have been prevented? If not, why was it put down so savagely?

These questions should be borne in mind when studying the events of the war. Its impact on the monarchy, the system of government and the economy are considered in Chapter 7.

WAR, 1585–8: THE COMING OF THE ARMADA

Though English aid to the Netherlands began in 1585, it did not lead to an immediate declaration of war by King Philip II of Spain. Indeed, negotiations between Elizabeth and the Duke of Parma continued right up to the arrival of the Spanish Armada in 1588. While on the Spanish side they were intended to lull the English into a false sense of security, Elizabeth was certainly ready to seek a solution to the Netherlands problem. It is hard to determine, therefore, the exact point at which war became inevitable.

Philip's reasons for sending the Armada

Estimating the venture. Preparations for the Armada began as early as October 1585 when the Marquis of Santa Cruz was asked to submit a plan for the invasion of England directly from Spain with estimates for the numbers of ships and men needed for such a venture.

Refining the plan. Between 1585 and 1587 this plan was refined to include an invasion force based in the Netherlands under Parma's command. Philip II, who was not called *Il re prudente* (the prudent king) for nothing, was finally persuaded to act, it seems by the execution of Mary Queen of Scots. He received a letter from the Spanish ambassador in France, Don Bernadino de Mendoza (expelled from England in 1584) which stated: 'For it would seem to be God's obvious design to bestow upon your Majesty the crowns of these two kingdoms [England and Scotland].' He had already received a letter from Mary herself, dated 20 May 1586, bequeathing her claims to the English and Scottish thrones to him.

Alexander Farnese, Duke of Parma.

Philip II of Spain.

Pope Sixtus V.

KEY PERSON

The Duke of Medina Sidonia
Blamed at the time for the defeat of the Armada, but recent historians have praised his judgement and leadership.

KEY TERM

Galleons A heavy square-rigged ship designed for fighting purposes. In 1588 galleons might have weighed as much as 1000 tons. They were designed for boarding enemy ships rather than fighting long-distance artillery duels, and carried large numbers of soldiers. Some Spanish galleons carried up to 34 guns, firing shot of up to 30 lbs in weight. The English ships were generally smaller and more manoeuvrable.

Support and security. Following Mary's execution, William Allen (now a Cardinal in Rome) offered his support to Philip in making a bid for the English throne. Whether Philip really aimed at such an objective is open to doubt. He was more concerned for the security of the Netherlands and the fate of English Catholics than acquiring more kingdoms. But he had no doubt about the holiness of the Enterprise, as it became known. The banner that accompanied the Armada had the words of the psalmist inscribed on a scroll: 'Exsurge, domine et vincia causam tuam' (Arise, O Lord, and vindicate thy cause). Pope Sixtus V had already given his blessing to the enterprise, offering one million ducats, but with characteristic prudence promising to send over the money only when he had confirmation that the Spanish had landed in England.

A promise fulfilled. On 29 July 1587, and as promised, one million ducats were duly transferred to two Roman bankers and an agreement reached for the government of England after the conquest. Philip would nominate, subject to Papal approval and investiture, a ruler pledged to restore and uphold the Catholic faith. In the meantime the administration of England would be entrusted to Cardinal Allen, assisted by his Jesuit pupils and local Catholics.

Events leading up to the Armada

March 1587. Preparations were already sufficiently advanced by March 1587 to cause alarm in England. In April, Francis Drake was sent on a pre-emptive strike to Cadiz.

- By his own account he destroyed 36 ships. (The Spanish admitted to a loss of 24.)
- He occupied the harbour at Sagres, where he burned quantities of barrel staves and other naval stores.
- His voyage ended on a lucrative note with the capture of a Portuguese merchant ship, the *San Felipe*, which had on board a huge cargo of spices – more than covering the costs of his expedition.

This 'singeing of the King of Spain's beard', as Drake described it, delayed the Armada for a year and later cost the lives of many Spanish sailors who would suffer from leaking water butts in 1588.

February 1588. In February 1588, the Spanish naval commander Santa Cruz died. His successor was the **Duke of Medina Sidonia**. It was his first naval command and he pleaded not to be appointed, but Philip insisted.

May 1588. By May, however, Medina Sidonia had assembled a huge fleet in the Tagus estuary off Lisbon. It included 65 **galleons** and an equal number of smaller vessels. On board were 7000 sailors and 18,000 soldiers. Should the planned rendezvous with Parma take place, they would be joined by another 17,000 battle-hardened troops. This was a greater force than Elizabeth could possibly muster. On the other hand, thanks to the reforms made by John Hawkins as Treasurer of the Navy, the English fleet had 34 well-armed and manoeuvrable ships with another 30 that could be pressed into service.

THE ARMADA

Events, 18 May to 28 July 1588
Setting sail. The Armada set sail on 20 May 1588 from Lisbon, Portugal (dates from the **Julian calendar** rather than the **Gregorian calendar**).

Encountering difficulties. Unfortunately, a storm forced the Armada to scatter, and it had to reassemble in the port of Corunna on Spain's north-west coast. After this experience, Medina Sidonia urged Philip either to negotiate with England or to postpone the Armada for another year. Philip insisted that he should sail again at the first opportunity.

A second attempt. On 12 July, the Armada began its slow progress again. On 19 July, it had reached the Lizard, the most southerly point on the English coastline. It maintained its crescent formation despite the efforts of the English fleet based at Plymouth to disrupt it, and reached Calais Roads by 27 July with the loss of only two ships.

Problems with embarking troops. It now became clear that Parma had no easy way of transporting his troops from the shore to the Spanish fleet. He lacked sufficient landing craft and, in any case, the Dutch controlled the coastline. Communications were not established with Medina Sidonia until 27 July, bringing the unwelcome news that Parma's troops would not be ready to embark for another five days.

English plans to cause disruption. The English commanders, **Howard of Effingham** and Drake, were none the less alarmed by the uninterrupted progress of the Armada, moored only 20 miles from England, and were determined to disrupt it. Eight fireships were despatched on the night of 28 July and their appearance forced the Spanish ships to leave their anchorages. In the ensuing chaos, two ships drifted ashore.

Events, 28 July to 3 September 1588
Continuing northward. Despite the disruptions, the Armada retained its cohesion and sailed northward. A day of hard fighting between the two fleets, known as the Battle of Gravelines, followed.

- The English did not lose any ships.
- The Spanish suffered from the more powerful English guns but only one of its galleons was sunk.

Gregorian and Julian calendars
Two calendars were being used in 1588. Protestant states, including England, were still using the Julian calendar, whereas Catholic states had mainly adopted the Gregorian calendar introduced by Pope Gregory XIII in 1582. This eliminated ten days from the Julian calendar in the interests of astronomical accuracy. This means that all dates in Spanish accounts of the Armada are ten days ahead of English dates. In this book, the old-style English dates have been used throughout.

Howard of Effingham
Appointed Lord High Admiral in 1585, partly on the strength of his relationship to the Queen (he was her cousin), but he did have some seafaring experience.

His handling of the English fleet in 1588 has been generally praised. He was created Earl of Nottingham in 1596 after the successful attack on Cadiz, where he shared command with the Earl of Essex.

At this point, Howard commented in a letter to Sir Francis Walsingham: 'Their force is wonderful great, strong; and yet we pluck their feathers little by little.'

It looked as though the Armada was to be blown onto the Flanders coast, but a fortunate shift of wind enabled it to turn northwards. Both sides were now almost out of powder and ammunition. The English fleet broke off the action.

Council of war. Medina Sidonia held a council of war on 31 July, at which it was decided to turn the fleet around and attempt a second junction with Parma if the wind permitted. However, the wind continued to blow from the south-west.

Return to Spain. Medina Sidonia, therefore, took the only sensible course open to him: to return to Spain, by sailing round the north coast of Scotland and the west coast of Ireland. Even in good weather this would have been a challenging undertaking. But 112 vessels out of the 130 that set out were still accounted for when the Spanish reached the north of Scotland. Unseasonable August storms then made it a fearful experience for ships already battered by gunfire, with provisions and water running dangerously short.

Damage to the Armada and its men. Estimates differ on the number of ships that made their landfall in Spain.

- Only 60 are known to have returned.
- Among that number were 34 of the 65 galleons that had set out.

Most losses were sustained on the rocky Irish coast. Those sailors who did survive were put to death if they encountered English forces. Sir William Fitzwilliam, the Lord Deputy in Ireland, pointed out to the Privy Council on 22 September that he had only 750 troops at his disposal. Orders went out to officers in the western provinces 'to apprehend and execute all Spaniards found, of what quality soever'. A fortunate few managed to make their way to Scotland where they were more kindly treated. Total loss of life on the Spanish side has been estimated at 15,000.

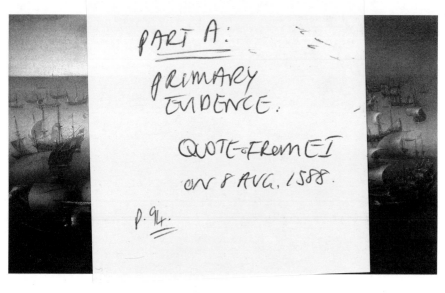

Truth and rumours. The fog of war concealed news of the Armada's fortunes until long after the event.

- Mendoza, relying on rumours from French fishing boats, was calling for a celebratory **Te Deum** to be said on 2 August.
- News of Drake's supposed capture reached Vienna (Austria).
- Even in England the perceived threat lasted much longer than the real one.

Elizabeth rallies her faithful. On 8 August, ten days after the Battle of Gravelines, Elizabeth visited her troops at **Tilbury** (on the River Thames, east of London), where they had assembled under the command of the Earl of Leicester. It was here that she made the **speech** for which she has been most remembered:

> *My loving people, we have been persuaded by some that are careful for our safety, to take heed how we commit ourselves to armed multitudes, for fear of treachery. But I assure you, I do not desire to live to distrust my faithful and loving people. Let tyrants fear. I have always so behaved myself that, under God, I have placed my chiefest strength and safeguard in the loyal hearts and goodwill of my subjects; and therefore I am come among you … to live or die amongst you all, and to lay down for my God and for my kingdom and for my people, my honour and my blood, even in the dust. I know I have the body of a weak and feeble woman, but I have the heart and stomach of a king, and of a king of England too, and think foul scorn that Parma or Spain or any prince of Europe should dare invade the borders of my realm …'*

KEY TERM

Te Deum This was a recognised form of Thanksgiving for events such as a military or naval victory for the Christian side. It began with the words 'Te Deum Laudamus' (We praise thee, O God).

KEY SPEECH

Elizabeth's speech at Tilbury There are several texts of this speech. William Camden refers to it in his history. This version dates from 1623 and derives from a copy made by Dr Lionel Sharp, one of Elizabeth's chaplains, who attended her at Tilbury.

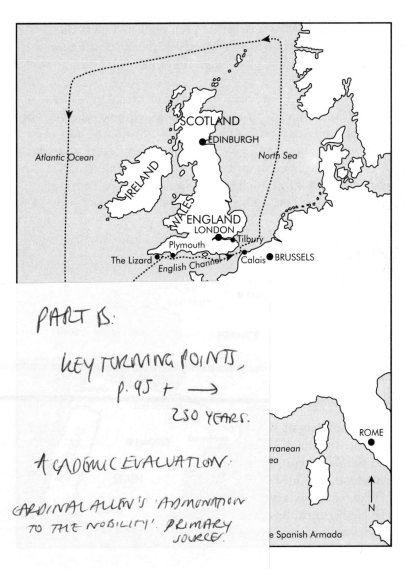

The route of the Spanish Armada, 1588.

Handwritten notes overlaid on map:

PART B:

KEY TURNING POINTS,
p. 95 + →
250 YEARS.

ACADEMIC EVALUATION:

CARDINAL ALLEN'S 'ADMONITION
TO THE NOBILITY'. PRIMARY
SOURCE.

AN ADMONITION
TO THE NOBILITY
AND PEOPLE OF ENG-
LAND AND IRELAND CON-
CERNINGE THE PRESENT WARRES
made for the execution of his Ho-
lines Sentence, by the highe
and mightie Kinge Ca-
tholike of Spaine.

By the CARDINAL of Englande.

Aº. M.D. LXXXVIII.

Cardinal Allen's 'Admonition to the Nobility'.

THE RESULTS OF THE ARMADA

The defeat of the Armada has been hailed as a major turning point in English and European history. It proved one thing. In June 1588, Cardinal Allen published *An Admonition to the Nobility and People of England* concerning the present wars. In it he urged that all must be ready 'at the arrival of his Catholic Majesty's forces … to join the said army … to help towards the restoring of the Catholic faith and deposing the usurper'.

Allen's advice was ignored. There was no English Catholic support for the Armada as it made its way up the Channel. While the legend of the Armada would be used to strengthen anti-Catholic sentiment in the years ahead, those Englishmen prepared to put their faith before their loyalty to the present queen were far fewer than had been predicted by Philip's supporters. The Armada greatly strengthened Elizabeth's position on the throne and there were no more plots to get rid of her.

However, the naval threat from Spain was far from over. On the news of the Armada's defeat, Philip gave the order to build ten new galleons. The struggle for naval supremacy between England and Spain had only just begun. The Protestant cause in the Netherlands and in France was still threatened. In the unlikely event of the Armada succeeding, Philip's power would have been immeasurably enhanced. As it was, he had suffered a major, but not fatal, setback.

WAR, 1589–1604

In the pages that follow, the war will be comprehensively covered. The foreign policy options are examined both at sea and on land. This section is followed by a study of the limitations on England's forces during this period. There is an account of the policies pursued; the naval expeditions against Spain; and English aid, both to the Netherlands and to the French Huguenots. Finally, there is an account of the Irish Rebellion and how it was suppressed.

Foreign policy options at sea

The defeat of the Armada did not mean an end to the threat from Spain. According to Burghley, writing in 1590, the King of Spain aimed 'to be lord, commander of all Christendom, jointly with the Pope, with no other associate'. He may have exaggerated Philip's ambitions, but with Spanish troops in the Netherlands, Brittany and Ireland, and the despatch of two further Armadas in 1596 and 1597 and the planning of a fourth in 1599, it is not surprising that English statesmen saw a coherent purpose – the destruction of England's independence – guiding Spanish policy throughout these years. It followed this assumption that there could be no peace with Spain until England was secure. This, in turn, required:

- an independent Netherlands;
- a well-disposed French king;
- the destruction of Spanish naval power.

These objectives were pursued consistently between 1589 and 1604, but the methods adopted varied according to circumstance and the limitations of cost and human resources. There were several possible strategies.

- Elizabeth could keep her fleet at home, ready to intercept any future Armada.

- Alternatively, she could wage a naval offensive, striking at Philip's naval bases as Drake had done in 1587.
- A variant on this strategy was to cripple Philip's financial resources by raiding the assembly points for the **Spanish silver fleets** in the New World, or intercepting them on their way back to Spain.

All these str_____ _____ _____ at one time _____ another and with varying suc_____

Foreign p_____

The foreign policy options _____

- aiding _____ Dutch _____
- aiding _____ Henry of _____

Aid to th_____ Dutch. After 1585, Eliz_____ and two allies _____ support on land:

- the D_____ rebels
- the F_____ Huguenots.

After the Treaty of Nonsuch (1585), England was committed indefinitely to keeping a body of troops in the Netherlands. In practice, the numbers varied, as did the reasons which they were employed. However, there were never fewer than 1000 soldiers, and initially they were paid for by Elizabeth. To begin with, England was the senior partner. But as the struggle continued the relationship changed and, in 1598 when the Dutch assumed responsibility for paying the English troops stationed there, England ceased to have a voice in how they were used.

Aid to Henry of Navarre. English aid to France was much more sporadic and dispersed, in keeping with the complexity of the power struggles that were waged there in the 1580s and 1590s. It should be remembered that under the Treaty of Joinville (signed in 1584), Philip II agreed to support the Guise faction in their bid to control the succession to the French monarchy.

- In May 1588, the Duke of Guise seized control of Paris.
- In August 1588, he forced Henry III to appoint him as Lieutenant-General of the Kingdom. But Henry had his revenge.
- On 23 December, Guise was murdered at Blois with Henry's connivance, and his brother, the Cardinal of Guise, was arrested and killed on the following day.

The removal of the Guise leaders did not end the Guise threat, however. The **Catholic League** continued to receive financial support from Philip II, and Henry III now came to terms with the Huguenot leader, Henry of Navarre, whom he recognised as his heir (see Chapter 5, page 86).

(see Chapter 5, page 86)

KEY TERMS

Spanish silver fleets By the 1560s, the Spanish had developed a very successful convoy system for transporting the huge quantity of silver now being mined in Mexico and Peru. Each year, two fleets would meet in the Caribbean to escort Spanish treasure ships back to Spain. Philip II was able to use the silver both to pay his armies directly and as security for the huge loans he was able to make from his Italian bankers.

The Catholic League Founded by Henry, Duke of Guise, in 1576 to oppose any concessions to the Huguenots. It was banned by Henry III, but gained a new lease of life with the Treaty of Jouiville in 1584 with aid from Philip II. It continued to oppose Henry of Navarre until his politic conversion to Catholicism in 1593.

All too soon, on 1 August 1589, Henry III was himself assassinated by a Catholic fanatic, Jacques Clement. Henry of Navarre now claimed his inheritance as Henry IV, and war broke out anew – this time between Henry and his Huguenot supporters and the Spanish-supported Catholic League. Henry put in an immediate bid for English assistance. Elizabeth and her ministers were faced by a suppliant to whom they found it hard to say no, and between 1589 and 1593 a succession of expeditions went to Henry's assistance. When Spanish forces occupied ports in Brittany (France) in 1591, they were seen as even more dangerous than when positioned in the Netherlands. Consequently, an English force spent more than three years there.

LIMITATIONS OF ENGLAND'S FORCES

The two main limitations of England's forces were:

- manpower;
- costs.

Manpower

Though England had no standing army at this stage in her history, every able-bodied man between the ages of sixteen and 60 was liable for military service.

- In 1575, 183,000 able-bodied men were recorded in the national musters in 37 counties.
- Of these, 12,000 were selected for special training.
- A further 63,000 were equipped but untrained.

Ironically, those men who were trained were exempted, where possible, from service abroad in case they were needed more urgently at home.

Every county was expected to make its contribution of manpower, and there was a reasonably effective mechanism for raising the necessary forces. Each county had:

- a Lord Lieutenant and several Deputy Lieutenants;
- a corps of Justices of the Peace;
- village-based constables who were charged with supplying the soldiers required.

It was usual practice to raise men in the localities nearest to the theatre of operations where they were needed. This meant that:

- the south-eastern counties were liable to provide the forces going to Brittany;

KEY TERMS

Muster masters
Professional organisers of the militia. It was their task to draw up muster rolls, and to ensure that when national musters

were held those who should be there 'passed muster' – that is, they were capable of taking part in all the activities of the company. The scope for corruption was considerable. It was not unknown for pay to be drawn for wholly fictional companies.

Pike A pole of about 18 feet long, tipped with metal. Its handling required considerable physical strength as well as skill.

Arquebus, calivar and musket
These were all types of firearm in use in the sixteenth century. They had a greater range than the longbow and did not require the same degree of skill. There was still considerable debate among the military experts on the respective merits of longbows and firearms, but in 1592 Sir Roger Williams, an experienced campaigner in the Netherlands, argued that 500 musketeers were far better than 1500 archers.

- the north-western counties and Wales were liable to provide those required for Ireland.

It was possible to buy exemptions and to bribe the **muster masters** so the bulk of the soldiers recruited came from the poorest section of the community. There was little likelihood that they would have received any adequate training before they were sent overseas. The standard weapons of the time, the **pike**, and early forms of fire-arm such as the **arquebus**, **caliver** or **musket**, required considerable skill if they were to be used effectively. Most casualties, however, were due to poor food, lack of hygiene and primitive medicine. In a poor and hostile environment such as Ireland, simply staying alive was challenge enough.

- Death and desertion probably accounted for at least one-third of any expeditionary force sent overseas.
- Approximately 8000 men out of 20,000 died on the great naval expedition sent to Spain and Portugal in 1589.
- The Earl of Essex's army in Ireland fell from 16,000 in the spring of 1599 to 11,250 by the autumn.
- In 1586, of 1100 recruits in the Netherlands 300 ran away.

A leading military historian, **C.G. Cruikshank**, states that the moment an Elizabethan soldier 'saw a chance of escape he was off like a shot and no oath dedicating his life to the state would stop him …'

Costs
The Elizabethan navy could call upon a larger pool of trained seamen, and a supply of well-found and well-armed ships. But the costs of maintaining them were enormous, and every major naval expedition was a combined enterprise to which private investors contributed, sometimes with money, sometimes with ships and commanders. This meant that the hope of booty often took precedence over strategic considerations, as in the expedition of 1587 (see page 91 of this chapter). It is a sad comment on the lack of care for the men who manned the ships that they were paid off as soon as possible to save on their wages. In 1588, after the Armada, Burghley commented: 'By death, by discharging of sick men and such like … there may be spared something in the general pay.'

It has been calculated that, between 1589 and 1595, Elizabeth spent roughly £200,000 per annum on the war at a time when her regular income was little more than that. The war had to be paid for by:

- Parliamentary subsidies;
- clerical subsidies;
- the sale of Crown lands.

War with Spain, 1585–1604   99

Though Parliament generally met the requests for funds, the amounts required rose steadily throughout the 1590s – particularly after the outbreak of the Irish Rebellion (see page 108 of this chapter). In the absence of any financial institution such as the Bank of England (which only came into existence in 1694), Elizabeth was dependent on foreign bankers and London merchants for loans. Between 1559 and 1574, she borrowed £1 million abroad, but therafter confined her borrowing to English lenders. In fact, when Elizabeth died, her debts of £364,000 were covered by the remaining instalments of a subsidy still to be collected. Thus, solvency was achieved at the price of stringent economy. In the account of English warfare that follows, the limitations on resources of men, material and money must be remembered.

NAVAL EXPEDITIONS

There were a number of naval expeditions that took place after the Armada, including:

- the huge expedition of 1589;
- the privateering expeditions of 1589–92;
- the major initiative of 1595–7 (which comprised three expeditions of war).

1589

The first naval expedition after the Armada was a massive undertaking. It included 83 ships and a force of 15,000 to 20,000 soldiers. The expedition's aims were dangerously open-ended.

- Elizabeth had certainly intended that it should be used to destroy the ships that had limped back to Santander (Spain) in the summer and autumn of 1588.
- It might then proceed to Lisbon (Portugal) and support a bid for the throne by Don Antonio.
- Finally, there was the prospect of seizing some of the islands of the Azores 'thereby to intercept the convoys of the treasure that do yearly pass that way to and from the West and East Indies'.

Progress of the fleet. Under the command of Sir John Norris and Sir Francis Drake, the fleet arrived at Corunna, well to the west of Santander, on 24 April, where they found only one galleon. Rather than risking being caught on a **lee shore**, Drake then sailed for Lisbon. The soldiers were landed some 45 miles north of Lisbon. However, when they got there, they lacked the siege equipment to force an entry. There was also little support for Don Antonio. A much depleted force re-embarked and headed for the Azores. The weather was unkind and all the ships eventually headed for home without seeing the Spanish treasure fleet.

The outcome. The only tangible fruits of the expedition were 60 merchant ships taken off the Tagus, and even these were restored to their owners.

The cost. The expedition is estimated to have cost £100,000, and the casualties of 11,000 far exceeded the forces sent to the Netherlands in 1585.

Privateering, 1589–92

For the next seven years, no expedition on the scale of that of 1589 was mounted and naval activity was restricted to commerce raiding, the main targets being:

- the Spanish treasure fleets from the Caribbean;
- the Portuguese **carracks** from the East Indies.

Much of this activity was privately financed and conducted. Some 236 ships have been identified as taking part in raids on Spanish ships between 1589 and 1591, during which time they took 300 prizes with a total value of £400,000. Government-approved and government-sponsored ventures also had limited success.

1590. In 1590, two squadrons under Sir Martin Frobisher and Sir John Hawkins cruised off the Spanish coast, visiting the Azores on their way home. They achieved nothing.

1591. In 1591, a larger expedition was planned by Lord Thomas Howard and **Sir Richard Grenville**. Its objective was to intercept the Spanish treasure fleet off the Azores. Unfortunately, a large and powerful Spanish fleet arrived at the Azores at the same time as the English one. All the English ships escaped, apart from the *Revenge* under Sir Richard Grenville. Rather than surrender, Grenville and his men took on the Spanish fleet, sinking four ships before capitulating. The Spanish treated the survivors honourably, despite the damage Grenville had inflicted. The Battle of Flores, as the encounter came to be named, proved that the chances of catching and defeating a well-defended treasure fleet were remote, to say the least. In addition, the Spanish had now adopted the tactic of shipping much of their silver in fast, smaller ships that did not need to call at the Azores.

1592. One success was achieved in 1592, more by luck than good judgement. An English force arrived at the Azores at the same time as two Portuguese carracks.

- One of the carracks was set on fire.

- The other – the *Madre de Dios* – was successfully intercepted and brought back to Plymouth. The total value of her cargo has been estimated at £500,000. The Queen gained £80,000 from the sale of the **pepper** carried.

The return to naval warfare, 1595–7

After the relatively small-scale operations of 1590–4, both England and Spain embarked on major initiatives in 1595.

- On the English side were the initiatives both from the old generation of sea dogs (Drake and Hawkins) and from new leaders like the Earl of Essex.
- On the Spanish side, Philip II hoped to exploit growing resistance to English rule in Ireland.

Expedition 1 (1595). The first of four major expeditions was to be directed initially at the Spanish coast, then at the Azores and finally at the Caribbean. It included:

- six first-line ships;
- 13 merchant men;
- 1000 soldiers.

Drake and Hawkins shared the command. Drake's preferred intention was to land at the Isthmus of Panama in the hope of repeating his success in 1572 in seizing Spanish silver, and the Queen finally allowed the expedition's third objective to take priority. The expedition set off in August 1595. The Spanish were forewarned. Both Drake and Hawkins died, and the fleet limped home in April 1596 with nothing gained.

Expedition 2 (1596). The next expedition was the largest mounted in Elizabeth's reign. The fleet numbered between 100 and 120 ships, and carried 12,000 to 15,000 soldiers. The expedition's objectives were dangerously vague: it was to use all means to destroy Spain's ships and supplies. This achieved, the commanders might then attempt the capture of a town incapable of defence. Command of the expedition was shared between Lord Howard (the sea commander) and Essex (the land commander). Cadiz became the destination and was captured in the most successful venture of the war, the English ships silencing the Spanish guns at the entrance to the harbour. They failed to prevent the Spanish from burning their own merchant fleet to prevent its falling into English hands. Essex wanted to hold the city, but Howard refused and the expedition returned to England. Two Spanish galleons had been captured, but this was hardly enough to dissuade Philip II from launching his own Armada in the autumn of 1596. Its probable destination was

Ireland, but it encountered storms in the Bay of Biscay, losing 24 of its 100 ships.

Expeditions 3 and 4. In 1597, there were further manoeuvrings, but this time no actual encounters. On 10 July, an English fleet set off with the aim of attacking the Spanish fleet at anchor in the port of Ferrol. It would have been a hazardous operation at the best of times, Ferrol having a narrow entrance with forts to defend it. Only one of the three English squadrons reached the Spanish coast in poor weather, and by 31 July the whole fleet was back in Plymouth. A second voyage later in the year detected a treasure fleet in the Azores, too well-defended to attack. Philip was equally unsuccessful. His third Armada, consisting of 136 ships and 12,000 men, was scattered off the Scilly Isles.

The 1597 voyages were the last of the war though there was an invasion scare in 1599, which led to the commissioning of the fleet. A Spanish fleet did assemble, but sailed to the Azores in pursuit of the Dutch. At the end of the day, honours were about even.

- Spanish naval power had not been destroyed, and such defeats as had been suffered were due as much to the weather as to English action.
- For its part the English navy, after the defeat of the Armada, had not succeeded in its two main goals – the destruction of the Spanish navy and the interception of the Spanish treasure fleets.

Despite occasional victories, English seapower had not yet shown its full potential.

INTERVENTION ON THE CONTINENT, 1585–1603

English soldiers were employed continuously on the continent of Europe from 1585 until the end of Elizabeth's reign, but their numbers varied considerably with the changing fortunes of war and the demands made by England's allies. There were three different theatres of operation:

- the boundary between the northern and southern Netherlands (roughly the border between Holland and Belgium today);
- Normandy;
- Brittany.

All were linked, both by land and sea, and not infrequently English troops were moved from one theatre to another. This explains the complexity of English military operations during the years concerned, as the chart on page 106 indicates.

INTERVENTION IN FRANCE

When Henry III of France was stabbed to death on 1 August 1589, Henry of Navarre immediately sought English assistance to make good his claim to the French throne. For the next six years, Elizabeth did her best to respond, aware that a friendly France would make a counterweight to Spanish power. How much difference English assistance made is hard to say, but English troops were present on several campaigns.

Normandy and Maine

In September 1589, 3600 men were sent under Lord Willoughby at Henry's prompting, and accompanied him on a wide sweep through Normandy and Maine. Conditions were hard and, by December 1589, only 800 men were fit for active service. Only 100 casualties were sustained in the fighting.

Brittany

In October 1590, a Spanish force occupied the port of Blavet in Brittany, and Elizabeth was faced with a new request for assistance in Brittany.

In response, Sir John Norris was sent with 4000 men to the port of Paimpol in May 1591. They lingered in Brittany for the next few months, wasted by desertion and disease, and by February 1592 Norris's army was down to 1700 men. At the same time, Henry IV wanted English assistance at the **Siege of Rouen**, which lasted, unsuccessfully, for eight months. Its only impact was to distract Parma from his campaign in the Netherlands.

Henry's return to Catholicism

Henry's lack of success finally convinced him that he would need to secure Catholic support, especially in Paris, if he was to overcome the Spanish-backed Catholic League. In July 1593, he made the tactical decision to return to the Catholic faith. This immediately altered the English attitude to their ally. Elizabeth ordered the return of all troops in France, except those still stationed in Brittany.

Events, 1593–8

So far as Henry was concerned, his return to Catholicism brought immediate benefits. Orleans and Lyon went over to him in 1593. Philip II none the less continued to support the Guise party.

KEY EVENT

The Siege of Rouen This began under Henry of Navarre's direction, in the autumn of 1591. It lasted until April 1592 and was then abandoned. The Duke of Parma successfully maintained supplies to the city and avoided the besieging forces. Altogether between 6000 and 8000 English soldiers took part in the siege at one time or another. The bulk of them died or were invalided home.

Date	Netherlands	Normandy and Paris	Brittany
1585	Treaty of Nonsuch 4500 troops to Netherlands		
1586	Unsuccessful attack on Zutphen		
1587	Deventer betrayed		
1588	Spanish Armada. Dutch prevent Parma's embarkation		
1589		Willoughby to France with 3600 troops	
1590	Dutch capture Breda		Arrival of Spanish troops at Blavet
1591		4000 troops under Williams to Siege of Rouen	4000 troops under Norris to Brittany
1592	Death of Parma	April, Siege lifted	
1593		July, Henry IV returns to Catholic faith Return of English troops in Normandy	
1594	Dutch capture Groningen		English troops to Brest Fall of Crozon
1595		All English troops withdrawn from France Henry IV declares war on Spain	
1596		Treaty of Greenwich between Henry IV and Elizabeth Spanish capture Calais	
1597		2000 troops to Amiens	
1598	August, English troops under Dutch command and pay; debts to Elizabeth to be repaid	May, Peace of Vervins between Henry IV and Philip II	
1601	Spanish besiege Ostend		
1604	Fall of Ostend Treaty of London		

A change in the character of the war. In March 1594, Henry occupied Paris and the war took on a changed complexion. This change was reflected in his formal declaration of war on Spain in January 1595, which changed Elizabeth's attitude too. In March 1596, Calais fell to the Spanish. Renewed negotiations for further assistance culminated in May with the **Treaty of Greenwich**, which committed Elizabeth to providing 2000 troops. They eventually arrived at Dieppe in November, but Henry had no use for them so late in the year and they suffered the usual hazards of army life in winter quarters. Henry was forced into action when Amiens fell to the Spanish in March 1597. He asked for another 2000 men to assist in its recovery. The most Elizabeth would do was to make up the depleted contingent already in France. Some 400 men duly arrived to take part in the recapture of Amiens in September.

The Spanish outcome. Meanwhile, the Spanish continued to be active in Brittany. In 1594, they began to fortify Crozon, a position opposite the strategic port of Brest. Some 1100 English soldiers were released from service in the Netherlands and in October, Crozon was captured. With its capture the threat of a Spanish presence there was ended. Elizabeth immediately ordered the withdrawal of English troops, who were then transferred to Ireland.

The end of war. The Franco-Spanish war came to an end in May 1598 with the **Treaty of Vervins**. Henry IV was recognised as the rightful French king and England had lost a demanding ally. She was now faced with the choice of making peace herself with Spain or continuing the war in alliance with the Dutch.

AID TO THE NETHERLANDS, 1585–1603

As we have already seen, Elizabeth was always reluctant to become too deeply drawn into Dutch affairs. But she, and more particularly her ministers, were never willing to tolerate an effective Spanish presence there. Thus, while she berated Leicester fiercely when he unwisely accepted the governor generalship of the Netherlands when it was offered to him in 1585, she never withdrew all English forces. How much they contributed to the Dutch success is also hard to compute. Under Leicester, English forces achieved very little.

- In 1586, there was an unwise attack on Zutphen, easily repulsed by the Spanish.
- In January 1587, two forts in English hands were betrayed to the Spanish by their commanders, Sir William Stanley and Rowland Yorke. This action was defended by William Allen on the grounds that it was the duty of Catholics to aid 'the greatest and justest monarch in the world [Philip II] and under a general so peerless [Parma]'. Leicester resigned his position shortly afterwards.
- Probably the greatest service England did the Netherlands was to distract Philip's and Parma's attention in 1587–8, when the Armada absorbed all Spanish energies.

Treaty of Greenwich
Signed in May 1596 between Elizabeth I and the Huguenot leader Henry Turenne. Spurred on by the loss of Calais, Elizabeth agreed in public to provide 4000 troops, though in private this was whittled down to 2000 because of the pressing demands of Ireland.

Treaty of Vervins
Signed between commissioners representing Henry IV of France and Philip II of Spain on 2 May 1598. It brought Spain's intervention in the French Wars of Religion to an end. It would have suited England to see Spanish troops tied down in France, but Elizabeth was not prepared to offer Henry IV any more assistance and he was not willing to continue the fight without it.

The Netherlands, Normandy and Brittany.

Thereafter England's role was very much an auxiliary one. Burghley lamented what he called 'this unhappy war with its infinite charges and an end that no man could see'. In 1592, 1800 troops in the Netherlands were diverted to the Siege of Rouen and, by 1593, the English force in the Netherlands had been reduced to 3400.

On the credit side, **Sir Francis Vere**, its new commander, had struck up a good working relationship with Prince Maurice, son of William of Orange, who was the best Dutch commander. The claims of Brittany in 1594, the Cadiz expedition in 1596 and Amiens in 1597 all helped to reduce the men and money available to the Dutch, but there were some English soldiers at the capture of Groningen in the north-east, in July 1594. This helped to seal the north-eastern frontier against the Spanish and was a landmark in the Dutch Revolt.

Elizabeth's position. With the ending of the Franco-Spanish war in 1598, Elizabeth was in a stronger position to renegotiate the terms of the Treaty of Nonsuch. In August 1598, a new agreement was reached under which the Dutch agreed to repay the £800,000 that Elizabeth had spent in aid to the Netherlands. Each partner was to offer mutual support at sea. The English contingent would now be directly controlled, and paid for, by the Dutch.

Achieving peace with Spain. Elizabeth and her ministers could not make peace with Spain, so they believed, until they were sure of the independence of the rebellious provinces. It would be left to Elizabeth's successor to end the war. Neither James I nor Philip III saw any purpose in continuing the conflict. A peace conference was held at Somerset House between 20 May and 16 July 1604, and the Treaty of London was signed on 28 August. Its terms gave Philip III much of what his father would have wanted.

- English intervention in the Netherlands was to cease (though English volunteers were still able to serve in the Netherlands, and England retained control of Brill and Flushing).
- Greater toleration would be shown to Catholics in England.
- Trade was renewed between the two countries.

THE SITUATION IN IRELAND

Possible policies
Elizabeth's relationship to Ireland was not unlike that of Philip II's to the Netherlands. In each case an alien ruler sought to maintain her or his authority over an area that had little sympathy for the mother country. The parallel goes further. Philip strove to remove heresy from the Netherlands, while Elizabeth and her ministers outlawed Catholicism in Ireland. Each ruler supported rebels in the other's problem province.

For Elizabeth, Ireland was always a tiresome distraction and a wasteful drain on her finances. It was not until the very end of her reign that she was prepared to devote the resources needed to make her authority effective.

Sir Francis Vere
Arrived in the Netherlands at the age of 26. After three years' service with the English contingent, he became its commander in 1589. He struck up a warm friendship with Prince Maurice, the most effective Dutch general, and in 1590 took part in the capture of Breda. He remained in the Netherlands until the end of Elizabeth's reign, playing a notable part in delaying the siege of Ostend in 1601.

Tudor Ireland.

KEY TERM

The Pale The area around Dublin under effective English jurisdiction.

- Initially, Elizabeth preferred to limit direct English rule to **the Pale**, and elsewhere to rely on the support of powerful Old English families who could be persuaded to recognise her authority.
- When this failed she was forced to send in armies. These might be employed to garrison strategic points and to defeat her enemies on the battlefield. If all else failed, they would resort to scorched earth policies, starving the hostile population into surrender.
- A third weapon was colonisation. It was hoped that English settlers might be attracted to fertile parts of the island and would provide the nucleus of a land-owning class favourable to Protestantism and English rule.

Each of these policies had their advocates, both at Court in England and in Dublin, and they were tried with varying success throughout the reign. But as **W.T. MacCaffrey** (in *Elizabeth I, War and Politics, 1588–1603*, 1992) has truly said: 'Both the actions of the English government and the Irish resistance to them were episodic, fitful, and confused.'

Periods of crisis

These periods covered the following years.

- 1566–9;
- 1579–81.

1566–9. The first serious challenge to English authority in Ireland came from **Shane O'Neill**, Lord of Ulster. Though he had been invited to Court by Queen Elizabeth in 1561 and recognised her authority, he continued to harass his neighbours. In 1566, he was known to be negotiating for support from Charles IX of France and Mary Queen of Scots. Elizabeth ordered the **Lord Deputy**, Sir Henry Sidney, to take action against him. Sidney sent a naval expedition to Lough Foyle and marched through Ulster to assert his authority. O'Neill was then defeated in a battle with his rival, Hugh O'Donnell, and murdered by Scots settlers in Antrim in 1567.

Sidney subsequently embarked on a programme of extending English rule over Munster and Connacht, where two presidencies were created, and grants of land were made to English settlers. This helped to provoke a rising led by James Fitzmaurice Fitzgerald, cousin to the imprisoned Earl of Desmond in the south. Cork and the area around Waterford were attacked, and Fitzgerald proclaimed the Catholic religion. The rebellion was quickly, and brutally, suppressed. Fitzgerald escaped to France. In 1571, Sir John Perrott was appointed President of Munster and he put a further 800 rebels to death.

Catholic conspiracies, 1579–81. The excommunication of Elizabeth in 1570 provided a further spur to Irish opposition.

- In 1578, Thomas Stukely set off from Italy with a ship, 600 men and arms provided by the Pope to invade Ireland. He got no further than Lisbon, where he was diverted to a North African crusade against the Moors.
- Another Papal champion was found in the person of James Fitzmaurice. He landed on the Dingle peninsula in July 1579, accompanied by a Papal **nuncio**, **Dr Nicholas Sander**. Fitzmaurice was killed almost at once, but the Earl of Desmond's brother and then the Earl himself took up the revolt.

Shane O'Neill
O'Neill was typical of the difficulties faced by Tudor governments in Ireland – too powerful to be ignored, but too dangerous to be trusted. In 1558 he had rebelled against the decision by Mary's government to confer the earldom of Tyrone upon his illegitimate half-brother, Matthew. Having had Matthew murdered, Shane proclaimed himself Earl of Tyrone. In a conciliatory gesture, condemned by her Irish advisers, Elizabeth invited Shane to Court, but, on his return to Ulster in 1561, he continued to make war on his neighbours.

Lord Deputy The Crown's chief officer in Ireland. He might also be the chief military commander, as was Lord Mountjoy in 1601. Other terms such as Lord Lieutenant were also used.

- The revolt was joined in 1580 by a Catholic peer, Lord Baltinglass, in Wicklow, and later in the year 600 Spanish and Italian troops landed at Smerwick on the Dingle peninsula.
- A new English Deputy, Lord Grey, marched to the fort where they had established themselves, secured their surrender and massacred them all. Grey continued a savage policy of devastation and, in 1583, Desmond was captured and killed.

The scale of these rebellions and the outside aid provided were too small to be a really serious threat to English rule, but at the time they were perceived as 'an universal conspiracy' in **Humphrey Gilbert**'s words, and the cruelty with which they were suppressed helped to alienate both the Old English and the Gaelic Irish from their new masters.

Tyrone's Rebellion, 1595–1603

Background to the Rebellion. The most serious challenge to English rule in Ireland was mounted from Ulster. It was led by Hugh O'Neill, who was created Earl of Tyrone in 1585. His motives and actions are still unclear, and for the first ten years of his earldom he was on relatively good terms with the authorities in Dublin. In 1591, however, he antagonised Sir Nicholas Bagenal, Marshall of the English army, by carrying off and marrying Bagenal's daughter, Mabel. Suspicion was also aroused when O'Neill's daughter, Rose, married Hugh Roe O'Donnell. The O'Donnells had previously been great rivals of the O'Neills and a useful counterbalance to them. By 1595, O'Neill had built up a substantial army comprising:

- 1000 cavalry;
- 1000 pikemen;
- 4000 musketeers.

Negotiations and campaigns. O'Neill was known to be negotiating with Philip II, and made no secret of the fact. But as late as 1594 he appeared at Dublin 'offering all service to Her Majesty as becometh a good subject and standing only upon his innocency'. Shortly after making this promise he refused to meet the English Deputy, Sir William Russell, at Cavan. He gave aid to his son-in-law, Hugh Maguire, who campaigned against English incursions in Fermanagh.

- In February 1595, Tyrone's brother captured the Blackwater Fort in Armagh, controlling the gateway to Tyrone's lands.
- In May, Enniskillen was lost to the rebels.
- In June, Bagenal was intercepted and his troops badly mauled at Clontibret by Tyrone's forces.

Not surprisingly, Elizabeth then declared Tyrone a traitor and the policy of indirect rule in Ulster came to an end.

Events, 1595–8. For the next seven years, Tyrone and his fellow Gaelic supporters posed the most serious challenge Elizabeth had to face during the course of her reign. Her immediate response was to transfer the 2000 troops stationed in Brittany, who arrived in 1596. Outnumbered by Tyrone's forces, they could not risk a battle, and truces were signed both in 1596 and 1597. In the summer of 1598, and with a reinforced army, Sir Henry Bagenal (son of Sir Nicholas) set out to relieve Blackwater Fort, but was defeated on 14 August at the Battle of Yellow Ford. The rebellion spread to the rest of Ireland. English settlers in Connacht and Munster were driven from their lands, and only the province of Leinster remained in English hands. A major expedition was clearly needed if English rule was to be restored. In January 1599, the Earl of Essex was appointed to lead an army of 16,000 men to Ireland, the largest force to leave English shores in Elizabeth's reign.

Essex's expedition, 1599. Essex, still basking in the glory of his expedition to Cadiz in 1596, was in one sense the obvious choice of commander, but he was totally unfamiliar with Ireland. His plan for a two-pronged attack on Ulster was never put into effect and, when he did confront Tyrone's army in August 1599, which greatly outnumbered the English army, he decided not to fight. Instead he made a truce, renewable every six weeks. On 24 September, he left Ireland, never to return. His successor, Charles Blount, Lord Mountjoy, was appointed in January 1600, and arrived in February.

Mountjoy's rule in Ireland. Mountjoy was the most successful of Elizabeth's generals. He planned a three-pronged attack on Ulster and won over two important Ulster Chiefs, Art O'Neill (Tyrone's brother) and Neill Garve O'Donnell. Sir George Carew was sent with 3000 men to subdue Munster. The campaigns were brutally fought. Sir Arthur Chichester, a tough and experienced soldier, reported that: 'We spare none of what quality or sex soever, and it hath bred much terror in the people.'

By the summer of 1601, most of the south-west was in English hands. Tyrone had appealed for Spanish help as early as 1595, and Philip II despatched Armadas in 1596 and 1597, both of them fruitless, as we have seen. Philip's death in 1598 brought a more conciliatory approach to Spanish foreign policy, and it was not until October 1601 that further aid was made available in the shape of an expeditionary force that landed at Kinsale in south-west Ireland.

Spanish landing at Kinsale. The landing was commanded by Don Juan del Aguila, a competent and experienced soldier, but he only had 4400 men at his disposal, too small a number to attract Irish support or to hold out on its own. Kinsale was besieged by Mountjoy, and Tyrone was forced to come south to its relief. Penned between Kinsale and Tyrone's army, Mountjoy was still able to defeat Tyrone on the battlefield in December

The Edict of Nantes was revoked in two stages. In 1629 Cardinal Richelieu removed its political clauses, and in 1685 Louis XIV swept away its remaining clauses. The Protestant religion remained banned thereafter in France until the French Revolution in 1789.

KEY DEBATE

Wernham and MacCaffrey R.B. Wernham has argued that English aid to the Dutch and the French Huguenots was vital to their success – England 'had played a very considerable part'. W.T. MacCaffrey concludes that England made 'only a marginal contribution to Dutch and French success'. See R.B. Wernham's *After the Armada, England and the Struggle for Western Europe* (1984) and W.T. MacCaffrey, *Elizabeth I, War and Politics, 1588–1603* (1992).

1601 and Aguila surrendered in January 1602. In June, Mountjoy crossed the Blackwater river into Tyrone's homeland. On 30 March 1603, Tyrone surrendered. Under the terms of the peace treaty that followed, he and his fellow earl, Tyrconnel, were allowed to retain their official titles, but were shorn of their powers. Both earls left Ireland in 1607.

THE EFFECTS OF ELIZABETH'S WARS

The total cost of Elizabeth's wars has been calculated at £4,500,000, of which £2,000,000 was spent in Ireland. Of the 50,000 English troops sent overseas between 1594 and 1603, the great majority went to Ireland. It was the most expensive theatre of operations, and it left the most bitter legacy in the hatred sown between the Catholic majority and their Protestant conquerors.

Thus Elizabeth survived all the external challenges to her security, and that of her realm. At her death there was still an English contingent in the Netherlands. The United Provinces would get their independence in two stages:

- through a nine-year truce in 1609;
- after the Thirty Years' War;
- through the **Peace of Westphalia** in 1648.

In France, even though Henry IV had converted to Catholicism in 1593, Huguenots were guaranteed freedom of worship under the **Edict of Nantes** in 1598. England's contribution to both of those outcomes should not be forgotten. Despite the failures in battle, and the costs in life and money, Elizabeth's foreign policy had achieved, at least, some of its goals.

SUMMARY QUESTIONS

1 Draw up a chronological table of English and Spanish conflicts at sea, indicating in each case the results of the encounter.
2 How much assistance did England give (a) to the Dutch and (b) to the French Huguenots between 1562 and 1603?
3 Summarise the changes in Elizabeth's policies towards Ireland during the course of her reign.

A2 QUESTION IN THE STYLE OF EDEXCEL

'If the late Queen would have believed her men of war as she did her scribes, we had in her time beaten that great empire in pieces … But her Majesty did all by halves, and by petty invasions taught the Spaniard how to defend himself, and to see his own weakness' (Sir Walter Ralegh). Is this a fair comment on Elizabeth's handling of her naval and military resources in the war with Spain?

Suggested approach to answering this question

The key phrase is 'her Majesty did all by halves' and thus by the small scale of her operations ('petty invasions') contributed to their failure. Your essay must test the fairness of this accusation. One way of doing this is to examine the arguments for and against it.

Arguments supporting the accusation

- The petty scale of assistance given to the Dutch rebels and the French Huguenots – for example, 5000 men to the Netherlands in 1585, 4000 men to Rouen in 1592, 4000 men to Brittany in 1592, 400 to Amiens in 1597. It is doubtful whether English intervention made very much difference.
- The failure either to destroy Spanish naval power in 1589 and 1596, or to intercept Spanish silver convoys in 1591.

Arguments to rebut the accusation

- The scale of naval expeditions of 1589 and 1596 – in each case over 80 ships and 15,000 men are involved. Failure was the fault of commanders, who disobeyed instructions in 1589, or who had no clear idea of what they wanted to achieve in 1596. The attempt to intercept Spanish silver convoys, always well protected, was never likely to succeed.
- Problems of recruitment and training. England had no standing army and simply to increase the scale of military operations would have led to increased casualties from hardship and disease, as is shown by death rates in the 1589 and 1596 expeditions.
- Lack of financial resources. Elizabeth spent about £4,000,000 on warfare when her ordinary income was only £200,000.
- The burden of Ireland. At the point when England might have spared more resources for the Netherlands the Irish Rebellion broke out in 1595.

Conclusion. Ralegh's accusation does not really stand up. Elizabeth did commit huge resources to some of her expeditions. It was their commanders who were to blame for failures. The destruction of Spanish power was, in any case, an unrealistic ambition.

CHAPTER 7

The end of the reign

INTRODUCTION

The final years of Elizabeth's reign have been increasingly portrayed in terms of decline. Indeed, one of her most recent biographers writes: 'She ended her days as an irascible old woman presiding over war and failure abroad and poverty and factionalism at home' (Christopher Haigh, *Elizabeth I*, second edition, 1998).

But how fair is this judgement? In Chapter 5 we examined Elizabeth's foreign policy and its consequences. In this chapter we shall look at the domestic scene in the years following the Armada until Elizabeth's death and the accession of her cousin, James VI of Scotland.

CHANGING PERCEPTIONS OF ELIZABETH

Her authority
Elizabeth's authority depended, to some degree at least, on the image she was able to portray. Her reputation probably stood at its height in the

The Armada portrait.

year of the Armada. A portrait, known as 'The Armada portrait', was specially commissioned. It shows Elizabeth with her right hand on the globe, dominating the world.

Celebrations of the date of her accession, 17 November 1558, were more frequent after 1588. The Parliament that met in February 1589 readily voted the subsidies requested, and speeches made by Elizabeth's ministers described her as 'a most gracious Lady' and referred to 'her invincible courage'.

The greatest Gloriana. The following year, **Edmund Spenser** published his great work *The Faerie Queen*. The work describes the land of Faerie and its queen, Gloriana. In an open letter to Sir Walter Ralegh, Spenser said: 'In that Faery Queen I mean glory in my general intention but in my particular I conceive the most excellent and glorious person of our sovereign …' The term 'that greatest Gloriana' was coined to describe her. Thus Elizabeth acquired the title.

Comparisons with others. Elizabeth was also likened to Diana, chaste goddess of the moon, and to Astraea, the Roman goddess of justice. One of her courtiers, Sir John Davies, wrote 26 **Hymns of Astraea in Ackrostic** verse in 1599, the first letters at the beginning of each line of the poems spelling out the words Elisabetha Regina. Each poem brings out various aspects of the Queen and praises her virtues. Perhaps the most far-fetched comparison was that made with the Virgin Mary. Soon after her death in 1603, an engraving of the late queen was inscribed:

She was, she is, (what more can there be said?)
In earth the first, in heaven the second Maid.

Those who were critical. However, both at Court and in the country at large, the audience was becoming more critical. Sir Walter Ralegh described Elizabeth as 'a lady whom time hath surprised', and Francis Bacon wrote cruelly that 'she imagined that the people, who are much influenced by externals, would be diverted by the glitter of her jewels, from noticing the decay of her personal attraction'. In October 1602, John Harington, Elizabeth's godson, described how 'the Queen stamps with her feet at ill news and thrusts her rusty sword at times into the arras [a tapestry screen] in great rage'. An Essex labourer was quoted as saying in 1591 'we shall never have a merry world while the Queen still liveth'.

Public opinion. Court gossip and tittle tattle were no more reliable as an index of public sentiment in the sixteenth century than they are today, but neither can they be ignored entirely. It would be surprising if Elizabeth, who had exploited her charm to the full when she was at her most attractive, did not suffer a corresponding loss of popularity as her

KEY PERSON

Edmund Spenser
A patriotic Protestant poet who was in the Earl of Leicester's circle. He served as secretary to Lord Deputy Grey in Ireland, and sought Elizabeth's patronage.

KEY POEM

Hymn of Astraea in Ackrostic A typical entry for one of the 26 Hymns would be as follows:

E xil'd Astraea is come againe,

L o here she doth all things maintaine

I n *number, weight, and measure*

S he rules us with delightful paine,

A nd we obey with pleasure.

B y *Love* she rules more than by *Law*

E ven her great mercy breedeth awe;

T his is her sword and scepter:

H erewith she hearts did ever draw,

A nd this guard ever kept her.

R eward doth sit at her right-hand,

E ach vertue thence takes her garland

G ather'd in Honor's garden;

I n her left hand (wherein should be

N ought but the sword) sits Clemency

A nd conquers Vice with pardon.

(Quoted in Francis Yates, *Astraea The Imperial Theme in the Sixteenth Century*, Routledge, 1976, p. 68.)

physical appearance deteriorated with age. Similarly, while her friendship with Robert Dudley, Earl of Leicester might have been indiscreet, it was never ridiculous. The same could not be said for the relationship that developed between Elizabeth and the Earl of Essex, who was born in 1567, 34 years after the queen.

ELIZABETH AND HER MINISTERS, 1588–1603

Fortunately for England, the years during which the country was most threatened by internal conspiracies and the threat of invasion saw the Privy Council function at its best, and least riven by faction. Four men dominated proceedings:

- William Cecil, now Lord Burghley;
- Sir Francis Walsingham;
- Sir Christopher Hatton;
- Robert Dudley, Earl of Leicester.

They all knew each other well, and while there were real differences over foreign policy, particularly in relation to the provision of aid to the Netherlands, these did not lead to an open rupture. This informal inner council broke down when Leicester took command of the Netherlands expedition in 1585. His return in 1586 did not lead to a return to royal favour, though Elizabeth's affection for him remained. Walsingham died in 1590, Hatton in 1591. Burghley soldiered on until 1598, combining the offices of Treasurer and Secretary until 1596, but he was increasingly frail and crippled. Thus the old guard gradually passed away.

The Cecils, father and son.

Replacements to the old guard. In several cases, replacements for these four men were sons of Councillors – most notably Robert Cecil, who joined the Privy Council in 1591 at the age of 26. He shadowed his father and did much of the work of the Secretary until 1596, when he was officially appointed to the post. On his father's death, Robert Cecil became Elizabeth's leading Councillor, though he still had to overcome his main rivals.

Robert Devereux, Earl of Essex

Robert Devereux, the Earl of Essex, was the most significant of Cecil's rivals.

Background. He came from a very different background to Cecil's. Though he was only the second Earl of Essex, he could trace his descent back to the royal line. His mother, Lettice Knollys, widowed in 1576, married Leicester in 1578, who then became Essex's stepfather. Essex himself married Walsingham's daughter in 1590. Thus he was doubly connected to the Leicester–Walsingham axis. He accompanied Leicester to the Netherlands in 1586, where he had his first taste of military action.

Meeting Elizabeth. He first attracted Elizabeth's attention in 1587, when, aged nineteen, he arrived at Court. He was tall, good looking and accomplished. He was also a brave soldier.

Promotion and ambition. He was promoted to his stepfather's post of Master of Horse and gained entry to the Household. He was soon recognised as Elizabeth's favourite, spending hours in her company. Always ambitious for military glory, he joined Sir Francis Drake's unsuccessful voyage to Lisbon in 1589. Thanks to Elizabeth's favour, his plea to be given command of the expedition to France in 1591 was granted, and he took part in the abortive Siege of Rouen in 1591–2.

At home. The next four years were spent in England. Essex joined the Privy Council in 1593 and by all accounts was a reasonably diligent attender when he was available. He attended 35 out of 57 meetings between July 1598 and March 1599, for instance.

Greatest success. In 1596, he achieved his greatest success as military commander of the huge expedition to Cadiz. He was also put in charge of English naval operations in 1597, failing to intercept the Spanish silver fleet as had been hoped.

Rivalry with Robert Cecil. While Lord Burghley lived, the rivalry between his son Robert and Essex was muted. Even so, by 1598 Essex had begun to show his insatiable ambition. There was also a serious division between Essex and both Cecils on foreign policy. Essex was anxious to continue the war with Spain, both because he did not trust Spanish overtures for peace, and because war offered the best chance of personal advancement and enrichment (despite his own disappointing track record). Burghley sent his son to France in the summer of 1598 to safeguard English interests in the Franco-Spanish negotiations then proceeding. Henry IV ignored English and Dutch concerns and signed the Treaty of Vervins. When Burghley argued in the Privy Council that this opened the way to an English peace with Spain, Essex strongly dissented. Burghley, opening his Bible, quoted the Psalmist: 'Men of blood shall not live out half their days.'

Rejection. More serious than this division was **Essex's quarrel with Elizabeth** in June that year. Always hyper-sensitive to an imagined slight, when she rejected Essex's suggestion of Sir George Carew to become Deputy in Ireland, he turned his back on her. Elizabeth then, according to Robert Cecil, boxed his ears and dismissed Essex from the Court. It was this episode that caused Essex to remark in a letter to Lord Keeper Egerton, who was trying to heal the breach: 'What, cannot princes err? Cannot subjects receive wrong? I have received wrong and I feel it.'

Reconciliation. Burghley's death on 4 August 1598 brought Essex back to Court and there was a reconciliation with Elizabeth. In September he was again taking his place in the Privy Council. By this stage, too, the Irish Rebellion was in full swing, and an army and a commander were needed to suppress it. Essex, both in his own eyes, and the Council's, was the obvious man for the job, but even he had his reservations. He wrote in a letter to Lord Willoughby: 'The Queen has irrevocably decreed it; the Council do passionately urge it; and I am tied by my reputation to use no tergiversation [turning his back].' Essex was duly appointed on 12 April 1599. As we have seen, he had little success in Ireland, and his return to England in September brought his political and military career to an end, though this was not obvious at the time.

Allegations and arrest. After his sudden arrival at Court, Elizabeth had Essex consigned first to the house of Lord Keeper Egerton, then placed under house arrest in his own home. In the summer of 1600, he was called before an enlarged meeting of the Privy Council to answer various charges, the most serious of which related to his private dealing with the Earl of Tyrone. Essex was stripped of all his offices except the mastership of horse, and placed under custody during the Queen's pleasure.

Planning to rebel. In August 1600, Essex was allowed his liberty, though he was still banned from the Court. Had he been content to retire into private life he would probably have died in his bed (Elizabeth did not share her father's vindictiveness against failed servants). Unfortunately, Essex dabbled in treason. This had begun even before his disgrace.

He entered a secret correspondence with James VI as early as 1593. When in Ireland, he broached to his subordinates, Sir Christopher Blount and the Earl of Southampton, the possibility of using part of his army to march on London and oust the Cecilian faction from the Council. When in confinement in 1600, he corresponded with his successor as Irish Deputy, Lord Mountjoy, to see whether James VI could be induced to intervene on Essex's behalf. Mountjoy very wisely refused to act without James's support.

Last bid for power. What seems to have prompted Essex's final bid for power was Elizabeth's refusal in September 1600 to renew the **patent** for sweet wines, which was an essential source of Essex's income. His debts stood at £16,000. But poverty was not the only motive. Essex had gathered a number of committed supporters, mainly military men of gentry and noble status. They included the Earl of Southampton, Sir John Davies, Sir Charles Danvers, Sir Christopher Blount and Sir John Lyttleton. Danvers, Blount and Lyttleton were also Roman Catholics. Their intentions were to force an entry into Elizabeth's Privy Chamber and take control over her person. The Privy Council would be purged of its 'caterpillars of the Commonwealth' (self-made men like Robert Cecil), Parliament summoned and James VI named as Elizabeth's successor.

Executing the Essex Rebellion. Essex's rebellion was planned for early February 1601. The initial plan to enter the Privy Chamber at Whitehall was abandoned when it became known that Elizabeth's Guards had been doubled there. Instead, Essex decided to seize the City. On Saturday night, 7 February, his supporters arranged for a performance of Shakespeare's *Richard II* to be performed at the Globe Theatre, including the famous deposition scene. On Sunday, four Privy Councillors sent to Essex House to summon Essex to Court were themselves taken hostage, and Essex and 300 of his followers processed into the City. They were surrounded by the London Trained Bands, summoned by the mayor. Essex returned by river to Essex House and surrendered on the promise of a fair trial. The whole rebellion lasted just twelve hours.

The outcome. Essex and five of his close adherents were tried for treason and executed on 25 February. Many were spared on payment of fines, including the Earl of Southampton. It is hard to see in the Essex Rebellion a serious challenge to Elizabethan government, nor was it one that had been provoked by government action. Sir John Harington's comment on Essex's conduct is a fair one: 'He shifteth from sorrow and repentance to rage and rebellion so suddenly as well proveth him devoid of good reason as of like mind.' With Essex's execution, Robert Cecil's hold on power was now unchallenged and he was able to turn his mind to other problems.

KEY TERM

Patent The equivalent to a monopoly (see page 121). Every importer of sweet wines would have had to pay the Earl of Essex for the right to do so (see also page 182).

THE CHALLENGE FROM ELIZABETH'S LAST PARLIAMENT

While the war with Spain endured and the Irish Rebellion raged, the government was desperately in need of money. A Parliament would probably have been called at the beginning of 1601, but Essex's Rebellion delayed its summons until October. At its first meeting on 27 October, the Lord Keeper dwelt on Elizabeth's urgent need for money and, on 7 November, Cecil spelled out her needs more precisely. He called for £300,000, to be raised by Easter. With the Spaniards entrenched at Kinsale, 'it is time to open our coffers'.

The House agreed in principle to vote for four subsidies, but there was considerable argument over the form and distribution of the payments to be made. Ralegh urged that men of smaller incomes should pay less while others urged that all Justices of the Peace should be assessed at £20 of land, the statutory qualification for the office. In the end, no changes were made and the subsidy bill gained unanimous assent on 5 December. But its passage was delayed by another issue that showed the Commons in one of its most contentious moods, and Elizabeth at her most conciliatory.

KEY TERMS

Monopoly The granting to an individual of the sole right to produce and/or sell a particular commodity.

Prerogative The rights of the sovereign that could not be infringed by Parliament.

Monopolies

Monopolies had long been used as a fiscal device to raise money. The Crown would sell this right, and the purchaser would then be in a position to fix the price of the commodity in question. This was a long-standing grievance, and had been raised in the 1597–8 Parliament. Elizabeth had promised redress, but no action had been taken.

Legality of monopolies. When the Commons met in 1601 it was not long before the grievance was raised again. On 18 November, a bill to examine the legality of monopolies was introduced by a private member and gained a groundswell of support. The Queen had made it plain in 1597 that she regarded such action as infringing her **prerogative**. Cecil attempted to persuade the House to drop the bill and to refer the matter to a special committee. But, when the Clerk called the Commons to give the subsidy bill its first reading on 24 November, 'the House cried it away and called for the report of the monopolies'. They had openly adopted the principle that redress of grievances should precede the granting of taxes.

Intervention and reformation. Elizabeth then intervened. She sent a message through the Speaker promising to take present order for reformation of anything evil and that some monopolies should be 'presently repealed, some suspended and none put in execution but such as should first have a trial according to the law for the good of the people'.

Proclamation. Cecil followed with a speech promising a proclamation and itemising the monopolies to be revoked – including salt, vinegar and **woad**. The House voted to send the Speaker and about twelve members to express their thanks to Elizabeth. The proclamation was printed on 28 November 1597 and, on 30 November, Elizabeth received a large deputation of between 140 and 160 members in the Council Chamber at Whitehall. She delivered to them what has come to be known as her Golden Speech. It deserves to be quoted in full, but the following excerpts perhaps convey its flavour and sentiments:

> *I do assure you there is no prince that loves his subjects better, or whose love can countervail our love …*

> *Of myself I must say this: I never was any greedy, scraping grasper, nor a strait, fast-holding Prince, nor yet a waster. My heart was never set on worldly goods, but only for my subjects' good. What you bestow on me, I will not hoard it up, but receive it to bestow on you again …*

> *Mr. Speaker, you give me thanks, but I doubt me I have a greater cause to give you thanks than you me … For, had I not received a knowledge from you, I might have fallen into the lapse of an error, only for lack of true information …*

> *To be a King and wear a crown is a thing more glorious to them that see it, than it is pleasant to them that bear it. For myself, I was never so much enticed with the glorious name of a King or royal authority of a Queen, as delighted that God hath made me His instrument to maintain His truth and glory, and to defend this Kingdom (as I said) from peril, dishonour, tyranny and oppression …*

Elizabeth's last speech to Parliament

The Golden Speech was not Elizabeth's final speech to Members of Parliament. On 19 December 1601, the House assembled to hear their Speaker, John Croke, deliver an oration. In it he expressed his gratitude to Elizabeth:

> *And we, your most bounden and devoted subjects and servants, with the bended knees of our heart, do offer all thanks to God and your Majesty for our conservation in true religion, in peace, and in all happiness, for our preservation from tyranny, from thraldom [slavery], from dishonour, from oppression, from being a prey and spoil to our malicious and cruel enemies, from which God and your Majesty have delivered us.*

Elizabeth gave a gracious reply and a description of her reign, almost as though she was aware that it was her final opportunity to render an account of her stewardship. In the course of this reply, she referred to the 'devices, practices and strategems' attempted against her and the invasion of the State itself. She included a long passage on foreign policy:

> *Now touching foreign courses, which do chiefly consist in the maintenance of war: I take God to witness that I never gave just cause of war to any prince – which the subjects of other States can testify – nor had any greater ambition than to maintain my own State in security and peace, without being guilty to my own self of offering or intending injury to any man: though no prince have been more unthankfully requited, whose intention hath been so harmless and whose actions so moderate.*

There followed a detailed justification of her policy in the Netherlands and her dealings with King Philip II of Spain. There was a brief reference to Philip III's intervention in Ireland, and Elizabeth concluded:

> *At this time it will be sufficient to let you know the grounds and nurtures of the war to which you contribute; that my care is neither to continue war nor conclude a peace, but for your good … This testimony I would have you carry hence for the world to know: that your Sovereign is more careful of your conservation than of herself, and will daily crave of God that they that wish you best may never wish in vain.*

These were hardly the words of an irascible old woman.

Popular challenges to the government
It has sometimes been argued that the last years of Elizabeth's reign saw mounting protests from the poor.

Poor harvests. It is certainly true that a succession of poor harvests from 1594 to 1597 saw a huge increase in food prices and a corresponding fall in **real wages.**

Food riots. There were food riots in London, the south-east and the south-west in 1595. Up to 1800 apprentices, disbanded soldiers and masterless men took part in the London riots. Similar disturbances, albeit on a smaller scale, took place in 1596 in East Anglia, the south-west and on the Kent–Sussex border.

The Oxfordshire Rising. However, the only overt challenge to the government, the so-called Oxfordshire Rising of November 1596, was a damp squib. This rising was led by three young men without family ties.

They aimed to pull down enclosures, seize weapons from the local Lord Lieutenant and march on London. Only four rebels turned up at the appointed rendezvous. The Privy Council reacted in alarm and a specially appointed committee tortured them. They were then sentenced to death for treason.

New laws and legislation. It is significant, however, that legislation against enclosures was enacted in the next Parliament of 1597–8, and that a new poor law was introduced at the same time (see Chapter 9). The evidence suggests that popular unrest was caused by economic unrest; it was not part of a general challenge to the regime.

THE SUCCESSION

By 1603, Elizabeth was in her 70th year and the prospect of her death had to be faced.

Raising the question

The succession had been a matter of concern ever since her reign began. The Commons, it will be remembered, urged her to name her successor as early as 1563. Elizabeth resolutely refused to do so, or to allow public discussion of the issue. Anyone who raised the question was likely to be silenced.

The fate of Peter Wentworth. In 1587, **Peter Wentworth**, a Member of Parliament with Puritan sympathies, drafted a pamphlet entitled *A Pithie Exhortation to her Majesty for Establishing her Successor to the Crowne* (which was not intended for publication). In 1590, he tried to get a copy to the Earl of Essex, but instead it fell into the hands of the Privy Council. After interrogation he was arrested in August 1591. Released in February 1592, he indiscreetly tried to interest fellow Members of Parliament in the cause and was sent once more to the Tower of London for his persistence. He remained there until his death.

Father Parsons's attempt. No resident Englishman dared to re-open the question. But in Rome, Father Robert Parsons wrote *The Book of Succession* in 1595 under the pseudonym R. Doleman in which he canvassed the claims of other candidates besides James VI of Scotland. This book caused James and Cecil some concern, and its publication showed that the Scottish king's accession was not a foregone conclusion. In fact, there were several candidates with a claim as valid as James's (see the genealogy chart on page 6).

Arabella Stuart

Her claim to the throne rested on her descent from her father, Charles Stuart, the younger brother of Lord Darnley. In 1574 Charles Stuart married Elizabeth Cavendish, daughter of the redoubtable Bess of Hardwick. Queen Elizabeth was furious at the match and summoned both mothers to London. Arabella was born in 1575 and was seen as a serious rival to James VI. Invited to Court in 1603 by James, she fell in love with William Seymour, who had a claim to the throne through the Suffolk line. In 1610 the two married secretly, against James's orders. Both were arrested. They escaped from the Tower, but Arabella was seized on board ship and confined to the Tower where she died in 1615.

The candidates

- **Lady Arabella Stuart** could trace her claim to the throne back to Henry VII, through his daughter Margaret, as could James.
- Edward Seymour was similarly related to Henry VII through his second daughter, Mary.
- Father Parsons's favoured claimant was Isabella, daughter of Philip II by his third marriage, and now Archduchess of the Spanish Netherlands. She could trace her ancestry back to John of Gaunt, one of the sons of Edward III. (See genealogy chart on page 27.)
- James VI of Scotland.

Cecil's support for James

In 1599, Robert Cecil commissioned portraits of Isabella and her husband, Albert, and it is possible that he was hedging his bets. However, with the death of Essex in 1601, Cecil decided to throw in his lot with James. A secret correspondence was opened with the Scottish king in March 1601, which was maintained until his arrival in England. James also won Catholic support. In 1601, his wife, Anne of Denmark, admitted her conversion to Catholicism. James did not object, provided she was discreet.

News of the queen's conversion reached the new Pope, Clement VIII. He was now prepared to support James's accession, as was Isabella, in the hope that James too might return to the Catholic fold. In Catholic eyes, unlike Elizabeth I, he was legitimate, not a usurper and not excommunicate.

Thus, when Elizabeth's health began to fail in February 1603, all that was needed was to stage-manage the change of dynasty.

- On 20 March, Cecil sent to James a draft of the Proclamation of his accession. James gave his unstinted approval.
- On 23 March, Elizabeth fell unconscious.
- Surrounded by her Privy Councillors and bishops she died at 3 am on 24 March 1603.

The text of the Proclamation was read at various sites in London and printed for distribution throughout the land. Whether Elizabeth gave her approval on her deathbed or not is immaterial. The evidence is inconclusive.

James came to the throne because he was the most acceptable candidate, with the best claim, and because the leading figures in the Council wanted him there. The ease with which the transition from Elizabeth Tudor to James Stuart was accomplished also reflects the stable political system that had taken root during Elizabeth's long reign.

SUMMARY QUESTIONS

1 Examine the evidence for and against the view that veneration for Queen Elizabeth I diminished in the last decade of her reign.

2 Write a brief account of the military and political career of the Earl of Essex and assess his significance.

3 What were monopolies, and why did they arouse so much resentment in 1597 and 1601?

4 Why did James VI of Scotland succeed so easily to the English throne?

AS QUESTION IN THE STYLE OF OCR

How serious were the challenges to Queen Elizabeth's authority in the last decade of her reign?

Suggested approach to answering this question
This question requires you to identify the challenges, and from where they came, and to assess their seriousness.

Challenges come from:

- within the Privy Council, notably the Earl of Essex;
- the House of Commons;
- from the lower orders.

Challenges from within the Privy Council
- The successful operation of the Privy Council broke down with the deaths of Hatton and Walsingham, and with Burghley's increasing feebleness.
- Essex challenged Burghley over peace negotiations in 1598 and quarrelled with Elizabeth.
- There was a growing rivalry between the Essex and Cecil factions at Court after Burghley's death.
- On his return from Ireland, Essex's dismissal from both his offices and the Court persuaded him to attempt to seize and control the Queen in February 1601.
- Also to be considered are the circumstances of the Essex Rebellion and its aftermath.
- You will need to discuss the purpose of the Rebellion, the forces involved and the nature of Essex's supporters.

Challenges from the House of Commons
- Discuss the opposition to monopolies, both in 1597 and 1601, and the delaying of the subsidy bill.
- Make reference to the way the dispute is resolved and the Golden Speech.

Challenges from the lower orders
- Discuss the reasons for discontent (compulsory military service, high food prices and so on), and the nature of opposition.
- Mention the Privy Council's alarm at the Oxfordshire Rising of 1596.

The seriousness of the challenges
Points that could be made are as follows.

- Lack of support for Essex within the Privy Council, but he did have the support of some aristocrats and military men outside it. A possible rift in the governing class.
- Parliament's protests occurred within a framework of loyalty to the Queen. The largest subsidy of the reign was voted without dissent once monopolies had been withdrawn.
- None of the popular protests enjoyed gentry support, unlike Kett's Rebellion or the Rebellion of the Northern Earls. On the other hand, they did provoke a constructive response in the anti-enclosure legislation and the revised Poor Law passed in 1598.
- Robert Cecil was able to stage-manage the accession of James VI without difficulty.

PART III: FEATURES OF THE REGIME

CHAPTER 8

The working of the religious settlement

INTRODUCTION

The making of the Elizabethan religious settlement was discussed at some length in Chapter 3. In this chapter we shall be looking at the way in which the Anglican Church evolved. What characteristic features did it acquire in Elizabeth's reign? How successful was it in attracting an effective episcopate and clergy? How was it viewed by the laity? In the second part of the chapter we examine those who wanted to reform the Church in a more Protestant direction, the Puritans, and those who refused to have anything to do with it, the committed Catholic community.

THE MAKING OF THE ANGLICAN CHURCH

Influences

It will be remembered that, under the Act of Supremacy, Elizabeth I adopted the title of Supreme Governor of the Church of England, and there can be little doubt that hers was the main influence on the way the Church of England developed.

Elizabeth's religious preferences. There has been much speculation over Elizabeth's own religious preferences. At the age of eleven she translated a work of piety, *Miroir de l'ame pechereuse* (Mirror of the sinful soul), and has been credited with the authorship of a **book of private prayers**, made about 1578, which provide evidence of her personal devotion and sincerity. One of these prayers concludes:

> Grant me grace to live godly and to govern justly: that so living to please thee, and reigning to serve thee I may ever glorify thee, the Father of all goodness and mercy.

Elizabeth's religious views may also be inferred from her actions.

- She insisted on keeping a cross and candlesticks on the altar in royal chapel.
- She attended services daily.
- She made no secret of her dislike of a married clergy.
- She had little time for preaching, and would have preferred her ministers to confine themselves to reading homilies.
- She waged a constant struggle against Puritans both in the Church and in Parliament.

At the same time, while Elizabeth may have tried to moderate the hostility shown by some of her Councillors and Parliament to Catholics, she was prepared to sanction the savage legislation and repression of Catholicism that marked the later years of her reign. Thus, while political and international circumstances forced her into the Protestant camp, her preferences were to retain the Elizabethan settlement of 1559 (see pages 47–50) as little changed as possible.

But Elizabeth was only one influence on the Church. She had to take into account the views of her archbishops and some of her bishops. It has been calculated that seventeen of 27 bishoprics were occupied by **Marian exiles**.

Her archbishops. Elizabeth's three archbishops of Canterbury were:

- Matthew Parker, 1559–75 – a scholarly-minded don from Corpus Christi College, Cambridge.
- Edmund Grindal, 1576–83 – a Marian exile, previously Bishop of London and Archbishop of York.
- John Whitgift, 1583–1604 – whose views were closest to Elizabeth's. He was the only cleric to sit on the Privy Council.

The two **Convocations** of Canterbury and York on occasion produced initiatives of their own.

Her ministers. Elizabeth's ministers, notably William Cecil, had to interpret and enforce her wishes, and enjoyed a certain discretion when it came to appointments. Puritan-minded Members of Parliament regularly came up with suggestions and bills to reform the Church.

Others with influence. Finally, there were the views of writers such as John Foxe, whose *Acts and Monuments*, better known as *The Book of Martyrs*, did much to shape public opinion.

Changes and additions to the Elizabethan settlement
The main structure of the Elizabethan settlement had been created in 1559 with the Acts of Supremacy and Uniformity, and the injunctions

KEY TERMS

Marian exiles
Committed Protestants who had taken refuge on the Continent during Mary's reign. The majority went to Zurich, Geneva, Basle, Frankfurt and Strasbourg. Some 788 have been identified, of whom 67 were clerics.

Convocations
Assemblies of clergy who met on various occasions. Since the Submission of the Clergy in 1532 their recommendations were subject to Parliamentary approval.

that followed them (see Chapter 3). There were a number of significant additions, however, the most important of which are:

- the Geneva Bible;
- the Thirty-nine Articles;
- Parker's *Book of Advertisements*;
- other publications.

Matthew Parker, Archbishop of Canterbury, 1559–75.

The Geneva Bible, 1560. The Geneva Bible was translated by William Whittingham in Geneva, and had **Calvinist** notes. It was divided into chapters and verses, and was printed in roman type. It was relatively cheap, and went through 60 editions by 1611.

The Thirty-nine Articles, 1563. When the Canterbury Convocation met in 1563, there was a flurry of opposition to the injunctions. There were objections to such religious symbols as the use of the sign of the cross, the giving of a ring in the marriage service, kneeling at Communion and the compulsory wearing of the surplice. Proposals to end these practices failed by only a handful of votes. But Convocation did give its approval to the Thirty-nine Articles, a statement of the doctrinal beliefs of the Anglican Church, based on Archbishop Thomas Cranmer's Forty-two Articles of 1552. In most respects, the text was unchanged and reflected the moderate but nonetheless firmly Protestant views of their author. Elizabeth made some minor changes, deleting Article 29 which referred to the Lord's Supper. In 1571 under the Subscription Act, they were finally approved by Parliament with Article 29 restored, and subscription to them was made compulsory for all ordained clergy.

Parker's Advertisements, 1566. Archbishop Parker became concerned about the variety of practices, especially in relation to clerical dress, that were brought to his notice. In March 1566, 37 London clergy were suspended for refusing to wear the surplice (see Chapter 3, page 51). Later in the year, Parker issued his *Book of Advertisements*. This publication laid down rules for the ordination of ministers, licensing of preachers and clerical apparel. The surplice was to be worn in church, and clerical dress outside. The *Advertisements* were issued without Elizabeth's approval because Parker did not insist on the wearing of copes for Communion services. The Vestiarian controversy, as it came to be called, rumbled on and no consistent policy was pursued.

Other publications. Three books also helped to shape the Elizabethan Church:

- *Book of Martyrs*;
- *An Apology of the Church of England*;
- *Of the Lawes of Ecclesiastical Politie*.

KEY TERM

Calvinist
Generally used to describe the followers of John Calvin, but in this context it has a more specific meaning. It applies to those clergy and laity who went to Calvin's Geneva during Mary's reign. William Whittingham was such a one. He stayed in Geneva until 1560 in order to complete his translation of the Bible. (For Calvin's ideas see Key person on p. 134.)

Author John Foxe.

- *Book of Martyrs*. The most popular, and therefore probably the most influential of these publications, was **John Foxe**'s *Book of Martyrs*. This ran through several editions and was continually expanded. By 1563 it ran to 2000 pages. It contained a history of all the martyrs of the Christian Church from its foundation. Foxe's accuracy, certainly so far as the Marian martyrs are concerned, has generally been supported. But he was writing from a committed Protestant viewpoint, and his identification of the Papacy as Antichrist rested on some very dubious calculations in relation to the number 666 in the Book of Revelation. Anti-Catholic sentiment was a pronounced feature of the Elizabethan Church, shared by many, if not all, of its adherents.

- *An Apology of the Church of England*. A more moderate defender of Anglicanism was John Jewel, Bishop of Salisbury, whose *Apology* was published in 1562. Jewel argued that the English had left the Roman obedience justly, because, since the Papacy of Pope Gregory VII (1073–1085), popes had claimed an unwarranted authority. Thus Elizabeth and Parliament had returned to 'the true Catholic Church founded by the Apostles and Fathers, the Scriptures and justified by Scripture'. Elizabeth had 'departed from that Church which these men call [Roman] catholic … and we are come, as near as we possibly could, to the church of the apostles and of the old catholic bishops and fathers'.

- *Of the Lawes of Ecclesiastical Politie*. The most acute defender of the Anglican Church was Richard Hooker, whose academic work *Of the Lawes of Ecclesiastical Politie*, which comprised eight books, was written in the 1590s. The first five books were published between 1594 and 1597. For Hooker, the Church and the Commonwealth were one, and laws for the Church must have the assent of the monarch, Convocation and Parliament. Hooker also identified three sources of authority: the Bible, tradition and reason. Though his publication was least read, it provided the most convincing defence of the Anglican Church.

It should not be forgotten that, as well as the changes listed above, the Anglican Church retained the traditional structure it inherited. It continued to be divided into the two provinces of York and Canterbury, and into their 25 **dioceses** (including the Welsh dioceses and the Isle of Man). The ecclesiastical courts continued almost without change, both in terms of their organisation and work. Thus by the end of Elizabeth's reign the Church of England had:

- a well-established organisation;
- a matchless liturgy in Cranmer's *Book of Common Prayer*;
- an accessible English translation of the Bible;
- a statement of its doctrinal position in the Thirty-nine Articles;
- two convincing defences of its separate identity.

The Anglican Church on the ground

Parishes. It is much harder to assess the impact of the Church of England at the parish level. There is plenty of **qualitative evidence**, taken from the records of visitations and ecclesiastical courts, the comments of bishops and clergy, and miscellaneous pieces of information. But there is a wide discrepancy of views on such basic questions as the number of clergy or church attendance.

Buildings. We are on relatively firm ground when it comes to church buildings. There was no such wholesale destruction of church property as had occurred under Henry VIII, but, according to one authority, there were only nineteen churches or chapels built or rebuilt in Elizabeth's reign. Many church interiors were stripped of their Catholic trimmings and wall paintings, where these had survived.

Material resources. The Church's material resources had suffered, too, from the dissolution of the monasteries and chantries in the reigns of Henry VIII and Edward VI. Elizabeth showed little concern for the Church's material needs. She kept dioceses vacant so that revenues due to the bishop would come to the Crown instead.

Land. Church lands were frequently rented out on long leases, making it impossible to increase rents in line with inflation. Church lands were exchanged for impropriated **tithes**. Whitgift calculated in 1584 that only 600 parishes out of almost 13,000 yielded an income sufficient to attract a graduate clergyman. (Though Whitgift grossly exaggerated the number of parishes in England. It was nearer 9000 than 13,000.)

Cathedrals. At the same time there was, surprisingly, no interference with Elizabethan cathedrals and the tradition of choral music flourished thanks to Elizabeth's patronage. The **Chapel Royal** continued to function and composers such as Thomas Tallis, William Byrd, Orlando Gibbons and Thomas Morley all wrote church music of superb quality under its auspices. Byrd's Catholic sympathies did not prevent his continued employment.

Bishops and archbishops. Elizabeth's archbishops and bishops probably compared well both with their predecessors and their successors. Cecil had a hand in the first appointments, and chose men of committed Protestant views, for the most part. Among the best were:

- John Jewel – Bishop of Salisbury;
- Richard Cox – Bishop of Norwich;
- William Alley – Bishop of Exeter;
- Richard Cheyney – Bishop of Gloucester.

KEY TERMS

Qualitative evidence Such matters as irreverent behaviour in church, the low calibre of preaching and the counter attractions of football and the ale house on Sundays.

Tithes Regular payments owing to the Church, in theory 10 per cent of income. When tithes were impropriated, they were paid, not to the Church, but to a layman, thus reducing the Church's income.

Chapel Royal This was not a building, but a body of clergy and musicians employed to attend the monarch.

John Jewel, Bishop of Salisbury.

There were few idle or careerist men among them, though Richard Fletcher, who became Bishop of London, was an exception. Unlike some of their medieval forbears, they stayed in their dioceses and stuck to their **episcopal** duties.

Ordinary clergy. So far as the ordinary clergy are concerned, there was an initial decline in the numbers seeking **ordination**. However, by the end of the century the situation had improved and there was a visible rise in the numbers of graduates. In Canterbury the proportion rose from 18 per cent in 1571 to 60 per cent in 1603, and most southern dioceses would have shown similar increases. Two Cambridge colleges – Emmanuel (1584) and Sidney Sussex (1594) – were founded to provide a learned ministry. How many of these men were good preachers and pastors it is impossible to say. There were certainly attempts to increase the numbers of **licensed preachers**, and many towns such as Ipswich funded their own lecturers. **Patrick Collinson**, a leading authority on Puritanism, has traced the growth of these preachers and concludes that, by the end of the reign, London parishes and most market towns could call upon their services. These initiatives were viewed unsympathetically by the Queen, and one of the major problems faced by the Church of England was that many of its most committed members shared the Puritan inclinations to which she was so opposed.

Laity. If it is hard to generalise about the clergy, it is impossible to do so about the laity. One of the few certain facts is that in 1603, according to a comprehensive episcopal census, 2,266,000 took Communion in an Anglican church. This compares with a figure of 8600 recusants.

Church attendance. Under successive Acts of Uniformity, attendance at an Anglican place of worship was compulsory every Sunday and on Saints' Days. Local records are full of complaints about non-attendance. Nicholas Bacon asked Parliament in 1563: 'How cometh it to pass that the common people in the country come so seldom to common prayer and divine service?' But few prosecutions were brought in the ecclesiastical courts for non-attendance, and, while Catholics might have to pay recusancy fines, none were levied on Protestants.

Bible reading and personal devotion. If church attendance figures cannot be measured with any precision, except on particular occasions such as Easter, it is even less easy to trace the extent of Bible reading and personal devotion. But the Bible, closely followed by Foxe's *Book of Martyrs*, were probably the two best-known and most-read books in Elizabethan England.

THE CHALLENGE OF PURITANISM

Who were the Puritans?
In a letter dated 1559 to a friend in Zurich, Bishop Jewel wrote:

Others are seeking after a golden, or as it rather seems to me, a leaden mediocrity; and are crying out that the half is better than the whole.

In one sense, the Puritans were all those who did not think that the Elizabethan settlement of 1559 had gone far enough.

- The first use of the term itself has been traced to a Catholic exile in 1565 who referred to 'the hot puritans of the new clergy'.
- By the end of the sixteenth century, 'puritan' came to be used to describe the overly religious and the killjoys who turned against what they saw as sinful pleasures.
- In 1602, a Puritan was described as 'one who loves God with all his soul and hateth his neighbour with all his heart'.

Thus, much depends on the context in which the word is used, and who is using it.

Two strands of Elizabethan Puritanism
Elizabethan Puritanism had two main strands.

The first strand. The first strand, who formed the majority, would have included those who were loyal to the Anglican Church, but who wished to purge it of what they saw as popish practices. Their wishes were reflected in the changes called for at the Convocation of 1563. In addition, they wanted the use of ordinary bread rather than wafers at the Communion service. They were opposed to the wearing of the surplice. They wished to see a greater emphasis on preaching and Bible reading. Many of Elizabeth's bishops were sympathetic to such requests, and if Puritanism had stopped there it would not have been a serious challenge.

The second strand. The second strand we may call Presbyterianism. These Puritans looked to **John Calvin** and Geneva for the true Church. This implied a much simpler form of service, relying chiefly on metrical psalms and the exposition of Scripture. The **Presbyterians** also believed in the parity (equality) of ministers, and therefore the abolition of bishops. Each congregation should have the right to elect elders, who in turn would choose their minister. Calvinists also held to the doctrine of **predestination**.

Both these strands believed in a national Church. They wanted to remodel it to suit their beliefs.

Predestination

The belief, in its simplest form, that because God is All-powerful and All-knowing, the fate of every human being has already been determined. It follows from this that human beings are divided into the 'elect' (the chosen) and the 'reprobate' (the damned). Calvin traced this doctrine back to St Augustine, but gave it a particular emphasis. Knowledge that one belonged to the 'elect', it has been argued, gave a strong sense of self-belief to Calvinists. This would be reflected in virtuous living. It was possible to believe in predestination without sharing Calvin's ideas about Church government. Archbishop Whitgift was in this position.

Edmund Grindal.

There was a third group, known as the Separatists or **sectaries** (see Key terms on page 136), who believed the national Church was past redemption. Salvation could only be found in individual congregations of like-minded believers.

Elizabeth and her bishops had to contend with opposition from each of these groups. The Queen herself would have no truck with any of them. Her first two archbishops were not unsympathetic to the first group but Whitgift, her third, was of the same mind as Elizabeth.

Puritan opposition

This came in the form of:

- attempts by moderates to end Catholic practices and introduce more preaching;
- attempts by Presbyterians to abolish the Prayer Book and bishops.

The moderates. Though their demands were narrowly defeated in the Convocation of 1563, the moderates continued to press their case at various points throughout the reign. Their views were reflected in the House of Commons, and in 1571 William Strickland introduced a bill to reform the Prayer Book by outlawing practices such as the use of the surplice, kneeling at Communion and the use of the ring in marriage. Elizabeth reacted furiously. Strickland was arrested and barred from the House. Every subsequent attempt to promote moderate changes through Parliament was successfully resisted.

Elizabeth also managed to suppress the exercise of **prophesyings** (see Key terms on page 136). Several dioceses had introduced them in the 1570s, and Grindal gave them his support when he became Archbishop of Canterbury in 1575. Elizabeth ordered him to end prophesyings. Grindal took the step of canvassing all of his dioceses, who reported favourably on the practice. The Queen refused to change her mind.

Grindal stuck to his guns. In a long letter to Elizabeth he argued that:

The said exercises for the interpretation and exposition of the Scriptures ... are both profitable to increase knowledge among the ministers and tendeth to the edifying of the hearers.

The letter concluded with the words:

Bear with me, I beseech you, Madam, if I choose rather to offend your earthly Majesty than the heavenly majesty of God.

In June 1577, Grindal was suspended from his office, though not actually deprived of it.

The Presbyterian challenge. The Presbyterian challenge surfaced in 1570 when Thomas Cartwright, Professor of Divinity at Cambridge, delivered a lecture advocating the parity of ministers. Cartwright was dismissed, but joined two others, John Field and Thomas Wilcox, in a Puritan campaign preparatory to the assembly of Parliament in 1572. Thomas Wilcox also produced *A First Admonition to the Parliament*. The *Admonition* did not mince its words. It described the Prayer Book as 'an unperfect book, culled and picked out of the popish dunghill, the mass book full of abominations'. It also called for the abolition of bishops and parity of ministers. Field and Wilcox were imprisoned, and Cartwright escaped to the Continent.

After his release and aided by Travers, Field continued to work for a Presbyterian system, but did so covertly. They set up what has been called the Classis system (*Classis* is Latin for 'fleet'). Parishes in East Anglia formed themselves into groups where like-minded ministers could meet together. In 1582, they held what amounted almost to a national **synod** at Cambridge. In the face of this challenge the new Archbishop of Canterbury, John Whitgift, who succeeded Grindal in 1583, launched a campaign to oust Presbyterian supporters. He required all ministers to subscribe to three articles.

- The first acknowledged the royal supremacy over the Church.
- The second demanded assent to the proposition that the 1559 Prayer Book contained nothing contrary to the word of God.
- The third required clergy to subscribe to all of the Thirty-nine Articles, not just the doctrinal ones as had been the case in 1571.

Between 300 and 400 clergy were suspended when they refused to give their assent. This provoked an angry reaction in Parliament and from some members of the Privy Council. Whitgift changed his tactics, offering instead to interrogate clergy on oath. Burghley complained that his proceedings 'savoureth of the **Romish inquisition**'.

From 1584 to 1586, Field and his supporters began to draw up a Survey of Ministry in an attempt to identify would-be Presbyterians and to place their supporters in livings where the patron was sympathetic. At this distance in time it is hard to assess what progress they made, and with Field's death in 1588 this initiative came to an end.

Synod A Church council attended by clergy and sometimes laity as well.

Romish inquisition The inquisition was an ecclesiastical tribunal for the suppression of heresy. The Spanish inquisition was first established in 1478 to deal with Moors and Jews. A separate tribunal was set up in Rome in 1542 to combat Protestantism.

Two further challenges

There were two more challenges to be faced:

* Cope's Bill and Book;
* *The Martin Marprelate Tracts*.

The Bill and Book. In the Parliament of 1586–7, summoned to support the execution of Mary Queen of Scots, a new Member of Parliament, Sir Anthony Cope, introduced a Bill and Book that would have completely transformed the Elizabethan Church.

* The first clause introduced the Genevan Prayer Book, which also incorporated a Presbyterian form of Church government.
* The second declared null and void all existing legislation relating to the Church of England.

This was a revolutionary document, and it commanded some support in the House of Commons. The bill was introduced on 27 February 1587. The Speaker begged members not to proceed, but some of them insisted on doing so. Two of them at least spoke in the bill's defence. Elizabeth immediately sent for the Bill and Book. This did not stop the House from debating the state of the Church the following day.

On 1 March, Peter Wentworth made a lengthy speech asserting the privilege of freedom of speech. The Speaker was summoned to Court. Wentworth was sent to the Tower where he was joined by Cope and his supporters on 2 March. There was a further debate on 4 March, when Privy Councillors Hatton, Egerton and Sir Walter Mildmay, a respected Puritan MP, delivered a massive attack on the Cope Bill. A message from Elizabeth made no concessions and concluded with the assertion that 'the full power, authority, jurisdiction and supremacy in church causes … should be united and annexed to the Imperial Crown of this realm'.

The Martin Marprelate Tracts. The last attack on the Church settlement took the form of a series of pamphlets known as *The Martin Marprelate Tracts*. As their title suggests their targets were bishops, who were described as 'profane, proud, paltry, popish, pestilent, pernicious, presumptious prelates'. The authors have never been identified, but may have been:

* Job Throckmorton (a Warwickshire MP who supported Cope's Bill),
* John Penry (a fiery Welsh preacher who was arrested for his part in circulating the *Tracts*).

Death penalties and punishments

Up to this point, no Puritan had suffered the death penalty, but in 1593 three men were put to death: **Henry Barrow**, **John Greenwood** and John Penry. Their offence was to challenge the royal supremacy and the crime they had committed was sedition.

In the same year, an Act to retain her Majesty's Subjects in Their True Obedience was passed in Parliament. This was directed particularly at the Separatists, known as sectaries. Those who could not accept the national Church were henceforth to be banished, with the loss of all their goods and **chattels**. Catholics were expressly excluded from banishment, indicating the change in the temper of Parliament, both to Catholics and Separatists.

Thus the Puritan challenge was held off. But, as James VI would find to his cost, it had not been crushed.

THE CHALLENGE FROM ROMAN CATHOLICISM

The nature of the challenge

The threat posed by Catholicism to Elizabeth's rule has already been discussed in Chapter 4. She was threatened by revolt, conspiracy and assassination. Her realm was prey to invasion. But there was another threat, a more subtle and in the long run, it might be argued, a more powerful one to the Elizabethan settlement. If the Catholic faith could be preserved in England, it might retain the loyalty of a faithful remnant who would provide a launching pad for the reconversion of the majority of Protestants, or heretics as they were seen in Catholic eyes. It was disastrous for Catholic fortunes that these two threats were so closely linked.

The seminary and Jesuit priests who risked, and often forfeited, their lives in their missionary endeavours would mostly have claimed that all they sought to do was to sustain the Catholic faith. But, as one historian, **A.G. Dickens**, has put it:

The fact remains that they were sent by superiors and rulers with every intention of arousing civil war and of using their work as a basis for the forcible imposition of a foreign Catholic monarch upon England (The English Reformation, second edition, 1989).

Henry Barrow and **John Greenwood** Both men were educated at Cambridge University. They co-operated in the production of Separatist publications attacking popery, episcopacy and Presbyterianism. Penry supported them.

KEY TERM

Chattels Movable goods.

Cardinal William Allen urged Englishmen to support the Spanish Armada. The Jesuit Robert Parsons actively canvassed the claims of Philip II and then of his daughter, Isabella, to the English throne. In these circumstances, the nurturing and spreading of Catholicism came to seem more and more like giving aid and comfort to the enemy.

The survival of Catholicism

It has recently been argued by several historians, notably **J. Scarisbrick**, **C. Haigh** and **E. Duffy**, that England was still, under the surface, a Catholic country in 1558.

In the north. In Lancashire and Yorkshire, Marian priests continued to say Mass without interference from the authorities. In Lancashire the Bishop of Chester reported that only five out of 25 Justices of the Peace supported the established Church. In 1564, a national survey of JPs for the Privy Council revealed that, in response to the religious changes that had occurred since 1558:

- 431 were favourable;
- 264 were indifferent (or neutral);
- 157 were hostile.

In the south and east. There were Catholic enclaves in the south too, in Sussex, Suffolk, Norfolk and Hampshire.

Nationally. In 1577, a hastily-conducted national survey that concentrated on the gentry and known malcontents listed 1500 recusants, but there were many more 'Church Papists' – that is, Catholic sympathisers who attended Anglican worship to stay clear of trouble.

It had been Elizabeth's hope that by tolerating such practices Catholicism would eventually die out, as Marian priests gave way to Protestant ministers and the advantages of conforming would win over the Catholic laity. In practice, it seems that this was not happening, or not as fast as the government would have liked.

When Pope Pius V first forbade Catholics from attending Protestant services in 1564 and then excommunicated Elizabeth in 1570, the dividing lines were sharply drawn. The possibility that Catholicism might be allowed to survive as a minority faith could not satisfy either side.

The impact of seminary and Jesuit priests

It has been calculated that about 470 priests, trained in the seminaries set up at Douai, Rheims, St Omer, Rome and Valladolid, came to England in the course of Elizabeth's reign. Of this number, 131 were put to death.

While no one disputes the devotion and heroism these priests showed, doubts have been expressed about the effectiveness of their work. **Haigh** argues that their efforts were misdirected. Over half of their number spent their time in Essex, London and the Thames valley where only one-fifth of recusants were to be found. At the same time, large groups of Catholics in the north of England were without the services of a priest, despite the fact that 66 seminary priests worked in Lancashire before 1603. Haigh also criticises the tendency for these priests to concentrate their efforts on noble and gentry families in the south at the expense of more numerous and poorer groups in the north and in Wales.

Haigh's criticism may have some validity. It was a Jesuit priest, Robert Southwell, who commented in 1586 that 'the priests actually working in the harvest betake themselves in great numbers to one or two counties, leaving the others devoid of pastors'. But one has only to read the autobiography of one of the most successful Jesuits, John Gerard, to realise how dependent they were on safe houses if they were to survive. In keeping the gentry loyal to Catholicism the seminary priests were at least ensuring that families of wealth and status could provide shelter for the faith in the future.

It may have been a **seigneurial** Catholicism that survived in England, but in the context of the sixteenth century it is hard to see what alternative was on offer.

Government responses

As we have seen in Chapter 4, the response of the Privy Council and Parliament to the growing number of seminary priests was to tighten the screw. The Treasons Act of 1571, the Act to retain her Majesty's Subjects in their True Obedience of 1581, the increase in recusancy fines to £20 a month (also in 1581), and the Act against Jesuit and Seminary Priests in 1585 could all be used to confine priests, and, in many cases, put them to death.

Under the Act of 1585, any Catholic priest ordained since 1585 was given 40 days to leave the kingdom. Thereafter he could be sentenced to death for high treason, merely for being a priest in England. It was under this statute that the majority of Catholic priests (123), were put to death. The Privy Council still claimed that the priests were sentenced not for their beliefs but for their implied treason.

At their trials they were faced with the **Bloody Question**:

> *Whose side would you take if the Bishop of Rome [the Pope] or other prince by his authority should invade the realm with an army ...?*

KEY TEXT

Haigh The view is expressed in his essay, 'The Church of England, the Catholics and the People' in *The Reign of Elizabeth I* (1984).

KEY TERMS

Seigneurial Associated with the landowning gentry, and dependent on their support.

The Bloody Question Strictly speaking, most missionary priests were put to death under the statute of 1585. Their mere presence amounted to treason. It became the practice to pose the Bloody Question or a variant of it so that the accused would also incriminate themselves as potential traitors.

Campion said that the Pope's power to depose sovereigns was a matter for discussion and that he accepted Elizabeth as his queen. But other Jesuits, such as those involved in the Throckmorton Conspiracy and Robert Parsons, were actively promoting the invasion of the realm.

Not surprisingly, there were many priests who disagreed with the policy of seeking to overthrow Elizabeth. In the 1590s, a serious dispute broke out on this question. The particular issue that brought it to a head was the Pope's appointment of George Blackwell to be archpriest, in effect bishop over all priests in England. Though not a Jesuit himself, Blackwell was known to be under their influence.

A group of priests, known as the Appellants, who favoured a policy of co-operation with the government and were jealous of the Jesuits, appealed to the Pope for Blackwell's replacement in 1598. They were initially unsuccessful, but in 1602 Blackwell was reprimanded and, in 1603, thirteen priests reached an agreement with the authorities. They were still not permitted to say Mass, but they continued to acknowledge the Pope's spiritual authority.

It is hard to judge how successful government measures were. It has been calculated that recusancy fines were only levied on 220 people between 1581 and 1593, though this number included men like Sir Thomas Tresham who paid £8000. The courage with which the victims faced their deaths could not but impress the bystanders, and might be compared with the example given by the Protestant martyrs in Mary's reign. Catholicism certainly survived, as the figures below show.

- A survey of Catholic recusants made by bishops in each of their dioceses in 1603 came to a total of 8630.
- A very careful census of recusants made in Yorkshire in 1604 produced a figure of 3500 in that county alone.
- A recent estimate suggests that there were as many as 30,000 recusants and Church Papists in England in 1604. (See P. Williams, *The Late Tudors, England 1547–1603*, 1995.) Among them was an intransigent minority who were still prepared to revert to violent conspiracy.

As with the Puritans, James VI was to find when he came to the throne that he had raised expectations he could not possibly meet. It was disillusion with his failure to relax the laws against Catholics that provoked the **Gunpowder Plot** in 1605, which, in its turn, led to an increase in the severity of the laws against Catholics.

KEY EVENT

The Gunpowder Plot A conspiracy organised by Robert Catesby and other Catholic gentry to blow up the House of Lords during the state opening of Parliament, at which King James I and other members of the royal family would be present.

Perhaps the best tribute that can be paid to the work of the Jesuit and seminary priests comes from one Anglican historian (**A.G. Dickens**):

> *That Catholicism survived in England as a minority religion has nevertheless proved in the long run a religious and cultural enrichment of the first order* (*The English Reformation*, second edition, 1989).

In the short run, that was not how Protestant Englishmen are likely to have seen it.

SUMMARY QUESTIONS

1 Summarise the additions made to the Elizabethan religious settlement between 1560 and 1603.

2 Describe the structure, doctrine and liturgy of the Anglican Church as they were in 1603.

3 Define, with examples, the main varieties of Puritanism.

4 Give a chronological account of Puritan challenges to the Elizabethan settlement and the government's responses to them.

5 Assess the strength of Catholicism in England in 1559 and in 1603.

A2 QUESTION IN THE STYLE OF AQA

Read the extracts below, then answer the questions that follow.

Source A

In no sense did the settlement [the Elizabethan religious settlement] arise from a compromise between Elizabethan Protestants and Marian Catholics. By a whole series of actions before Parliament met, Elizabeth showed her personal and independent desire for a non-Catholic settlement. Pending Parliamentary recognition she kept open her claim to the Royal Supremacy by adding '&' after her royal titles. She chose William Bill, a noted Protestant, to be the first preacher at Paul's Cross and she imprisoned a Catholic who answered him too fiercely. On the Christmas Sunday she commanded Bishop Oglethorpe to omit the elevation of the host at mass, and on his refusal she withdrew before it occurred … Already on 31 January Feria was writing to Philip that 'the Catholics are very fearful of the measures to be taken in this Parliament'. All these hints were deliberately given by Elizabeth before she began to encounter any Parliamentary pressure. However remote from Geneva, she intended from the first to figure in the character of a Protestant monarch. Whatever her pretences, one finds it almost impossible to believe that at any stage she seriously contemplated a concordat with Rome or even a return to her father's brand of conservative orthodoxy.

Source: A.G. Dickens, *The English Reformation,* Batsford, second edition, 1989.

Source B

Elizabeth could not admit that she was afraid of Catholics, indeed she behaved in ways that made some of her advisers think she was insufficiently afraid of them. But many of her policies were framed with at least half an eye to English Catholic opinion (and perhaps a glance towards Spain). Elizabeth's liturgical conservatism, her enforcement of clerical conformity, her reluctance to support Protestant rebels abroad, her restraint of Protestant preaching, and her moderation of the persecution of Catholics, all suggest a determination not to drive Catholics into outright opposition. The same may be true of the burning of two Dutch Anabaptists at Smithfield in 1575: the Queen herself signed the warrant and specified the traditional place of execution, thus emphasising her personal hostility to heresy.

Elizabeth wanted to be Queen of the English, not Queen of the Protestants, and she tried to associate conservatives with her regime. In 1558 she kept the more moderate (and, it is true more powerful) of Mary's Catholic councillors in office, Winchester, Arundel, Derby and Shrewsbury … Elizabeth was almost proud of her loyal Catholic subjects. When travelling on progress in 1568, Elizabeth heard an elderly bystander call out 'Vivat Regina'; she beamed, and told her companion, the Spanish ambassador, 'This good old man is a clergyman of the old religion.'

Source: C. Haigh, *Elizabeth I,* Longman second edition, 1988.

Questions

> 1 Study Sources A and B. How far do the authors of these two extracts agree on Elizabeth's attitude to Catholicism?

Suggested approach to answering this question

In any question that invites a comparison you are being asked to find differences and similarities. You should also refer directly and specifically to key phrases and statements in the text.

Both authors acknowledge Elizabeth's determination to have the kind of settlement she wanted. There is no dispute on Elizabeth's belief in the royal supremacy. The differences arise in their interpretation of her wishes.

In Source A, the author states that Elizabeth 'showed her personal and independent desire for a non-Catholic settlement'. She intended from the first 'to figure in the character of a Protestant monarch'. She was also willing to antagonise Catholic sentiment, as in the choice of William Bill as a preacher and her behaviour at the Christmas Sunday Mass.

Source B, on the other hand, stresses that Elizabeth wanted to be Queen of the English, not Queen of the Protestants, and emphasises the conciliatory policies she pursued towards Catholicism in the first part of the reign, and her anxiety to get Catholic sentiment on her side – for example, through her keeping some of Mary's Catholic Councillors.

You might use your further knowledge to comment on these disagreements.

Certainly the settlement that emerged in 1559 was undeniably Protestant, but such Catholic features that do survive – for example, the use of vestments – may owe something to Elizabeth's intervention. Source A makes it clear that Elizabeth had little sympathy for Calvinism – 'however remote from Geneva'. While in the first part of the reign Elizabeth was willing to conciliate Catholics, after 1570 and the Papal Bull of Excommunication she accepted most of the harsh legislation initiated by the Privy Council against Catholics.

> 2 Study Sources A and B and, using your own knowledge, discuss the validity of the following statement.

'Elizabeth was less tolerant of Puritanism than she was of Catholicism.'

Suggested approach to answering this question

In any question that asks you to discuss a historical judgement, you are expected to weigh the evidence for or against that judgement. The conclusion you reach is immaterial, providing you have considered the arguments on both sides. It is wise to decide on the conclusion you intend to reach before you begin the essay. In this question you are expected to use the sources, but also to use your further knowledge.

Your essay should include reference to at least most of the following points:

Treatment of Puritans
- Elizabeth's lack of sympathy for moderate reforms – for example, on the use of vestments;
- her opposition to clerical marriage;
- her opposition to preaching, the suppression of exercises of prophesyings and the suspension of Grindal;
- her vetoing of Parliamentary debates on Puritan proposals – for example, Strickland's and Cope's bill;
- her appointment of Whitgift and support of his insistence on conformity;
- the banishing of sectaries in 1593;
- the executions of Penry, Barrow and Greenwood.

If you refer to the Anabaptists put to death in 1575, it would be sensible to point out that they would probably have met the same fate anywhere else in Europe, Catholic or Protestant.

Treatment of Catholics
- the comparatively lenient treatment given to Catholics until 1570 when the Papal Bull of Excommunication changed the status of Catholics, making them potential rebels;
- the harsh legislation of 1571, 1581 and 1585;
- the raising of recusancy fines;
- the campaign to discover Jesuit and seminary priests, and the savage treatment they received.

When comparing Elizabeth's attitudes to Puritans and Catholics you will probably want to distinguish between different periods of the reign, and between Elizabeth's personal preferences and the policies into which she was forced by changing circumstances.

A2 QUESTION IN THE STYLE OF OCR

How successful were the measures adopted by Elizabeth and her ministers to contain the threat posed by Roman Catholics during her reign?

Suggested approach to answering this question
The key words are 'how successful'. You are being asked to assess the success of Elizabeth's measures in containing the threat from Catholics. This means that you must:

- analyse the threat;
- describe the measures adopted;
- assess their success.

The essay falls naturally into these three parts. You will also need to work out how you judge success.

Part 1: the two-fold nature of the threat. This came from extreme Catholics like Parsons and Allen who wanted to see the Catholic faith restored, and following the Papal Bull of 1570 were prepared to condone the assassination of Elizabeth (mention plots) and replace her by Mary Queen of Scots. Ultimately the threat came from Philip II and the Armadas of 1588, 1596 and 1597.

It also came from the work of seminary priests and Jesuits who wanted to keep the Catholic faith alive and, by their zeal, weaken the appeal of the Church of England to Church Papists, thus preparing the way for the re-conversion of England once a Catholic regime had been established. After the Papal Bull of 1570, the government found it impossible to separate the two threats.

Part 2: measures taken to deal with the threats
- Threat 1: measures taken included Walsingham's intelligence service, Bond of Association, the execution of Mary, and the navy.
- Threat 2: measures taken included legislation against recusants and seminary priests (1571, 1581, 1585) whereby around 187 priests were put to death or died in prison. Levying of recusancy fines hit the fortunes of 200 Catholic families.

Part 3: assessment of success. The political threat was contained. Plots were discovered, Mary was executed, and Armadas were defeated or lost through bad weather.

The threat to the Church of England was reduced but not ended. Recusancy survived, even if it was confined to noble households. One estimate suggested that there were 30,000 recusants and Church Papists in England in 1604 – mostly concentrated in Lancashire and Yorkshire. A determined minority survived, prepared to take part in the Gunpowder Plot in 1605.

CHAPTER 9

The working of Elizabethan government

INTRODUCTION

KEY TEXTS

C. Haigh
Elizabeth I (1998)
for a critical view
of Elizabeth.

J.E. Neale *The
Elizabethan House
of Commons*
(1949), *Elizabeth
and Her
Parliaments,
1559–81* (1953)
and *Elizabeth and
Her Parliaments,
1584–1601*
(1957).

G.R. Elton *The
Parliament of
England, 1559–81*
(1986) for
conflicting views
on the role and
importance of the
Elizabethan House
of Commons.

The institutions of government in Elizabethan England have already been described in this book (see Chapter 1). It is the purpose of this chapter, therefore, to study their operation and to see how well they worked in practice. Recent research and the work of revisionist historians such as **C. Haigh** have cast doubt, particularly, over the success of Elizabeth herself in handling the issues that confronted her. The pioneering work of **J.E. Neale** on Elizabethan Parliaments, in which he argued that 'the House of Commons reached maturity in Elizabeth's reign' has also come in for serious criticism from **G.R. Elton**, who sees no significant changes taking place during the reign of Elizabeth in the role and status of Parliament. You should bear these differences of view in mind when looking at the evidence presented in this chapter.

THE WORKING OF THE MONARCHY

Elizabeth inherited a number of recognised powers. In his book entitled *Of the Commonwealth of England* published in 1583, Sir Thomas Smith, one of her Privy Councillors (and therefore well placed to know), observed that 'the prince is the life, the head and the authority of all things that be done in the realm of England'.

- Elizabeth had the power of appointment to all offices, both in State and Church.
- She could veto any act of Parliament.
- Hers was the final voice on any question of foreign policy.
- In war she determined what forces were to be raised and where they were to be deployed, and where her ships were to sail – at least in theory.
- She could order the punishment of rebels without trial.
- Equally, her consent was needed before distinguished traitors, such as the Duke of Norfolk, could be put to death.

However, there were limits to her powers.

- Her Councillors could ask to be relieved of particular responsibilities, as Cecil did in relation to Scotland in 1560.

- Parliament's consent was needed for the passage of legislation and the voting of subsidies.
- The enforcement of her policies depended on the willing acquiescence of the **Lords Lieutenant** and **Justices of the Peace** who represented her authority in the shires and towns of England and Wales.
- In Ireland her rule rested in the last resort on military power.

How well did Elizabeth exercise these powers?

Appointments

By the standards of her predecessors Elizabeth seems to have been well served.

William Cecil. Her reliance on William Cecil, and later on his second son, Robert, showed a shrewd awareness of where her true interests lay. She took Cecil's advice on sending an expedition to Scotland in 1560, and in relinquishing Robert Dudley as a possible husband in 1560. This showed her strong, practical streak. Few things in her life are more touching than the devotion she showed to Lord Burghley (as Cecil had then become) during his final illness in 1598 when she attended his bedside. Burghley complained not infrequently at her inability to make up her mind. Elizabeth banned him from the Court in 1587 after the execution of Mary Queen of Scots. But the partnership endured, to the credit of both.

Other successful appointees. Most of Elizabeth's other appointments seem to have been successful. Sir Francis Walsingham, Sir Christopher Hatton, Sir Walter Mildmay, Sir Francis Knollys and Lord Howard of Effingham all showed their competence and loyalty.

Some difficulties. Elizabeth's relationship with the Earl of Leicester was never straightforward, and his failure in the Netherlands showed a lack of mutual trust. These weaknesses were magnified in the case of the Earl of Essex, which ended in disaster. It is arguable that the Rebellion of the Northern Earls might have been averted if Elizabeth had treated the Earls of Westmoreland and Northumberland with greater sensitivity. Elizabeth could show ingratitude, too. The rejection of her Secretary William Davison in 1587 was unfair, to say the least. That said, she never showed the vindictiveness of her father towards Cardinal Thomas Wolsey, Sir Thomas More and Thomas Cromwell, nor the dependence on favourites that characterised the rule of James I.

The making of policy

It is hard to assess Elizabeth's influence on the making of policy. It is rare to see her taking an initiative on her own. She was much more likely to to appoint muster masters and, within the limits of the county, to repress and if necessary kill the enemies of the Crown. Deputy Lieutenants might also be appointed, but they were nominated by the Crown.

Justices of the Peace The office of Justice of the Peace was well established by Elizabeth's reign. Duties of JPs were both legal and administrative. JPs were expected to deal with petty crime and to enforce a huge variety of statutes, ranging from the licensing of ale houses to the levying of poor rates and the collection of recusancy fines. In 1580 there were no fewer than 1738 JPs, mainly drawn from the ranks of the gentry, calculated at this time to include about 16,000. There were between 40 and 90 JPs in each county. They were appointed by the Crown and Burghley kept a series of county

frustrate those of others. Here the record is clearer. A few examples must suffice.

- In domestic policy, as we have seen, the religious settlement of 1559 owed a good deal to Elizabeth's intervention.
- The retention of many Catholic features (such as altars and clerical dress) were at Elizabeth's prompting.
- It was Elizabeth who insisted that the oath of supremacy should not be tended more than once to the Marian bishops, and who toned down the anti-Catholic legislation of 1581.
- Whether for reasons of state or out of genuine compassion, she opposed the execution of Mary Queen of Scots right up until 1587, notably in her rejection of a bill put forward by Parliament in 1572 calling for Mary to be executed, which had the full support of her bishops as well as the House of Commons.

On the other hand, Elizabeth suppressed perfectly reasonable Puritan practices, notably exercises and prophesyings and her suspension of Grindal, one of her most dedicated bishops, was hard to justify. Her refusal to permit discussion of her successor was maintained throughout the reign, and Peter Wentworth died in the Tower of London for prompting her to allow it. She was equally insistent that public discussion of her marriage should not be allowed. When **John Stubbs** wrote a pamphlet entitled 'The discovery of a gaping gulf, wherein England is likely to be swallowed by another French marriage …' opposing Elizabeth's marriage to Anjou in 1579, he was sentenced to have his right hand cut off.

Where Elizabeth excelled was in the politics of gesture and symbol. Right from the start of her reign she played the role of queen.

- She regularly appeared at the opening and closing of Parliamentary sessions, not infrequently using the opportunity to deliver her own speeches.
- Her knighting of Sir Francis Drake on his own flagship in 1580 may not have been the most tactful thing to do, but it enhanced her popularity.
- Her public appearance at Tilbury in August 1588, where she was dressed in a breastplate, contributed greatly to her prestige.
- Her reputation was also enhanced by her Golden Speech to a deputation from the Commons on the occasion of the monopolies debate in 1601 (see Chapter 7, page 122).

As the last example suggests, Elizabeth's success or failure as queen cannot be separated from the other institutions through which she ruled, notably the Privy Council and Parliament.

THE PRIVY COUNCIL

The Privy Council played an increasingly important role in the Elizabethan system of government for a variety of reasons:

- continuity of membership;
- a long period of warfare;
- an increase in its sphere of responsibility.

The following section examines:

- its composition;
- its functions;
- its activities;
- its operations;
- its ability to use enforcement and persuasion.

Composition

The Privy Council in Elizabeth's reign drew its membership from three social groups:

- the magnates who belonged to the hereditary peerage – such as the Duke of Norfolk, the Marquess of Winchester and the Earl of Worcester;
- the country gentry – men like Sir Francis Knollys and Sir Christopher Hatton;
- the men of business – men recruited for their abilities rather than their birth, such as William Cecil, Nicholas Bacon, Sir Thomas Smith and Thomas Wilson.

It should be pointed out that these three groups overlapped, and that progress could be, and frequently was, made from one to the other. Many of Elizabeth's Councillors were sons of peers, and not infrequently followed their fathers into the Privy Council. William Cecil was Secretary to Protector Somerset in 1551, knighted in 1553 and ennobled as Lord Burghley in 1571. Elizabeth created few new **peers of the realm** but most of her Councillors could at least expect knighthoods and entry into the gentry even if they did not belong to it when their careers began.

In total, 58 men served as Privy Councillors during the course of Elizabeth's reign. They formed a tight and homogeneous group.

- Of the 25 members between 1568 and 1582, eighteen were related to each other or to the Queen.
- Numbers varied between 20 in 1558 and ten in 1591, rising again to thirteen in 1601.

maps on which he plotted gentry families on whom he could rely. Courtiers, Councillors, MPs and JPs were all drawn from the same social grouping and this homogeneity undoubtedly smoothed the working of government.

KEY PERSON

John Stubbs An outspoken critic of the French marriage but, as with many Puritans, also extravagantly loyal to the Queen. After the amputation of his right hand he held up the bloodied stump and called out 'God save Queen Elizabeth'. He later sat in the Parliament of 1589.

Sir Nicholas Bacon.

Sir Christopher Hatton.

Peers of the Realm These people had a variety of titles including Duke, Marquess, Earl and Baron. They enjoyed two vital privileges:

- the right to pass on their title to their heirs;
- automatic membership of the House of Lords.

Elizabeth promoted Robert Dudley to be Earl of Leicester, his brother Ambrose Dudley to be Earl of Warwick, Henry Carey to be Lord Hunsdon and William Cecil to be Lord Burghley.

KEY TEXTS

C. Haigh *Elizabeth I* (1998)

M. Pulman *The Elizabethan Privy Council in the Fifteen-seventies* (1971)

- There was a shift towards a more professional Council in the course of the reign. Whereas in 1558 there were six magnates who owed their position to their territorial power, in 1591 the peers represented – Lord Burghley, the second Baron Effingham, Lord Hunsdon, Lord Buckhurst, the fourth Earl of Derby and the tenth Lord Cobham – were there on their merits and occupied important positions.

One historian, **Christopher Haigh**, has argued that 'from 1572 to 1601 Elizabeth's Council was dangerously narrow and weak in its membership', and that the Essex Rebellion of 1601 may have prompted the recall of the Earl of Shrewsbury and the promotion of the Earl of Worcester to the Privy Council.

What was remarkable about the Privy Council, seen in perspective, is how united its membership was on the great issues of the day and how little riven it was by personal or factional quarrels – at least until the division between the Earl of Essex and Robert Cecil. It compares very favourably with some twentieth-century cabinets. **Michael Pulman**, who has made a detailed examination of the Privy Council in the 1570s, comments that 'there is no evidence that bouts of huffiness interfered with the smooth running of the machinery of state'. Elizabeth's Privy Council enjoyed a further advantage. All of its members were JPs in the localities from which they came, sometimes in several. Members of the peerage were usually Lords Lieutenant as well; Privy Councillors might also be. Sir Christopher Hatton was Lord Lieutenant of Northamptonshire. In these ways members of the Privy Council kept closely in touch with the communities they directed.

Functions of the Privy Council

There were two main functions of the Privy Council:

- to advise Elizabeth;
- to act as a centre from which almost all instructions to the provinces emanated.

Advice. The Privy Council's most important function was to advise Elizabeth, without fear or favour. The view put by Cecil to Ralph Sadler in 1572 was that: 'Our part is to counsel. The Queen's Majesty hath no surety but as she hath been counselled.' Elizabeth was not bound to take advice, as Cecil delicately put it:

> *I do hold and will always this course in such matters as I differ in opinion from her Majesty: as long as I may be allowed to give advice, I will not change my opinion by affirming the contrary, for that were to offend God, to whom I am sworn first; but as a servant I will obey her Majesty's commandment …*

Sir Francis Knollys was more outspoken. In 1569, he told the Queen:

> *It is not possible for your Majesty's Councillors to govern your estate unless you shall resolutely follow their opinion in weighty matters.*

Whether Elizabeth took their advice or not, she did at least consult with her Privy Council. She attended many of its meetings in person in the first month of the reign, and again when contentious matters were to be discussed, such as:

- the French war in 1562;
- Mary Queen of Scots in 1568–70;
- the French marriage in 1579–81;
- Ireland in 1598.

On other occasions she preferred to face her ministers singly, or in twos or threes. The record shows that, where there were serious disagreements, the honours were evenly divided.

- Elizabeth refused to nominate her successor or to take the Council's advice to marry.
- On the other hand, she eventually agreed to send aid to the Netherlands and to the execution of Mary Queen of Scots, though with reluctance and an ill-grace in both cases.

Not surprisingly, her Councillors complained not infrequently about her refusal to make up her mind. Walsingham wrote in 1575, 'For the love of God, Madam, let not the cure of your diseased estate hang any longer in deliberation!', and again in 1581, in connection with the Anjou marriage negotiations, 'If your Majesty mean it, remember that by the delay your Highness useth therein you lose the benefit of time ...'. But Elizabeth was not to be rushed into any course of action against her will. When she did give way it was due as much to exhaustion as to persuasion.

The Privy Council as an executive board. The Privy Council was the centre from which almost all instructions to the provinces emanated. Every week, if not every day, State papers signed by a few Privy Councillors would be despatched to JPs, Lords Lieutenant, bishops, judges on assize, subsidy commissioners – in short, all those whose responsibility it was to see the royal will enforced.

The range of the Council's responsibilities was enormous, and not far short in compass from that of a modern cabinet.

- The maintenance of law and order required the punishment of vagrants.
- Religious uniformity had to be enforced.
- Plots against Elizabeth had to be detected.
- Soldiers had to be raised for expeditions overseas and defence at home.
- The navy had to be kept in a good state of repair.
- Taxes had to be raised and expenditure controlled.
- Provision had to be made for the deserving poor.
- Steps had to be taken to deal with the consequences of poor harvests or the loss of overseas markets.

The sheer volume of work that Cecil handled makes it clear just how extensive the Council's responsibilities were. A few examples (given below) must suffice to indicate the Council's activities.

Illustrations of the Council's activities
- In 1572, instructions were issued for musters to be held in each county, following the Massacre of St Bartholomew.
- In the same year, instructions were given to fortify the Isle of Sheppey, which guarded the harbour at Gravesend.
- It was the Privy Council that ordered the construction of the beacons that warned of the approach of the Armada.
- Following the anti-Catholic legislation of 1581 and 1585, it was the Privy Council that appointed Recusancy Commissioners to collect recusancy fines and paid informers to track down seminary priests.

- The Privy Council tried to control emigration and to make provision for the religious refugees who poured into England as a consequence of religious persecution on the Continent.
- It was the Privy Council's responsibility to control wages and prices. In 1572, instructions were given to the importers of wine from Bordeaux (in France) to keep their prices down.
- Miscellaneous matters of all kinds came to the Council's attention. In 1574, orders were given to restrict the number of badgers. In 1583, a serious fire in Nantwich led the Council to write to all bishops and JPs in England and Wales urging the collection of money to assist in the rebuilding of the town.
- The Privy Council also supervised the administration of justice and adjudicated differences between individuals, many of them apparently trivial – for instance, the complaint of one Richard Knight that Thomas Blagrave and son had stolen his corn and cattle fodder.

The operation of the Council

Evidence of the Council's operations has survived in the Privy Council Registers, which were started in Mary's reign. Three, sometimes four, clerks were employed to record the Council's activities. In the five years from 1570 to 1575, 412 meetings were recorded. There may well have been more. The majority took place at Greenwich, Hampton Court and Westminster. The average attendance was between eight and nine people. During these years, the Council has fairly been described by **Michael Pulman** as 'a body of men working hard and regularly at the business of the state in an essentially professional manner' (*The Elizabeth Privy Council in the Fifteen-seventies*, 1971).

Enforcement

The Privy Council had two essential powers:

- it could imprison;
- it could submit men and women to torture.

Imprisonment. Notorious recusants might be summoned to London (because it was the seat of government) and sentenced to prison until they agreed to conform. This happened in a small number of cases.

Torture. Torture was used not as a punishment but to extract information. Walsingham wrote to Burghley in 1575 in the case of a man named Corkin, 'without torture I know we shall not prevail'. The record does not say whether he did. There were only eleven cases between 1558 and 1575, but with the arrival of seminary priests in large numbers, and in many cases their arrest, torture was used more frequently.

Persuasion

Apart from these harsh powers, the Privy Council's only other power was to persuade. The execution of Privy Council orders depended on the compliance of Lords Lieutenant, JPs, bishops, subsidy commissioners, muster masters and so on. There were no paid civil servants outside London. Roads were poor and communications slow. The number of reminders that had to be sent is proof that response to Privy Council instructions was far from automatic. In some cases, as with the control of immigration and emigration along a coastline as long and indented as England's, the task was impossible. The Privy Council could no more control wages and prices in the face of changes in supply and demand than could twentieth-century governments.

The Privy Council occupied an intermediate position between a powerful queen and an independent-minded gentry. Neither could be coerced. For most of Elizabeth's reign, however, members of the Privy Council shared the concerns of the gentry to which many of them belonged. While there were differences between the Queen and more Protestant-inclined members such as Walsingham, they shared the same fundamental objectives – the safety and unity of the realm. It is true that this harmony between Elizabeth and her Councillors was broken in the period 1598 to 1601 when the rivalry between Sir Robert Cecil and the Earl of Essex came to a head. But this did not interrupt the normal processes of government and, in the final years of the reign, the Privy Council despatched the largest army of the reign to Ireland and raised the largest subsidy to pay for it.

KEY TERM

Puritan choir
Neale's three books attach great weight to Puritan activities in the House of Commons and he suggests that Puritan MPs concentrated their attacks on the Elizabethan settlement. There is little evidence for this in 1559, but in the 1560s and 1570s there was some co-operation between like-minded MPs.

PARLIAMENT: AN INTRODUCTION

The role and importance of Parliament in Elizabeth's reign have been the subject of much controversy in recent years and students need to be aware of the background to the current debate. Between 1949 and 1957 one eminent historian, **Sir John Neale** (then Professor of History at London University) produced three ground-breaking books on Elizabeth's Parliaments (see page 146). As a result of his research he concluded that during the reign of Elizabeth the House of Commons radically changed its membership, as the borough seats were progressively taken over by the country gentry. In consequence, the House of Commons developed a greater sense of its own importance and mounted a succession of challenges to the Crown, claiming a larger share in the making of policy. In the sphere of religion, in particular, the attack on the Crown's policies was led by what Neale christened a **Puritan choir** of about 40 MPs who co-ordinated their activities both inside and outside Parliament.

Though Elizabeth succeeded in facing down this opposition, she only did so by exercising her rhetorical skills and giving way when she had to. Thus, she bequeathed to James VI an institution that had flexed its muscles and would immediately pose a challenge that the less adept Stuarts would prove incapable of handling. Neale claimed that the House of Commons 'reached maturity in Elizabeth's reign. The instrument was tempered with which the Crown was to be resisted and conquered.'

This view was generally accepted until the 1960s. It has come under attack from several quarters. In 1964, J.M. Roskell, a medieval historian, argued that Elizabethan Parliaments were less threatening than their fourteenth- and fifteenth-century predecessors, which had deposed kings (Edward II and Richard II), and **impeached** their ministers. **G.R. Elton**, who had initially supported the Neale interpretation, has, in recent years, rejected many of his findings. He has argued that the real change in the role of Parliament occurred in Henry VIII's reign with the Reformation Parliament, 1529–36, which established its sovereignty.

Elton asserts that in Elizabeth's reign there was no institutional development. The Puritan choir did not exist. So far from Puritans leading the challenge to the Crown, it was rather the Privy Council who used the House of Commons to bring pressure to bear on the Queen. Neale also greatly underestimated the continuing power and influence of the House of Lords. Elton's views have been echoed by **M.A.R. Graves**, who concludes his book on Tudor Parliaments with this verdict: 'Parliament continued to be a source of strength to the Tudors until the death of Queen Elizabeth, the last of the line.'

One final twist in the story comes from some seventeenth-century historians. Whereas Neale argued that the outbreak of the English Civil War in 1642 could be traced back to the growing self-confidence of the Elizabethan House of Commons, **Conrad Russell** maintains that there was no high road to Civil War. This happened, he would say, only because of a breakdown in trust between Charles I and Parliament in the years 1637–42. What happened to Parliament in Elizabeth's reign therefore has little relevance to the great constitutional struggles of the seventeenth century. You need to bear these complex arguments in mind when considering the evidence that follows.

THE COMPOSITION OF PARLIAMENT

Strictly speaking, Parliament consisted of three elements:

- the Crown;
- the House of Lords;
- the House of Commons.

KEY TERM

Impeachment A process by which a minister could be removed from office by a vote in the House of Commons. It was resurrected in the reign of James I to get rid of unpopular ministers.

KEY TEXTS

G.R. Elton *The Parliament of England, 1559–81* (1986)

M.A.R. Graves *The Tudor Parliaments* (1985)

Conrad Russell (ed.) *The Origins of the English Civil War* (1973)

The participation and assent of each was needed for the passage of legislation. Only the Queen could summon, prorogue and dissolve Parliament.

The House of Lords

Total membership of the House of Lords fluctuated between 75 and 88 members in Elizabeth's reign. All of the 27 archbishops and bishops were entitled to sit, as were the 55 or so hereditary peers. At any one time there were certain to be vacancies on the bench of bishops and some peerages died out while a few new ones were created. Attendance fluctuated, but most of the bishops in post were usually there, at least at the start of the session. The Lords' journals indicate that there were never fewer than 40 peers at the start of any Parliamentary session. Those peers on the Privy Council attended automatically, unless their duties prevented them. The Lord Keeper, though a commoner, usually presided.

The House of Commons

There were two noticeable changes in the **composition of the House of Commons**:

- a substantial increase in membership;
- change in the the character of the membership.

An increase in membership. At Elizabeth's accession it was already established practice for each county to be represented by two **knights of the shire**. County MPs were elected by 40 shilling freeholders – that is to say those who owned, as opposed to renting, land worth 40 shillings a year. As there were 45 counties, including the Welsh ones, they were represented by 90 MPs. Since the thirteenth century it had also been the practice to allow each chartered borough to elect two burgesses to the House of Commons. In 1558, there were 153 such boroughs. London had the right to elect four MPs. Thus Elizabeth's first House of Commons contained 400 MPs. Another 32 boroughs were given charters in the course of her reign. In practically every case, it would seem, this was at the behest of her Privy Councillors or courtiers. The Isle of Wight, for instance, gained six new members at the request of Sir George Carey, son of Lord Hunsdon. The Earl of Leicester secured representation for Andover, the last borough to be enfranchised, in 1586. Thus membership of the House rose by 64 to 462.

The character of membership. More significant was the change in the character of the borough members.

- Strictly speaking, out of a membership of 462, 90 seats should have been held by the country gentry, with 372 by burgesses and merchants.

KEY FACT

Composition of the House of Commons

Neale's figures have been superceded by P.W. Hasler's *The History of Parliament: The House of Commons, 1588–1603* (1981) in some respects. He points out that we only have details of educational qualifications for two-thirds of MPs, though the trends are still clear.

KEY POSITION

Knights of the shire

These people did not have to be 'knighted', but they did have to belong to the gentry. They would have had the right to a coat of arms and been expected to own land, preferably in the county they represented.

- Such was the demand for Parliamentary seats that, in the Parliament of 1584–5, only 77 MPs out of a total membership of 460 could be classified as merchants, borough officials or lawyers, which left 383 members drawn from the gentry.
- Instead of one gentleman to four townsmen, the proportions were reversed, such was the pressure from the country gentry to get into Parliament.
- Country gentry did not need to draw wages, which had to be raised by the boroughs concerned, and, in many cases, so few were the voters that nomination of borough members rested in the hands of the local landowner.
- This invasion of the boroughs by the country gentry also saw an improvement in the educational qualifications of MPs. In 1563, 63 MPs out of 420 had been to Oxford and Cambridge (the only universities in England); by 1593 the figure had risen to 161 out of 462.
- The number of MPs who had been to the **Inns of Court** showed a corresponding increase, from 108 in 1563 to 197 in 1593.

It should be noted that, while peers in the Privy Council sat automatically in the House of Lords, gentry members of the Privy Council nearly always contrived to gain a seat in the House of Commons. William Cecil also took pains to see that both his sons, Thomas and Robert, were elected to Parliament.

Attendance in Parliament

While the rise in the social and educational status of MPs is indisputable and reflects a growing competition to get into Parliament, many MPs showed little enthusiasm for the work of Parliament once elected. Attendance figures are not given in the Commons journals, so have to be inferred from the voting figures when the House divided. On this basis the highest votes recorded were:

- 276 out of 411 in 1563;
- 345 out of 462 in 1593.

The Privy Council complained frequently about poor attendance. In 1571, fines were introduced for the following:

- failure to attend prayers at 8.30 am (fourpence, to be paid to the poor box);
- failure to attend a session.

Penalties of £20 for country members and £10 for borough members were also to be levied. Those who put in an appearance and then departed without the Speaker's licence would lose their wages.

KEY TERM

Inns of Court (for example, Middle Temple or Gray's Inn) These provided a professional training for common lawyers, and also a general legal education for the gentry, many of whom would become JPs and MPs.

THE MEETINGS OF PARLIAMENT

Parliaments were summoned at Elizabeth's discretion, usually on the advice of the Privy Council.

- There had to be a Parliament at the start of a new reign so that customs duties, known as tunnage and poundage, could be voted for life.
- Subsequent Parliaments were usually summoned to vote taxes.

Of the thirteen meetings of Parliament during Elizabeth's reign, only one – the 1572 Parliament summoned to deal with the Ridolfi Plot and Mary Queen of Scots (see Chapter 4, pages 69 and 73) – was not asked to vote a subsidy. Once elected, a Parliament could last for several sessions. In this case it would be prorogued at the end of each session. If the Queen and Council wanted a new Parliament the old one would have to be dissolved. The table below lists Elizabeth's ten Parliaments and the sessions into which they were divided. Election writs were usually sent out six weeks or so before the election took place.

Year	Date of election writ	Dates of sessions	Date of dissolution
1559	5 December 1558	25 January to 8 May 1559	8 May 1559
1563–7	10 November 1562	(i) 12 January to 10 April 1563	
		(ii) 30 September 1566 to 2 January 1567	2 January 1567
1571	Unknown	2 April to 29 May 1571	19 May 1571
1572–81	28 March 1572	(i) 8 May to 30 June 1572	
		(ii) 8 February to 15 March 1576	
		(iii) 16 January to 18 March 1581	19 April 1583
1584–6	12 October 1584	23 November 1584 to 29 March 1585	14 September 1585
1586–7	15 September 1586	29 October 1586 to 23 March 1587	23 March 1587
1589	18 September 1588	4 February to 29 March 1589	29 March 1589
1593	4 January 1593	19 February to 10 April 1593	10 April 1593
1597–8	23 August 1597	24 October 1597 to 9 February 1598	9 February 1598
1601	11 September 1601	27 October to 19 December 1601	19 December 1601

Source: Neale's *The Elizabethan House of Commons* (1949)

Elizabeth's ten Parliaments.

Much may be learned from this table. For a start, Parliament met much less frequently than it did during the reigns of Edward and Mary.

- In Edward's reign it met in 1547, 1549, 1550, 1552 and 1553.
- In Mary's reign it met in 1553, 1554–5 and 1558.

In both these reigns, England was at war with France and Scotland for much of the time, and there were major religious changes that required Parliamentary authority. The fact that Parliament did not meet between 1567 and 1571, between 1572 and 1576, or between 1576 and 1581 is an indication that it was not needed. The collection of subsidies might well be spread over two or three years and unless there was an urgent need for money Elizabeth saw no reason to summon Parliament.

Once Parliament had voted the taxes required, which it usually did without demur, the Queen would happily have prorogued or dissolved it. Sessions were kept as short as possible, usually less than three months. The exceptions – the sessions of 1559, 1566–7, 1584–5, 1586–7 and 1597–8 – can be explained by the complexity of the religious settlement in 1559, the problem of the succession in 1566–7, and the threatening domestic and international scene in the later Parliaments of the reign.

THE BUSINESS OF PARLIAMENT

The business of Parliament can be divided into two areas:

- dealing with taxation;
- dealing with legislation.

Taxation

Taxes were levied in the form of **subsidies**, a tax on land and on property. The assessment was undertaken in each county by subsidy commissioners, drawn from the gentry. As might be expected, the assessments were skewed in favour of the wealthy, who were generally assessed at much less than their true worth. No attempt was made to allow for inflation with the result that subsidies were worth much less at the end of the reign than they had been at the beginning. Though MPs in the later part of the reign drew attention to these anomalies, no action was taken to remedy them. It is still the case that once the subsidies had been voted they were duly collected. The short falls were made good by voting several subsidies at once, as happened in the 1590s.

According to precedent, subsidy bills always started in the House of Commons. Again, according to precedent the request for money was usually made by a private member of the House rather than a Privy Councillor. From 1576 onwards it became the practice for the Lord Chancellor to spell out to the House the need for money.

Queen
Elizabeth I in
Parliament.

The subsidy bill would then usually be passed within a matter of weeks. Delaying the passage of the subsidy bill could be used as a deliberate tactic. The record indicates that this was done on three occasions:

- first in 1566;
- then in 1587;
- finally in 1593.

1566. In 1566 the Commons, almost certainly with the consent of the Privy Council, tried to link the subsidy bill to a promise by Elizabeth to marry, or at least name her successor. After prolonged argument, she agreed to remit one-third of the subsidy providing the bill was passed without any undertaking on her part. She still protested at the preamble to the bill: 'I know no reason why any my private answers to the realm should serve for prologue to a subsidies book.' The preamble had to be amended.

1587. As we have seen, there were delays to the passage of the subsidy bill in 1587 until Cope's Bill and Book had been considered.

1593. Finally, in 1593, there was a brief tussle with the House of Lords. The Commons voted a double subsidy, but Lord Burghley urged the House of Lords to vote a treble subsidy to be collected in three years. Several MPs objected to the Lords' initiative on the grounds that money bills had to start in the Commons. A conference between the two Houses was eventually agreed, and a compromise reached. Three subsidies were voted, but collection of the final one was to be spread over two years. The Commons did not succeed in asserting the principle that redress of grievances should precede the voting of taxes, but some of their members did at least toy with the idea.

Legislation

Acts of Parliament took two forms:

- public acts;
- private acts.

Public acts (such as the Act of Supremacy) would normally be promoted by the Privy Council. Private acts would be introduced by individual MPs, usually on behalf of their localities or an interest group. In the 1584–5 session of Parliament, for instance, a bill was passed to diminish the statutory width of cloth. But the distinction was not a hard and fast one. Private bills to promote the public interest were often introduced – for instance, a bill to prevent perjury and unnecessary suits in law, in 1601. Its sponsor, Hayward Townsend, showed his concern for the public well-being by remarking: 'Mr Speaker, I take every man to be bound in conscience to remove a little mischief from the Commonwealth.'

In fact, the only clear distinctions between public and private bills were formal ones. Fees were paid to clerks during the passage of **private bills**, and **public bills** were printed in full at the end of the session, while private bills were simply listed. By far the greatest number of bills introduced were private ones. In the first seven sessions of Elizabeth's Parliaments, 283 private bills were introduced:

- 22 of these became public acts;
- 98 bills became private acts;
- 163 bills failed.

Bills, apart from money bills, might start in either House. The success rate for bills introduced into the Lords was generally greater than for those that began life in the Commons. It was already accepted practice for bills to be given three readings.

First reading. Here, the bill would be read aloud. In the case of a subsidy bill this might take as long as two hours.

Second reading. The bill would be debated, after which it might be sent to a committee for further amendments. This practice became more common as the reign went on.

Third reading. Finally, the committee would report its amendments back to the full House, Lords or Commons, as the case might be. The amendments would be approved or rejected and the bill would then have its third reading.

At this point, the bill would pass to the other House, where it would undergo the same procedure. Usually, but not always, bills passed more rapidly through the second chamber. At the end of the session all bills that had passed both Houses had to go to the Queen for the royal assent. This was given in the Norman French form:

- for public bills it was 'la royne le veult' (the Queen wishes it).
- for private bills it was 'soit fait comme il est désiré' (may it be done as is wished).
- should the Queen wish to veto a bill the accepted formula was 'la royne s'avisera' (the Queen takes note).

In 1572, when vetoing the act to have Mary Queen of Scots banned from the succession, Elizabeth indicated that the veto was not necessarily a permanent one.

Elizabeth vetoed bills in every session of her Parliaments. Apart from the one concerned with Mary Queen of Scots in 1572, the most important were bills dealing with religion that Elizabeth regarded as trespassing on her prerogative, or because they were too hostile to Catholics.

In 1571, for instance, she vetoed a bill to make receiving Communion in an Anglican church compulsory. In the course of her reign she gave the royal assent to 429 acts, one-third of which were private. She exercised the veto at least 35 times, usually it would seem on the advice of her Privy Councillors (at least where private bills were concerned).

PARLIAMENTARY PRIVILEGE

Members of Parliament had secured two vital privileges by 1559.

- They enjoyed the right not to be arrested for civil suits (getting into debt, for instance) when Parliament was sitting. This privilege extended to their servants.
- They also enjoyed freedom of speech, within certain limits. Those limits were undefined.

To some MPs (Peter Wentworth, for instance), freedom of speech meant the right to debate any matter of common concern. To the Queen, on the other hand, the privilege was confined to matters that the Commons might legitimately debate. Elizabeth drew a distinction between:

- matters affecting the common weal – such as poverty and vagrancy, and
- matters that lay within her prerogative – the succession, foreign policy and religion.

These were not to be debated without the Queen's consent. At the opening of each Parliament, the Speaker requested both privileges.

CONFLICT OR CO-OPERATION

Some historians, notably **G.R. Elton** and **M.A.R. Graves**, have stressed the high degree of co-operation between Elizabeth and her Parliaments. This was exercised through the Privy Council, whose members sat in both Houses. They often used men of business, such as **Thomas Norton**, to assist in the passage of legislation. It was only, so it has been argued, when the Privy Council and MPs were in agreement against the Queen, that serious conflict occurred. This happened in the following instances:

- 1566–7, over the succession;
- 1572, over attempts by the Privy Council to exclude Mary Queen of Scots from the succession;
- 1586–7, over the execution of Mary Queen of Scots.

On each occasion Elizabeth won, though she did finally relent in the case of Mary. But the impression of harmony may be misleading. The Queen

KEY TEXTS

G.R. Elton *The Parliament of England, 1559–81* (1986)

M.A.R. Graves *The Tudor Parliaments* (1985)

KEY PERSON

Thomas Norton
An active MP in the Parliaments of the 1570s. He was used by members of the Privy Council to urge courses of action they wished to see followed. It was Norton, among others, who argued for the execution of the Duke of Norfolk in 1572.

dismissed the Parliament of 1566–7 with the words: 'Let this my discipline stand you in stead of sorer strokes, never to tempt too far a Prince's patience.' In the 1576 session, there was a very outspoken attack from Peter Wentworth on the Queen's attempts to prevent discussion of the succession. When he became critical of the Queen, Privy Councillors in the house intervened. Wentworth was examined by the Privy Council and sent to the Tower. He was released after a month, but Sir Walter Mildmay, Chancellor of the Exchequer, reminded the Commons that 'we may not forget to put a difference between liberty of speech and **licentious** speech'. Cope and his allies were sent to the Tower in 1587 for trespassing on the royal prerogative by introducing religious legislation. The attacks on monopolies in 1597 and 1601 showed the House in a fractious mood, with Robert Cecil complaining that their behaviour was more fit for a grammar school than a court of Parliament.

Thus while the Puritan choir may have disappeared and there is little evidence of co-ordinated opposition to the Queen, the automatic assent of the House of Commons to royal wishes could not be taken for granted. Fortunately for Elizabeth, she had skilled Parliamentary managers in both Houses of Parliament and, on set-piece occasions, her own rhetorical abilities helped her to get her way without arousing unnecessary hostility.

It is hard to chart the changes that occurred to Parliament in the course of Elizabeth's reign; in terms of procedure and function little that is new seems to have happened. But there can be little doubt that the invasion of the boroughs by the gentry and the improved qualifications of MPs had a subtle but pervasive effect on the self-confidence and aspirations of MPs. When James I's first Parliament met in 1604 there was a dispute over the right of the Commons to decide on a disputed election. At the end of the session, a group of MPs drew up a document called *An Apology of the Commons,* in which they claimed that 'the prerogatives of princes may easily and do daily grow; the privileges of the subject are for the most part at an everlasting stand'.

Whether an Elizabethan House of Commons would have made the same accusation is impossible to say. That it was made at all is surely evidence that the House of Commons, in the perception of its members at least, in 1604 was not what it had been in 1558.

KEY TERM

Licentious In this context it means disregarding accepted rules.

SUMMARY QUESTIONS

1 List the occasions when Queen Elizabeth can clearly be seen to have had a decisive influence on policy.

2 Analyse the composition of the Privy Council during Elizabeth's reign. Were there any significant changes in how it was made up?

3 Summarise the functions of the Privy Council.

4 Describe the changes made to the composition of both Houses of Parliament during Elizabeth's reign.

5 For what reasons were Parliaments summoned and what did they achieve?

A2 QUESTION IN THE STYLE OF OCR

Before answering the following questions, read the relevant pages on Parliament in Chapters 1 and 8, then read the sources below. It is essential in a source-based question to make frequent and specific reference to all the sources.

Source A

The most high and absolute power of the realm of England is in the Parliament … The Parliament abrogateth [repeals] old laws, maketh new … establisheth forms of religion, giveth forms of succession to the Crown, appointeth subsidies, condemneth or absolveth them whom the Prince will put to the trial … It representeth and hath the power of the whole realm both the head and the body. For every Englishman is intended to be there present either in person or by procuration and attornies [representatives] … from the Prince (be he King or Queen) to the lowest person of England.

Source: Sir Thomas Smith, *De Republica Anglorum,* 1583, printed in G.R. Elton, *The Tudor Constitution,* 1962, pp. 234–5.

Source B

Birth and education, expert knowledge, practical experience, and corporate solidarity – all were present in abundant measure in the Elizabethan House of Commons. And so was character. It was an assembly which never failed to display high and independent spirit, moral and religious fervour, and patriotism. By a paradox [contradiction] which must be accounted one of the supreme felicities in the history of the Mother of Parliaments, flagrant violation of the law and of medieval representative principles, resulted in assembling in Parliament the elite of the country – 'the flower and choice of the Realm' … The House of Commons reached maturity in Elizabeth's reign. The instrument was tempered with which the Crown was to be resisted and conquered. It was not from the Stygian [murky] darkness of Tudor despotism that early Stuart Parliaments emerged. They succeeded to a rich heritage, to great traditions.

Source: J.E. Neale, *The Elizabethan House of Commons,* Cape, 1949.

Source C

Parliament continued to exercise that function which had induced Edward I to summon it: it made the government of the realm more smoothly effective. And it also continued a function which the baronage of Edward II's reign had found so useful: it enabled an exasperated governing order to turn the king's instrument against him. But all talk of the rise of Parliament as an institution, or, worse, the rise of the House of Commons, into political prominence is balderdash.

In the reign of Henry VIII, politics in Parliament achieved their aim because the monarch, proprietor of Parliaments, took the lead. In the reign of Elizabeth, political debates in Parliament, and especially in the Commons never achieved anything because the monarch was entirely free to ignore them and usually did so. In both reigns, politics in Parliament reflected the purpose of non-Parliamentary agencies, resorting thither either because laws enforceable in the courts were needed or because failure had attended action in the normal places of debate and strife. The old established search, beloved by historians, for some growth or development in the political power and authority of Parliament and especially of the Commons is chimerical [fanciful] because in fact that power never changed in its fundamental characteristics:

Source: G.R. Elton, *The Parliament of England, 1559–1581,* Cambridge University Press, 1986.

Source D

Perhaps the Council could control the Commons, but could the Queen control the Council? The problem of Queen Elizabeth's dealings with Parliament has changed since Sir John Neale wrote his classic account in the 1950s … The real difficulties arose when Privy Councillors permitted, or through their business managers, organised Commons agitation to press the Queen to accept policies she disliked – as over marriage and the succession in 1563 and 1566, over religious reform in 1571, over the execution of Norfolk in 1572, over anti-Catholic laws in 1581 and over the execution of Mary Stewart in 1586. Elizabeth's problem of controlling her Parliament was thus part of her problem of controlling her Council: just as councillors tried to manipulate information to force policies upon the Queen, so they sought to manipulate Parliament to force policies on her.

Source: C. Haigh, *Elizabeth I,* Longman second edition, 1998.

Questions

1 Compare the views expressed in Sources B and C about the role of the House of Commons in Elizabeth's reign, and account for the differences between them.

Suggested approach to answering this question

Pick out key phrases to pinpoint the differences – for instance, Neale's reference to the 'high and independent spirit' shown by the Commons, whereas Elton dismisses their debates as achieving nothing. Neale draws attention to the high calibre of Members of Parliament, 'the flower and choice of the Realm', whereas Elton ignores this feature altogether. Neale stresses the maturity achieved by the Commons in Elizabeth's reign, paving the way for the struggle that is to come between Crown and Parliament in James's reign; Elton denies that there has been any development.

When explaining the differences it would be sensible to compare the dates when each source was written, and the new evidence Elton has uncovered, especially the role of the House of Lords, the importance of private bills and the leading role of Privy Councillors in managing the Commons. Neale was the first historian to investigate Elizabeth's Parliaments seriously and may have exaggerated the significance of the Puritan opposition.

2 What can be learned from Sources A to D about the role of the House of Commons in Elizabeth's reign?

Suggested approach to answering this question

You need to distinguish carefully between Parliament (Queen, Lords and Commons) and the House of Commons.

Source A is largely concerned with Parliament and brings out its extensive powers over legislation, religion, the succession and taxation. It also brings out its representative function.

Source B brings out the high calibre of Elizabethan MPs and refers indirectly to the invasion of the boroughs by the country gentry ('flagrant violation of medieval representative principles'). You might compare this with Sir Thomas Smith's claims. Source B emphasises the independence of the House of Commons and suggests that it was developing into an institution ready to challenge the Crown in the next reign.

Sources C and D suggest different roles for the House of Commons. Source C argues that Parliament was needed by non-Parliamentary agencies – for example, the city of London or the Merchant Adventurers, to secure legislation enforceable in the courts. Alternatively it was used when 'failure had attended action in the normal places of political debate and strife'. Here, Elton is referring to the quarrels between Elizabeth and the Privy Council – for instance, over the succession or Mary Queen of Scots.

Source D amplifies and supports this argument. The House of Commons is brought in by members of the Privy Council to force Elizabeth to 'accept policies she disliked', as in the examples given in 1563, 1566, 1571, 1572 , 1581 and 1586.

You might conclude by bringing out the very different perceptions of the House of Commons revealed in Source B compared with Sources C and D, and indicating where you think the truth lies.

CHAPTER 10

Government and the economy

INTRODUCTION: THE CONCERNS OF THE GOVERNMENT

In or around 1549 a book was written entitled *Discourse of the Commonweal of this Realm of England*. It was first published in 1581. Its authorship has been ascribed both to John Hales and to Sir Thomas Smith, one of Elizabeth's Secretaries of State. In any event, it is as good a contemporary guide as can be found to the social and economic problems facing Tudor governments, and to the responses of government to them.

In sixteenth-century language, *Commonweal* implied common welfare, the good of the community. One of the main objectives of more enlightened Tudor statesmen was to promote that welfare. It can be seen in men as different as Sir Thomas More, Thomas Cromwell, Protector Somerset, Sir Thomas Smith and William Cecil. There were naturally other objectives, too. All members of the governing class wanted to maintain social stability and internal peace. Economic objectives were not so very different from those of present-day governments:

- price stability;
- full employment;
- economic independence;
- a favourable trade balance;
- a solvent government;
- low taxes.

Where sixteenth-century statesmen would have differed most noticeably from their present-day successors is, curiously enough, in their belief that governments had the power to determine wages and prices, employment practices, eating habits and dress regulations for instance. It was not until **Adam Smith** published *The Wealth of Nations* in 1776 that belief in the beneficial operation of market forces, unregulated by government, challenged the accepted wisdom that it was the duty of government to promote the people's well-being by active intervention.

THE ECONOMIC CONTEXT

The main features of the English economy have already been described (see Chapter 1, page 3). Two important trends had an important bearing on the economy throughout the century:

- the first was the rise in population;
- the second, the rise in prices.

The rise in population

The first accurate census of the population was not made until 1801 and before that date all estimates of the population are a matter of guesswork. But it is now possible to make fairly precise calculations on the basis of a variety of records, parish registers, subsidy returns and numbers of **Easter Communicants** for instance. Careful analysis of all the available evidence suggests that the population of England and Wales in 1558 was slightly less than 3 million, increasing to about 4.2 million in 1603, a rise of some 35 per cent. Over half the population would have been under 25 years of age in 1603. Life expectancy for those who survived the high infant mortality was about 47 in healthy areas.

Fluctuations in population. The rise in the overall population conceals some serious fluctuations, arising from epidemics and bad harvests. There were bad harvests in 1586–8 and 1596–8. The death rate is calculated to have risen by 21 per cent in 1596–7 and by a further 5 per cent in 1597–8, though food shortages were really acute only in the north of England. Epidemics were, similarly, mainly local. In London, burials were twice the normal plague-free level in 1563, 1578–9, 1582, 1592–3 and 1603. In 1563, 24 per cent of Londoners may have died and, in 1603, 23 per cent. It is noteworthy that the sessions of Elizabeth's Parliaments always avoided high summer.

Comparisons. By present-day standards in underdeveloped countries the rise in population was relatively slow – about 0.52 per cent per annum in the period 1541–1656, as compared to the 1.3 per cent achieved in England during the early nineteenth century, or 2–3 per cent in underdeveloped countries today. But it followed a period of decline, due to the Black Death and a serious epidemic at the end of Mary's reign. To contemporaries like **Richard Hakluyt** the rise in population was self-evident: 'Through our long peace and seldom sickness we are grown more populous than ever heretofore.'

Effect on living standards. Whether the rise in population had a serious effect on living standards is hard to judge. There were more mouths to feed, but also more hands to work. **David Palliser** argues that by European standards Englishmen had a greater margin of subsistence than many other Europeans at this time, and even by 1603 England 'was supporting perhaps only three-quarters of the population it had sustained before the Great Pestilence [the Black Death] in 1348' (*The Age of Elizabeth*, second edition, 1992).

Price inflation

There are numerous problems in measuring price changes.

The measurement and extent of price changes. All historians agree that prices rose during the sixteenth century. Disagreements abound about how much, why and with what effects.

- There are few accurate sources.
- It is necessary to know prices for the same products over a considerable period of time if a reliable price series is to be constructed. Although this can be done for some agricultural products in England (for example, wheat), there are still considerable local variations. Prices of other consumer products are much harder to come by.

When it comes to determining wage rates evidence is in even shorter supply. None the less, economic historians have produced price indices for agricultural products. They have also produced indices for the wages of building workers in Oxford and Cambridge colleges and in London, which are reliable as far as they go.

A price or wage index measures percentage changes from a base year or years. In the table on page 173, the base years are 1471–99. A figure 100 represents, for example, grain prices during those years. If the figure rises to 160 in 1546, grain prices will have risen on average by 60 per cent since the base years. To see whether wages have kept pace with prices it is necessary to relate them to changes in the prices of a typical 'basket' of consumer goods. The table on page 173 is based on the most recently available figures, which are reliable so far as they go. Column 1 indicates the kind of harvest, column 2 indicates changes in grain prices (wheat, barley, rye and oats), column 3 indicates changes in the price of consumables and column 4 indicates changes in equivalent real wages.

As can be seen, the most marked fluctuations in grain prices occurred during the years of bad or deficient harvests, as is to be expected, and it is probably true to say that the harvest was the biggest determinant of the level of food prices, which in turn had the biggest impact on living standards.

Other causes of inflation

Prices of all commodities rose during the sixteenth century and, even in the good harvest year of 1603, prices of consumables had risen from

Year	Harvest	Grain prices	Consumables	Real wages
1558–9	Average	284	255	–
1563–4	Average	343	–	–
1564–5	Good	258	290	58
1565–6	Average	335	287	58
1571–2	Good	305	270	62
1573–4	Deficient	478	374	–
1586–7	Bad	684	491	41
1594–5	Deficient	621	515	39
1595–6	Deficient	681	505	40
1596–7	Dearth	1039	685	29
1597–8	Bad	778	579	35
1598–9	Average	518	474	42
1599–1600	Average	557	459	44
1600–1	Bad	768	536	37
1601–2	Average	555	471	42
1602–3	Good	480	448	45

Government and the economy.

(Source: adapted from D.M. Palliser, *Age of Elizabeth, 1547–1603*, Longman, 1992.)

255 in 1558–9 to 448 in 1602–3. Two main explanations have been suggested to account for these changes:

- changes in consumer demand;
- changes in the money supply.

Changes in consumer demand. Economists have explained that when demand exceeds available supply, prices inevitably rise where the supply of goods is inelastic – that is, cannot be easily increased. The rise in population, so it has been argued, exercised an increasing demand for consumer goods that could not immediately be met. Hence prices were bound to increase.

Changes in the money supply. An alternative explanation for price rises centres upon the supply of money. If the volume of goods and services remains constant and the supply of money rises, then prices are also bound to rise. In the sixteenth century, money largely took the form of gold and silver coins. The money supply could be increased by **debasing the coinage** or by increasing the supply of **precious metals**. In the reigns of both Henry VIII and Edward VI, debasement of the coinage occurred, which led to a doubling of the quantity of money in circulation by 1551. In 1552, Northumberland made an attempt to repair the damage, calling in some (but not all) of the debased coins.

KEY TERM

Debasing the coinage
Debasement could take two forms:

- ordering existing coins to circulate at a higher value with the same bullion content, or
- reducing the bullion content of the coinage.

INFLATION IN ELIZABETH'S REIGN

Debasement of the coinage can be ruled out as an explanation for the Elizabethan inflation. One of the most successful initiatives of her reign was the recoinage of the currency. It seems that Cecil and Sir Thomas Smith were largely responsible. In 1560–1, all the remaining debased money was called in and re-issued at the gold and silver standards prevailing before 1544. The Elizabethan coinage retained its integrity throughout the reign, becoming the envy of Europe. On the other hand, its supply did increase, virtually doubling in the course of the reign. This was partly due to increased production from the mint and partly to the influx of Spanish silver. Drake's voyage of 1577–80 yielded £600,000 in silver coins.

These explanations are not mutually exclusive. It seems likely that both may have been responsible in causing the general increase in prices, as distinct from the years of dearth that led to the large fluctuations between 1596 and 1601.

The effects of inflation

It is generally accepted that inflation:

- harms those living on fixed incomes and those who are owed money (creditors);
- benefits those whose incomes increase faster than living costs, and those who owe money (debtors).

If we apply these tests to Elizabethan society, the Crown is clearly seen to have suffered.

- The receipts from the rents on Crown lands went down in real terms because they were not raised in line with inflation.
- Similarly, as was pointed out in the debate on the subsidy bill in 1601, subsidies did not increase in line with inflation as the assessments of individual wealth remained unchanged.
- Bishops, whose lands were often rented out on long leases, were also net sufferers, and had no easy way of increasing their incomes.
- Most obviously, the landless or urban labourer, whose money wages did not rise in line with prices, suffered severely, though there were mitigating effects. Few of those living in the country would have been dependent on money wages alone. The wage index only records wages per day, not the number of days worked.

It has been argued by **H.R. Trevor-Roper** that those of the landed gentry who were unskilled at managing their estates would have suffered from the decreasing value of their rent rolls, rather like the bishops. In this way

Precious metals
Gold and silver were precious metals. In the sixteenth century the supply of silver was greatly increased, both by the production of the silver mines in central Europe, reckoned to have increased by five times between 1460 and 1530, and by the import of silver by the Spanish from the New World between 1520 and 1600, equivalent perhaps to half of Europe's supply of precious metals.

KEY DEBATE

H.R. Trevor-Roper 'The Gentry, 1540–1640' in *Economic History Review* (1953). This ground-breaking article led to a major historical debate well-summarised by J.H. Hexter in 'Storm over the Gentry' in *Reappraisals in History* (1961).

See also: **G. Batho** 'Landlords in England: Noblemen, Gentlemen and Yeoman', cited in D.M. Palliser, *The Age of Elizabeth*, second edition (1992).

a dissatisfied group, identified as the Declining Gentry, supposedly emerged, who helped to staff such different enterprises as the Gunpowder Plot and the anti-royalist element among the gentry who opposed Charles I. This was never a very convincing thesis and recent research by **G. Batho** has shown that most landowners' incomes increased, at least in line with inflation. Those gentry who got into economic difficulties, unless they were among the minority of recusants who were heavily fined, had only themselves to blame.

Thus, the beneficiaries of inflation in Elizabethan England almost certainly included the landowners.

- Higher food prices yielded higher incomes.
- Competition for land increased its sale value.
- Most rental incomes kept pace with inflation.
- In the same way, English landowners benefited from the reduced tax burden they had to pay.

Therefore, the economic context in which Elizabeth's ministers had to operate was not too unfavourable. Both the increase in population and the increase in prices were moderate, by comparison with other European countries, though there was a period at the end of the reign when the food supply was seriously threatened and prices rose to unprecedented levels.

THE ROLE OF GOVERNMENT: AN INTRODUCTION

As we saw at the start of this chapter, Elizabeth's ministers took a wide view of their responsibilities. They certainly included:

- control of public expenditure and raising the necessary revenue to meet it;
- control of wages and prices;
- relief of poverty and the maintenance of public order;
- promotion and protection of overseas trade.

While each of these responsibilities will be examined separately, it is worth remembering that in Tudor eyes they were closely related. Above all, what Tudor statesmen sought was social and economic stability. Shakespeare's lines in *Troilus and Cressida* have often been quoted:

> *Take but degree [the social hierarchy] away, untune that string,*
> *And hark what discord follows!*

Queen Elizabeth tried to end a quarrel between the Earl of Oxford and Philip Sidney in 1579 by urging Sidney to remember the difference between earls and gentlemen and the respect inferiors owed to their superiors. Also, the link between poverty and vagrancy was recognised in almost every act concerned with poor relief. The search for overseas markets for English cloth was motivated by the fear of unemployment in England's largest industry.

Government finance

Government revenue came from two sources:

- the Crown's ordinary revenue;
- Parliamentary taxes.

At the beginning of the reign, Elizabeth's ordinary revenue amounted to about £200,000 a year, made up of:

- £83,000 from customs duties;
- £88,000 from the rents of Crown lands;
- the remainder from feudal dues such as wardship, monopolies, the sale of offices, and income from the Church.

The value of a Parliamentary subsidy stood at £140,000.

Elizabeth began the practice of asking for Parliamentary subsidies in peacetime as well as war time – for instance, in 1566 and 1571. Her first two military ventures, to Scotland in 1560 and France in 1562–3, cost £750,000 and she was not free of debt until 1574. Ten years of peace thereafter meant that by 1584 she enjoyed a credit balance of £300,000.

The nineteen years of warfare from 1585 to 1604 are calculated to have cost Elizabeth £4.5 million. Even so, when she died in 1603 she was in debt only to the tune of £350,000, and there were two subsidies still to be collected. **Solvency** was maintained by a variety of expedients.

- The sale of Crown lands yielded about £40,000 a year in the last twelve years of the reign.
- Prizes taken at sea averaged £15,000.
- Elizabeth's ordinary revenue reached £300,000, Parliamentary taxes £135,000.

The value of the subsidy had fallen, but more were voted; the sales of monopolies increased. War expenditure could also be met by local taxes such as:

- ship money (levied on coastal towns);

- coat and conduct money (levied on the localities to meet the costs of uniforms and getting soldiers to the ports of embarkation);
- purveyance (the requisitioning of goods and transport below market prices).

There is some evidence that these local taxes aroused more resentment than subsidies. Both in London and in Suffolk there were angry protests at ship money in 1596.

Thus solvency was maintained by a series of hand-to-mouth measures, rather than, for instance, a realistic assessment of incomes on which subsidies were calculated. For example, the rental income of peers was assessed at half its true figure. England remained, by continental standards, an under-taxed country, another problem that James I had to face.

VAGRANCY AND POVERTY

KEY TEXT

Paul Slack
'Poverty and Social Regulation in Elizabethan England' in *The Reign of Elizabeth*, ed. Haigh (1988)

The extent of the problem

In any pre-industrialised economy there is likely to be a high level of seasonal unemployment and under-employment. Inflation and dearth certainly hit the poor harder than the rich. In the view of one economic historian, **Paul Slack**:

> There is no doubt that the standard of living of wage-earners and labourers declined ... According to the available indices, the real value of wages fell by about a quarter in the course of Elizabeth's reign.

KEY TERM

Vagrant The Tudor term for the able unemployed man, or woman, who had no fixed abode. He or she might also be referred to as a rogue or vagabond. Initially he was to be treated as a criminal: he could be whipped, imprisoned and, in extreme circumstances, be put to death.

The **vagrant** was the product of poverty. The unemployed naturally made their way to the nearest provincial town or the capital. Soldiers discharged from the various expeditions for which they had been recruited also helped to swell the numbers of vagrants. Some 500 unpaid soldiers descended on London in 1589; and 96 vagrants were whipped out of Salisbury in 1598. Despite such illustrations it is impossible to say how many vagrants there were at any one time. In 1566, one author listed 215 male rogues in Essex, Middlesex, Surrey, Sussex and Kent. In 1577, another commentator, William Harrison, estimated that thieves and idle beggars of both sexes amounted to 10,000 in England. A recent estimate suggests a total of 20,000 – or one in 400 of the population.

When it comes to the extent of poverty as a whole, we are dependent on random pieces of evidence. The best comes from a survey undertaken in Norwich in 1570 by the enlightened municipality there.

A census was taken of all persons living within the town's boundaries. The poor who needed assistance numbered:

- 504 men;
- 831 women;
- 1007 children. (In all, about 25 per cent of the city's population.)

On the basis of such estimates, it has been calculated that about 10 per cent of the rural population and 20 per cent of the urban population, could be classified as poor. These figures would have been much worse during years of famine and epidemics.

Local and national responses

It was in the towns that the first serious attempts were made to deal with the problem of poverty.

London. In London between 1546 and 1557, five **hospitals** were founded or re-founded by the London Corporation. This was part of a coherent scheme advocated by Bishop Nicholas Ridley, Bishop of London, from 1549 to 1553.

The city of London thus began distinguishing between:

- the 'poor by impotence' (orphans, the sick and the aged);
- the 'poor by casualty' (wounded soldiers, decayed householders [resident poor]);
- the 'thriftless poor' (vagabonds, wastrels, prostitutes and so on).

York. In 1561, York imposed a poor rate to provide for the 'impotent poor'.

Ipswich. In 1569, Ipswich established a combined hospital and house of correction, an asylum for the old and a training school for the young.

Norwich. In 1570, Norwich imposed a compulsory poor rate. Work was provided for the able-bodied; those who needed relief were given it. For the next ten years the scheme worked as intended.

Nationally. The government lagged behind such enlightened schemes, but borrowed from them. By the time of Elizabeth's accession some initial steps had been taken.

- An act of 1536 ordered parish and municipal authorities to collect voluntary alms to maintain the impotent poor.
- An act of 1536 authorised the whipping of vagrants found outside the parishes where they were born.

London hospitals These were St Bartholomew's and St Thomas's for the sick and impotent; Christ's Hospital for orphans; Bethlehem (hence 'Bedlam') for the mentally ill; and Bridewell for the vagabonds, a house of correction. By the end of the century, 4000 people a year were being treated or punished.

These measures were supplemented in various ways.

- In 1563, penalties of imprisonment could be imposed for those refusing to contribute to poor relief, and fines for those refusing to assist in its collection.
- In 1572, a savage act against vagrancy was passed. Penalties were whipping and boring through the ear for a first offence, the penalties for felony for a second, and hanging for a third.
- In 1576, an act for the setting of the poor on work and for the avoiding of idleness required stocks of wool, flax, hemp and iron to be set aside to provide employment. Those refusing to work were to be sent to houses of correction.

The most significant measures to deal with the problem of poverty were passed in the 1597–8 session of Parliament in response to the poor harvests of 1594–7, and the unrest they had provoked.

- The 1598 Act for the relief of the poor required all parishes to appoint overseers of the poor, whose duties were to employ the able poor and to provide relief to those unable to work.
- Churchwardens were to enforce payment of the poor rates.
- County treasurers were to be appointed to administer funds to be paid for the relief of prisoners, soldiers and mariners passing through the county.

A further act, also passed in 1598, repealed all previous legislation dealing with vagrants.

- Houses of correction were to be set up in all counties and cities.
- Incorrigible rogues were to be sent overseas.
- Convicted vagabonds were to be whipped and returned to the parishes of their birth or last residence.

An act of 1601 simply codified the provisions of the 1598 legislation.

In 1593, Parliament had repealed all acts against the conversion of arable to pasture 'by reason of the great plenty and cheapness of grain', but here, too, the years of dearth and the Oxfordshire Rising of 1596 brought a reversal of policy. Two statutes were passed in 1598:

- one to prevent conversion of arable to pasture in 23 English and Welsh counties;
- the other to prevent the engrossing of farms – the joining together of farms to economise on the use of labour.

The execution of legislation

There is some evidence to show that the penalties for vagrancy were imposed. Numerous houses of correction were built, once they became compulsory. From 1569 to 1582, reports from eighteen counties list 750 vagrants seized. The Privy Council remained alert to any threat of disorder. When, in November 1596, a plan came to their notice that men in Oxfordshire were threatening to seize arms from the local Lord Lieutenant and to march on London to protest about enclosures, the four rebels who turned up were tortured and executed.

How widely the poor rate was collected is harder to judge. **A.L. Beier** argues that even in rural areas the poor rate was being levied. He quotes William Harrison as saying in 1577: 'There is order taken throughout every parish in the realm that weekly collections shall be made for their help and sustentation.'

In Wiltshire, a number of persons were fined for not paying rates and for refusing to be collectors. In two areas of Warwickshire in 1605 only eleven out of 100 parishes were reported as delinquent in administration. However, **John Guy** is more doubtful. He points out that the estimated cash yield of endowed charities for poor relief by 1600 totalled £11,776 per annum – 0.25 per cent of the national income, 'Yet the estimated amount raised by poor rates was smaller.' If only 10 per cent of the rural population were living in poverty, this would still amount to at least 300,000. The amount of £12,000 would not have gone very far towards their relief, particularly in the bad years from 1596 to 1598 when real wages fell to their lowest level in the reign and as many as two-fifths of the population may have been living below the margin of subsistence.

Action by the Privy Council

The Privy Council also took action to deal with two particular threats to living conditions:

- outbreaks of plague;
- bad harvests.

All JPs were issued with Books of Orders with instructions on what they should do. Plague orders were issued on three occasions – 1587, 1592 and 1593. The sick and their families were to be **quarantined**, watchmen appointed and special rates levied to support the sick. Dearth orders were also sent out in 1586, 1592 and 1593, formalising the methods to be used to locate grain supplies and authorising the compulsory sale of grain surpluses.

It is impossible to gauge the success of these initiatives, which must have varied from one place to another. In Newcastle, nine people died in the

KEY TEXTS

A.L. Beier *The Problem of the Poor in Tudor and Stuart England* (1983)

John Guy *Tudor England* (1990)

KEY TERM

Quarantined
Kept in isolation.

streets in September 1597 and sixteen in October from starvation, but such events were presumably rare enough to deserve special mention.

The control of employment

Just as vagrancy was seen as a threat to public order, so employment was seen as a guarantee of stability. The Privy Council wanted a labour market where wages were fixed and conditions of employment were regulated. A bill for husbandmen (agricultural workers) and artificers (craftsmen) had been prepared for the 1559 Parliament, but time pressure prevented its enactment.

At the next Parliament in 1563 a wide ranging act, known as the Statute of Apprentices and Artificers, was duly passed. Its purpose was conservative and its immediate purpose was to deal with a supposed shortage of labour following a serious epidemic of the plague in 1562. Its main provisions made apprenticeship compulsory in all urban crafts. This was to last seven years, and could not be completed before the age of 24. But entry to apprenticeships required a property qualification, excluding the poor from entry to skilled trades. The act also stated that contracts of labour were to last for a minimum of a year, and that men could be forced to work, especially at harvest time.

The most important provisions related to wage levels. JPs were given the power to fix maximum, but not minimum, wages. JPs were to meet at county level at Easter to agree on wage rates, having regard to price levels, and these would be approved by the Privy Council. There was a huge variety in the way these instructions were interpreted. The Rutland JPs were issuing most of the rates they had promulgated in 1563 as late as 1610. The Chester city JPs, on the other hand, regularly and substantially increased the rates, and in 1597 made explicit reference to 'the great dearth and scarcity of things at this present'. As with so much Tudor legislation, the impact of the Statute of Apprentices Artificers is very hard to judge, even where its intentions are clear.

The encouragement of industry and trade

England was still a pre-industrialised economy – that is to say, most manufacturing processes were carried on within the home. The only sources of power were water and wind power: the factory system of production was yet to come. Yet there were a number of well-established craft industries.

Textiles. The main craft industry was the textile industry, which included the processes of spinning, weaving, dyeing, tailoring and hatting, and was much the biggest source of employment after agriculture.

A typical town such as Worcester listed these additional occupations:

- brewers;
- shoemakers;
- butchers;
- tanners;
- barbers;
- smiths.

Metal working. Metal working was beginning to develop around Sheffield and Birmingham.

Coal and iron. The production of coal and iron was well established by 1558. The coal industry was producing about 170,000 tons annually in the 1550s. Coal shipments from Newcastle to London reached 163,000 in 1597–8, though this should be read as an indication of the growth of London's population rather than any new application of coal as an industrial fuel.

Lead production and copper. Lead production expanded rapidly and the mining of copper was introduced in the 1560s. The table on page 183 gives some idea of the quantities involved.

Government encouragement of domestic industry was largely confined to the cloth industry where the protection and development of overseas markets was a prime consideration. The Privy Council was also anxious to encourage foreign textile workers to settle in England if they had relevant skills. This applied especially to the Flemish Protestants who fled the Netherlands after the Duke of Alva's invasion in 1567. They settled in the towns of Kent, Essex and East Anglia, and helped to establish what were called the New Draperies, a cheaper and lighter cloth that could use the coarse wool less suited for high-quality **broadcloth** and **worsted**. It is noteworthy that Queen Elizabeth was shown a display of seven different types of weaving when she visited Norwich in 1578.

The Privy Council also encouraged foreigners with special skills by giving them **patents** or monopolies. For example, the copper industry in Cumbria was first developed by Daniel Hochstetter from the Tyrol in Austria. Together with an Englishman, Thomas Thurland, he was given a patent in 1564 to discover copper.

Overseas trade

It was the objective of all sixteenth-century governments to promote exports and to reduce imports to create a favourable trade balance. A **trade surplus** would be reflected in an addition to the gold and silver

KEY TERMS

Broadcloth and worsted
Broadcloth was made from fine, short-staple wool and owed its strength to being matted, or felted together. Worsted cloth was woven from longer wool.

Patents Licences to inventors and entrepreneurs giving them sole right of manufacture. The intention was to promote innovation. First introduced in 1552, the issue of patents also became a convenient device for rewarding courtiers and officials. Sir Walter Ralegh enjoyed a patent for the manufacture of playing cards.

Trade surplus
Arises when the value of exports exceeds the value of imports.

English and Welsh mining output 1500–1600 (in tonnes).	Lead	Tin	Iron	Copper	
	1500	625	600	3.300	nil
	1580	3,300	660	9,620	35
	1600	12,400	550	11,860	71

(Source: adapted from D.M. Palliser, *Age of Elizabeth, 1547–1603*, Longman, 1992.)

reserves, which represented a vital financial resource. King Philip II of Spain was able to continue borrowing huge sums of money from his Italian bankers, for instance, on the security of the silver he imported from the New World.

The Privy Council was naturally most concerned about the cloth industry, which provided 90 per cent of English exports throughout Elizabeth's reign. Cloth exports were controlled by the Merchant Adventurers, a **regulated company**. Throughout the first half of the sixteenth century practically all cloth exports went to Antwerp. As we have seen, this trade suffered its first interruption in 1563 (see Chapter 2, page 56).

The Antwerp market collapsed again in 1568, 1572, 1576 and finally in 1585 when the Anglo-Spanish war began. Much energy was expended in finding alternative outlets. The first one was the port of Emden in 1563, just north of Holland. This was too close to Alva's army for comfort, and in 1569 a deal was struck with the port of Hamburg. From 1569, until the privilege was withdrawn in 1578, annual fleets escorted by royal ships sailed to Hamburg on the river Elbe. Hamburg was a member town of the **Hanseatic League**.

For the next eight years, the Merchant Adventurers returned to Emden. But as the war with Spain approached they returned to the Elbe, this time to Stade, close to Hamburg but outside the jurisdiction of the Hanseatic League. Relations with the Hanseatic League worsened during the Anglo-Spanish war when Elizabeth imposed a blockade on naval stores destined for Philip II in 1589. But the market for English cloth at Stade was unaffected, apart from a brief interval in 1599 to 1602, when there was a brief return to Emden. The maintenance of the European market for English cloth thus enjoyed a high priority as an objective of Elizabeth's foreign policy, and was by all accounts achieved. Traditional cloth exports averaged 100,000 cloths a year, worth about £750,000, and by the end of the reign the New Draperies were also bringing in about £250,000 a year.

English traders and merchants also ventured into the Mediterranean, the Atlantic Ocean and the Indian Ocean.

- In 1573, English ships reached Livorno (Leghorn).
- In 1579, an English agent, William Harborne, reached Constantinople where he made contact with Sultan Murad III. The Sultan granted a safe conduct and trading facilities to all Englishmen.
- In 1581, the Turkey Company was set up, merging with the Venice Company in 1592 to form the Levant Company.
- Voyages to Morocco began in 1551, and extended down the coast of Africa as far as Guinea. John Hawkins picked up his first cargo of slaves there in 1562.
- In 1588, the Africa Company was established. Its members were given a monopoly of the trade between the Senegal and Gambia rivers.

The last company to be founded in Elizabeth's reign was the one with most significance for the future. It was the East India Company, founded by 218 London merchants in 1600, with a view to trading directly with the East Indies.

Impact of the new ventures

The impact of these new ventures initially was small. Cloth exports dominated external trade in 1603 as they had in 1558, and the share taken by traditional European markets also remained constant. The loss of the Spanish and Portuguese markets had a damaging effect on England's exports, though privateering helped to make good the losses. Receipts from this source have been calculated at £100,000 per annum. It may be that the founding of trading companies restricted the development of overseas trade rather than fostering it, by creating monopolies.

There is one area, however, where government action seems clearly to have been beneficial. In 1563, Parliament made Wednesday an additional **fish day**, at Cecil's behest, 'for the maintenance of the navy'.

- Within thirteen years, 140 more fishing boats were said to have been operating from 20 ports as a result of the statute.
- The size of the English carrying fleet also grew.
- By 1582, the country possessed about 177 ships of over 100 tons and most English exports were carried in English ships.

CONCLUSION

When trying to assess the success or failure of government intervention in the economy during Elizabeth's reign it is tempting, but misleading, to apply present-day standards. The limitations on government policy in the sixteenth century were considerable. There were no reliable statistics.

KEY TERM

Fish day The Catholic Church expected its members not to eat meat on Fridays, as a form of fasting. However, eating fish was permissible. In 1549, Saturday was also made a fish day with the aim of fostering the fishing industry.

There were no balance of payments figures, no census of the population, no wage or price indices.

We have already noted the problems of enforcing any policy in the absence of a paid civil service in the provinces and in London, and with a slow and haphazard system of communication. There was also nothing any government could do to prevent bad harvests or the rise in population.

Bearing these limitations in mind, it is perhaps the occasional successes of government policy that deserve to be remembered:

- the re-coinage of 1561;
- the achievement of solvency for much of the reign and the smallness of the debt which Elizabeth passed on to her successor;
- the machinery put in place for the relief of the poor;
- the successful search for alternatives to Antwerp as markets for English cloth.

On the debit side, one might note:

- the inhumane treatment of vagrants for much of the reign;
- the backward-looking provisions of the Statute of Apprentices and Artificers;
- the continued under-assessment of the wealthy when it came to Parliamentary subsidies. (Cecil was himself a prime example of this; his income for tax purposes remained at £133 when his real income was £4000. In this, as in much else, he was a man of his age.)

It is hardly surprising, with political power confined to the 2000 or so peerage and gentry from whom Parliament, the Privy Council, Lords Lieutenant and JPs were drawn, and a monarch as conservative in her political views as Queen Elizabeth, that there were no radical initiatives in social policy from the Privy Council. It was in towns like Norwich and Ipswich that a genuine concern for the poor was first manifested. It is nonetheless to the credit of the government that it was prepared to adopt at least some of their ideas.

SUMMARY QUESTIONS

1 Describe and account for the growth in England's population during the sixteenth century.

2 Summarise the various explanations given for the rise in prices in England during the sixteenth century.

3 Draw up a balance sheet of those who benefited from inflation and those who suffered from it.

4 What were the costs faced by Elizabethan governments and how were they met?

5 List any evidence given in this chapter on the extent of vagrancy and the extent of poverty.

6 Summarise the efforts made by Elizabeth and her ministers to deal both with vagrants and with the 'impotent poor'.

AS QUESTION IN THE STYLE OF OCR

1 What were the main causes of poverty in Elizabethan England?

2 How successful were government measures to solve the problem of vagrancy?

Suggested approach to answering these questions

1 This appears to be a descriptive question, but in fact you are being asked to explain the poverty that existed in Elizabethan England. You need to attempt to quantify the extent and degree of poverty before explaining it. Reference might be made to recent estimates and the variation in the incidence of poverty, depending on harvests and so on. Included in your explanation should be at least some reference to the effects of a rising population, rising prices and bad harvests. You might also point out that for the majority of the population who lived on the land many were on the edge of subsistence most of the time, as were the elderly and many town-dwellers.

2 Again the problem of vagrancy needs to be defined, with some reference to contemporary and recent estimates. You will need to make specific reference to particular measures – the Vagrancy Act of 1572, for example – and it is sensible to distinguish punitive policies from those that sought to provide employment. It is obviously hard to make any precise assessment of success, but you should refer to the detailed provision made by some cities such as York and Norwich, compared with the broad-brush approach of the 1598 Act.

BIBLIOGRAPHY

This bibliography lists those books that the author has found particularly helpful, those that have been quoted from and those that he would recommend to any student of the period. Dates of publication are usually those of the first editions of the books cited except in the case of significant revisions. Those marked with an asterisk are particularly recommended for introductory reading.

GENERAL

J. Guy, *Tudor England*, OUP (1990)*

J. Guy (ed.), *The Tudor Monarchy*, Arnold (1997)

C. Haigh (ed.), *The Reign of Elizabeth I*, Macmillan (1984)*

J. Hurstfield, *Elizabeth I and the Unity of England*, English Universities Press (1964)*

N. Jones, 'Elizabeth's First Year', in C. Haigh (ed.), *The Reign of Elizabeth I*, Macmillan (1984)

J.M. Levine, *Elizabeth I*, Prentice-Hall, New Jersey (1969)

W. MacCaffrey, *The Shaping of the Elizabethan Regime*, Cape (1974)

R. O'Day, *The Longman Companion to the Tudor Age*, Longman (1995)*

P. Ramsay, *Tudor Economic Problems*, Gollancz (1963)

G. Regan, *Elizabeth I*, CUP (1988)*

A.L. Rowse, *The England of Elizabeth*, Macmillan (1961)

T.C. Smout, *A History of the Scottish People*, Collins (1969)

P. Williams, *The Later Tudors, England 1547–1603*, Clarendon Press (1995)*

BIOGRAPHIES OF ELIZABETH I

C. Haigh, *Elizabeth I*, Longman, second edition (1998)*

J.E. Neale, *Elizabeth I*, Cape (1934)

D. Starkey, *Elizabeth: Apprenticeship*, Chatto & Windus (2000)*

A. Weir, *Elizabeth the Queen*, Pimlico (1999)*

N. Williams, *Elizabeth, Queen of England*, Weidenfeld & Nicolson (1967)*

OTHER BIOGRAPHIES

A. Fraser, *Mary Queen of Scots*, Weidenfeld & Nicolson (1969)*

M.A.R. Graves, *Burghley*, Longman (1998)*

FOREIGN POLICY AND WAR

W.T. MacCaffrey, *Elizabeth I, War and Politics, 1588–1603*, Princeton UP (1992)

C. Martin and G. Parker, *The Spanish Armada*, Hamish Hamilton (1988)*

G. Mattingley, *The Defeat of the Spanish Armada*, Cape (1959)*

R.B. Wernham, *Before the Armada*, Cape (1966)

R.B. Wernham, *After the Armada, England and the Struggle for Western Europe*, Clarendon Press (1984)

C. Wilson, *Queen Elizabeth and the Revolt of the Netherlands*, Macmillan (1970)

RELIGION

J. Bossy, *The English Catholic Community, 1570–1850*, London (1975)

P. Collinson, *Archbishop Grindal*, Cape (1979)

P. Collinson, *The Elizabethan Puritan Movement*, Cape (1967)

P. Collinson, 'The Church and the New Religion', in C. Haigh (ed.), *The Reign of Elizabeth I*, Macmillan (1988)*

P. Collinson, *Elizabethan Essays*, Hambledon Press (1994)

C. Cross, *The Royal Supremacy in the Elizabethan Church*, Allen & Unwin (1994)

A.G. Dickens, *The English Reformation*, Batsford, second edition (1989)*

E. Duffy, *The Stripping of the Altars: Traditional Religion in England, 1400–1580*, Yale University Press (1992)

C. Haigh, *Reformation and Resistance in Tudor Lancashire*, Cambridge University Press (1975)

C. Haigh, *English Reformations: Religion, Politics and Society under the Tudors*, Oxford University Press (1993)

W. Haugaard, *Elizabeth and the English Reformation*, Cambridge University Press (1968)

F. Heal, *Of Prelates and Princes, A Study of the Economic and Social Position of the Tudor Episcopate*, Cambridge University Press (1980)

D. MacCulloch, *The Later Reformation in England, 1547–1603*, Macmillan (1990)*

P. McGrath, *Papists and Puritans under Elizabeth I*, Blandford Press (1967)*

A. Plowden, *Danger to Elizabeth, The Catholics under Elizabeth I*, Macmillan (1973)*

J. Warren, *Religion and Foreign Affairs*, Longman (1993)*

GOVERNMENT AND PARLIAMENT

G.R. Elton, *The Tudor Constitution*, Cambridge University Press (1962)

G.R. Elton, *The Parliament of England, 1559–1581*, Cambridge University Press (1986)

M.A.R. Graves, *The Tudor Parliaments*, Longman (1985)*

J.E. Neale, *The Elizabethan House of Commons*, Cape (1949)

J.E. Neale, *Elizabeth and Her Parliaments, 1559–1581*, Cape (1953)

J.E. Neale, *Elizabeth and Her Parliaments, 1584–1601*, Cape (1957)

M.B. Pulman, *The Elizabethan Privy Council in the Fifteen-seventies*, University of California Press (1971)

Conyers Read, *Mr. Secretary Walsingham and the Policy of Queen Elizabeth*, Oxford University Press (1925)

Conyers Read, *Mr. Secretary Cecil and Queen Elizabeth*, Cape (1955)

Conyers Read, *Lord Burghley and Queen Elizabeth*, Cape (1960)

A.G.R. Smith, *The Government of Elizabethan England*, Arnold (1967)*

P. Williams, *The Tudor Regime*, Oxford University Press (1979)

ECONOMY AND SOCIETY

A.L. Beier, *The Problem of the Poor in Tudor and Stuart England*, Methuen (1983)*

B. Coward, *Social Change and Continuity in Early Modern England*, Longman, second edition (1988)

R.B. Outhwaite, *Inflation in Tudor and Stuart England*, Macmillan (1982)*

D.M. Palliser, *The Age of Elizabeth, 1547–1603*, Longman, second edition (1992)

P. Slack, 'Poverty and Regulation', in C. Haigh (ed.), *The Reign of Elizabeth I*, Macmillan (1984)

L. Stone, *The Crisis of the Aristocracy, 1558–1641*, Oxford University Press (1965)

H.R. Trevor-Roper, 'The Gentry, 1540–1640', *Economic History Review* (1953)

MISCELLANEOUS

C.G. Cruikshank, *Elizabeth's Army*, Clarendon Press (1966)*

J. Hurstfield, *Freedom, Corruption and Government in Elizabethan England*, Cape (1973)

R. Strong, *Gloriana, the Portraits of Queen Elizabeth*, Thames & Hudson (1987)

N. Williams, *All the Queen's Men, Elizabeth and her Courtiers*, Cardinal Books (1974)*

INDEX

States General **83**
Stuart, Arabella **124–5**
Stuart dynasty 6, 41, 64
Stubbs, John 149, **150**
Succession Act **43–4**
Supremacy, Act of 49, 51, 128
surplices **51**
synods 136, **137**

Tallis, Thomas 41, 132
taxation 160–2, 176–7
Te Deum **94**
theologians **18**
Thirty-Nine Articles 130, 131
Throckmorton plot 38, 71, 80, 85,
    141
tithes **132**
torture 154
Tower of London 44
Towton, Battle of 5
trade 182–4
trade surpluses **182**
transubstantiation **17**, 48
Treasons Act 38, 140
Troyes, Treaty of 56
Tudor dynasty 6, 64
Tyrone's rebellion 111–13, 119

Uniformity, Act of 49, 51, 129, 133
usurpers **62**
Utrecht, Union of 78, 83, 85, 86

vagrants **177**, 178–84
Valor Ecclesiasticus **19**
Vere, Sir Francis 107, **108**
Vervins, Treaty of **106**
vestments **18**, 49

Wales 22
Walsingham, Sir Francis **10**, 12
    foreign policy 81, 86, 93
    Privy Council 117–18, 148, 153–5
    security 71–2
War of Three Henries 86
Wars of the Roses **5**
Wentworth, Peter **124**, 164–5
Wernham, R. B. 89, **113**
Westphalia, Peace of **112**, 113
William of Orange 86
woad **122**
worsted **182**
Wyatt's Rebellion **21**, 43, 67

York, House of 5, 44